SAMUEL GOBAT, BISHOP OF JERUSALEM, HIS LIFE AND WORK : A BIOGRAPHICAL SKETCH

SAMUEL GOBAT, BISHOP OF JERUSALEM, HIS LIFE AND WORK : A BIOGRAPHICAL SKETCH

Gobat, Samuel, 1799-1879 and roehrich, L., Mme

www.General-Books.net

Publication Data:

Title: Samuel Gobat, Bishop of Jerusalem, His Life and Work : a Biographical Sketch
Author: Gobat, Samuel, 1799-1879 and roehrich, L., Mme
Reprinted: 2010, General Books, Memphis, Tennessee, USA
Publisher: London : J. Nisbet
Publication date: 1884
Subjects: Gobat, Samuel, 1799-1879
Missions
Missions
Missionaries

SAMUEL GOBAT, BISHOP OF JERUSALEM, HIS LIFE AND WORK : A BIOGRAPHICAL SKETCH

PREFACE.

This volume lias one great merit to begin with. It is short, compact, and very full of the most interesting and useful information. Autobiographies and private journals (specially in modern days) are open to a good deal of suspicion. In autobiographies we cannot generally expect that the writer will disclose what is really descriptive of himself, if it be not to his honour; and in journals, kept during the last forty years (so frequent has become the issue of such things), almost every one who makes his entries, acts, consciously or unconsciously, under an impression that liis thoughts will certainly in some cases, and possibly in otliers be revealed to the public.

But the autobiography of this excellent Bishop Gobat is transparent as glass. He says what he thought, he states what he felt; he goes through all the various phases of his opinions and actions witli child-like simplicity, writing only for himself, and for none other; having nothing that he wishes to divulge, and nothing that he wishes to conceal. All this is striking and in-structive, because it is manifestly true. It shows, too, tlie history of the workmgs of an able and ingenuous mind: its forward and its backward movements, its difficulties and its doubts, and how by God's mercy it was kept steady in its course by the one great object he had ever before him, the advent of the kingdom of Christ.

Not only those who are to go out on missionary enterprise, but those who are to battle with all the evils of the world at large, may learn a very great deal from the life of this admirable servant of our Lord.

The Bishop, in pp. 189 and 190 of his Memoirs, makes a comment which in these days is well worthy of special attention. He says:

"I remember one circumstance in connection with my work at Malta which would have convinced me, had I not already been convinced, of the Divine inspiration of tlie whole Bible.

"Whilst translating Keith on the Bullilment of Prophecy, the two chief translators, Phares Shidiak of Mount Lebanon, and the Rev. Mr. Badjer, both very good Arabic scholars, were puzzled continually, not knowing how to render the imagery in which the meaning was clothed in the English original, because that imagery consisted chiefly, or at least in great part, of terms derived from divers kinds of mechanism, the works of men, of which the uncivilised Arabs have no idea, and therefore possess no words to express them, especially when employed in a non-natural or immaterial sense. But the imagery of the Bible is nearly all taken from nature, the work of God, and thus intelligible to all, and can consequently be translated into all human languages. However, the pains taken in the translation of the work has rendered it acceptable to the best-educated Moslems; for of all the works published in modern times by the missionaries, Keith on Prophecy is to this day the most highly appreciated among them. My chief part in that translation, as in other ones, was to see that the meaning was correct."

This is confirmed by wlmt the writer of this Preface heard from a large body of young Indians who had come to England from all parts of Hindostan to study for various professionsj such as medicine, law, engineering, c. " Many of Dr. Colenso's objections to the Old Testament," said they, " are no objections to us; nor would they be to any one who lived in the East."

The later part of the Bishop's life, his career in Jerusalem, has been completed by other hands. It is, however, of real value and importance; and Bishops, both present and to come, may learn much from his episcopal example. He was a man misrepresented by some, and misunderstood by many more. Eew have had such obstacles to overcome and such trials to undergo. Calumny, and even actual indignity, were heaped upon him.

Of all this a good deal has been suppressed, and perhaps wisely. Little would be gained by reviving the memory of bitter conflicts when all the parties are dead and gone. He himself, were he alive, would be the last to desire it; and he would no doubt rest satisfied with the verdict of the public, that the Bishop in the Holy City was not, in wisdom, piety, and truth, inferior to the missionary in Abyssinia.

SHAETESBUEY.

October 31, 1884.

CONTENTS.

CHAPTER V.

PAGE

KETUEN TO EUKOPE MAEKIAGE SECOND MISSIONARY TOUR IN ABYSSINIA SERIOUS ILLNESS (1834-1837) I5S

CHAPTER VI.
A YEAR OP WAITING MISSIONARY WORK IN SWITZERLAND; AMONG THE DRUSES; IN ITALY; AND AT MALTA (1838-1845). 186
CHAPTER VII.
NOMINATION AND CONSECRATION AS BISHOP ARRIVAL AT JERUSALEM (1846) 207
PAET IL
HIS WORK AS BISHOP AT JERUSALEM (1846-1S79).
CHAPTER I.
RETROSPECTIVE GLANCE AT THE ORIGIN OF THE EVANGELICAL BISHOPRIC AT JERUSALEM 221
CHAPTER IL
DEVELOPMENT OF THE MISSION, AND OP SCHOLASTIC MATTERS UN-DER
BISHOP GOBAT (1846-1851) 232
CHAPTER in.
PROTEST FROM SOME OP THE ANGLICAN CLERGY AGAINST BISHOP CONTENTS.
CHAPTER IV.
PAGE IMMEDIATE CONSEQUENCES OF THE CRIMEAN WAR GROWING HOSTILITY OF THE MOHAMMEDANS RESUMPTION OF THE ABYSSINIAN MISSION (1854-1857) 297
CHAPTER V.
DEVELOPMENT OF THE CONGREGATION THEIR PRESERVATION AT THE TIME OF THE MASSACRE OP THE CHRISTIANS IN SYRIA (1859-1860) 322
CHAPTER VI.
y UNINTERRUPTED WORK CALAMITIES IN PALESTINE THE ABYSSINIAN WAR (1861-I871) 332
CHAPTER YII.
THE bishop's jubilee THE LAST SEVEN YEARS OF HIS WORK, AND HIS ENTRANCE INTO REST (187I-1879) 37O
PAGE In Peril by Water i8o
Mosque of Omar, Jerusalem 215
Street of the Bazaar, Jerusalem, with Mount of Olives IN Background 235
Encampment at Lifta 319
Bishop Gobat's House; Christ Church; David's Steeple 367
Old Mission-House, Basle; Bishop Gobat's Tomb; St. Julian's Mission-Hall Malta 390

PAET I.
FROM CHILDHOOD UNTIL HIS ENTRANCE UPON HIS EPISCOPAL FUNCTIONS AT JERUSALEM.
(1799-1846.)
FROM HIS OWN JOURNALS.
CHAPTEE I.

EARLY HOME AND BOYHOOD AT CREMINE CONVERSION TO CHRIST, AND COMMENCEMENT OF LABOURS AS TEACHER. 1799-1820.)

I WAS born on the 26th of January 1799 at Cremine, a small village in the beautiful Miinsterthal, in the Jura, then under the government of the French Eepublic, but now, since the fall of the first Napoleon, belonging to the Canton of Berne, in Switzerland.

My father and mother, especially the latter, had from their youth up been religiously inclined. They never, unless compelled to do so, failed to attend divine service on the Lord's day, while they usually passed the remainder of that day in reading, together with their children, the Bible and other good books, particularly the excellent sermons of Nardin. They also had daily family prayer, though during the busy season in the fields this duty was sometimes neglected. They loved each other most tenderly, and I never observed anything like a misunderstanding between them.

During the days of my infancy and early youth, my mother laboured under an almost continual sense of sin and guilt. Yet deep as was this melancholy consciousness, it was not so deep as to deprive her of the hope of making herself fit to receive the Saviour. My father shared her feelings; and thus, although exemplary in their conduct, they were both destitute of spiritual comfort. Nevertheless, when I reflect upon the wisdom they displayed in the training of their children, I feel convinced that even at that period they were, without knowing it, under the influence of the Spirit of God. They combined with the most devoted, self- denying, parental love the most untiring, inexhaustible patience, though they on all occasions exacted prompt and implicit obedience. They could bear with childish faults of thoughtlessness without excusing them, but they were uncompromisingly severe towards wilful sins, such as untruth, pilfering, or disobedience.

Having originally been in easy circumstances, but having, soon after their marriage, lost the greater part of their property through the French Eevolution, they contracted a character of reserve, which, together with a tender conscience, rendered them almost unfit to cope with the world. Their occupation consisted in the cultivation of their own estate until the year 1818, when my father, burdened with debts, resolved to sell as much land as would suffice to pay off his obligations, so that but little of it remained in his possession. This was very humiliating to the whole family. But the curse which had seemed to rest on all my father's enterprises disappeared with the sale of the property. Thenceforward my parents, though in a lowlier condition, enjoyed peaceful and happy days until they entered into everlasting rest. Spiritual blessings were showered upon us; and it pleased God in after years to choose several of us as instruments to lead fellow-sinners to that same Saviour, whom to know and to love we had found to be true happiness and Eternal Life.

In my earliest infancy I learned to look up to God for every blessing, and I was happy in the thought that our Lord Jesus, whom I believe I sincerely loved, was ever near me, like a faithful Friend. It was my greatest enjoyment to read the Word of God, especially the Gospels, and then to withdraw for secret prayer. In my seventh year I was nearly as well acquainted with the ISTew Testament and the historical parts of the Old as I am now, though there were many passages that I did not understand; and I frequently prayed to God that He would make me a minister of the Gospel, chiefly because I thought that I should then understand everything in the Bible which at that time was obscure to me.

This early piety, however, proved to be as a cloud of the morning; for in my ninth year I began to doubt about several portions of Scripture. A few years later, my doubts extended even to the immortality of the soul and the divinity of Christ; and at last, my heart being alienated from Christ and devoid of peace, I tried hard to persuade myself that there is no personal righteous God; but in this I could never succeed.

This melancholy state was brought about, as far as I remember, by the following circumstances.

From my fourth year I had been reading over and over again a book called " Le Berger dartois." It was a small controversial work, treating of the discussions between a simple shepherd who had been converted to Protestantism and his Eoman Catholic priest. By means of this book I learned to know all the leading errors of the Church of Eome, her tricks and her cruelty on the one hand, and on the other the essential truths of the "Word of God, as opposed to those errors and practices. This made an impression on my mind against Popery whicli never has been, and I trust never will be effaced, subsequent experience having only deepened it. But the contents of the book had also excited my compassion for the poor deluded Eoman Catholics, and I was seized with the desire to convert them. This brought me into contact with a Eoman Catholic priest, who began to come frequently to our house in order to discuss the question with me. But as he was ignorant of the contents of the Bible, and as I would not allow him to bring forward any argument not drawn from the Word of God, I was easily able to silence him, sometimes in the presence of many witnesses, who praised me for my skill in controversy. In consequence of this I grew vain and conceited.

From that time, when I read my Bible, instead of receiving, as formerly, all that I could understand in simple faith, I began to murmur against God for having caused things to be written which I could not comprehend; for I still believed, as I believe now, that the whole Bible was the Word of God. I began to read chiefly those parts of the Scriptures which were least intelligible to me, till by degrees I became disgusted, and began to doubt whether the Bible really was the Word of God, and to lose all relish for it; until at last I fell into complete scepticism. But I must confess that the love of sin had quite as much to do with producing this state of mind as my own ignorance.

Here it may not be out of place to say a few words respecting my boyhood, though on this head I have but little to relate.

From the age of about four to fifteen, I went to school for four months and a half in the year, during which time I had the credit of being a good boy, and was never punished but once, and that in part unjustly. It happened thus: It had for some time past formed part of the routine of my class to write from dictation; and the schoolmaster, who generally made too free a use of his cane, was wont to strike the boys' fingers for every mistake a very painful mode of correction. Now for a good while I had made no error and received no caning, in consequence of which the master was accused of partiality towards me. But on this particular occasion, I had left out one word of five letters, which, according to rule, ought only to have been considered as one mistake; now the master counted it as five, which, as I had a strong sense of justice, exasperated me; therefore, when he prepared to cane me, I received the first stroke submissively, but at the second I looked him in the face, and said in a resolute tone, "May God requite you" (Bieio vous le rende), and the same for each of the remaining strokes. My next neighbour, who, like myself, had been spared until then, had made a blunder similar to mine; and when he was to be punished I whispered in his ear, "Do as I have done," which he did; and from that moment every boy received his caning with an emphatic " JDicic vous le Te7ide! At last the master threw his cane out of the window, exclaiming in a kind of despair, "No more caning! If I cannot manage you without a cane, I will cease to be your teacher." On going out of school, we elder boys took counsel, and then, gathering all the children together, we agreed that in case the master kept his word and abolished the cane, we would all be docile and endeavour to please him; and that if any one should offend him, we would punish the culprit out of school. From that day forward the school was a model of order and good behaviour.

During the seven months and a half when there was no school, I used, when not required by my parents, to go fishing or to play with other boys, and I forgot much of what I had learned till the school was reopened in November. The only branches taught were reading, writing, arithmetic, and singing, with Ostervald's catechism and a little Scripture history. But as, during my last school year, I knew about as much as my master, I was induced by my parents to learn a number of psalms and chapters of the Bible, besides numerous prayers. This plan has proved very useful to me in after years, and is much to be commended, not only for strengthening the memory, but chiefly because it is the means of depositing in the mind many important truths which may lie dormant for a season, but which will most likely make their power to be felt sooner or later.

In the course of my boyhood I experienced great deliverances from imminent dangers, which, however, failed at the time to make a due impression upon me. On one occasion, when I was between six and seven years old, I climbed a loose wall of great stones after a lieavy fall of rain. Upon my reaching the top of it, the entire pile fell down with a terrible crash, and I with it. My left hand was crushed and the right seriously hurt; the bones of two fingers of my left hand were laid completely bare. The surgeon to whom my father took me was not at home, but his wife said that in similar cases her husband was accustomed to wash the wound with oil of vitriol, which must cause very great pain, for strong men to whom it was applied would cry out with all their might. She then asked me if I could bear it without crying out; to which I answered, that if it would cure me, I would endure it. She accordingly bathed my wounds with that liquid, thereby causing me excessive pain; yet I kept perfectly quiet. When the surgeon returned in the evening and saw my injuries, he declared that if he had been at home, he would not have had the courage to apply the vitriol, but would have cut off my hand, or at least several lingers; but now he hojded that I should be cured without amputation. For several weeks I went every morning to have my hand dressed, and frequently cried aloud, though the surgeon did all he could to soothe me. Thanks be to God, I was cured.

I could mention several similar perils from which the good providence of God has saved me, both in my boyhood and beyond it, when I was most unfit to be removed from this world; and for this I never can be sufficiently thankful to God my Saviour.

It had been the original desire of my parents, who at my birth had dedicated me to the service of God and of His Church, that I should study theology. But by the time I was old enough to begin the preliminary course, they had had such a succession of misfortunes that they were no longer able to afford the necessary expenses; and when, in my eleventh year, a friend of my father offered to defray all the cost of my studies, I was not disposed to devote myself to the ministry of the Gospel. I still cherished the conviction that a minister ought to be pious and self-denying, like the apostles and their companions, and for such a mode of life I no longer had any inclination. From that time up to my twentieth year I was an infidel not an avowed one, because I would not let my parents know it for fear of causing them sorrow. For the same reason my outward conduct was orderly; so much so, that I was frequently held up as a model to other young men. Still I could not prevent my parents observing that a great change for the worse had taken place in me.

Meanwhile I worked with my father and mother, but I did so merely to avoid displeasing them; for I did not like any kind of serious occupation. My heart was full lo LIFE OF SAMUEL GOB AT.

of the love of the vanities of the world. Happily I did not drink wine or any other intoxicating beverage; hence my control over my outward conduct. But whenever I could escape the eyes of my parents and their friends, I spent my time in frivolities, especially in card-playing.

During this period several persons in our neighbourhood had been converted, and among them my eldest sister; but as she had always been of a retiring and devout disposition, her conversion did not attract much attention. As for me, notwithstanding my utter destitution of religious faith, I loved and respected the newly-converted as well as other genuinely pious people, although in general I avoided them as much as politeness would allow. When the worldly and profane mocked or spoke evil of them, whether in their presence or their absence, I took their part so warmly that I was sometimes insulted for it; for I respected their sincerity and the harmony between their faith and their conduct, while I despised those who professed to believe the Bible, and yet lived not in accordance with their profession.

For several years I do not remember having felt the need of a Saviour or any desire after God. The first incident which availed to touch my heart happened as follows:

My parents had invited a zealous minister, the now well-known M. Bost, sen., then curate in a neighbouring parish, to come at a certain hour for the purpose of talking seriously with me. I was not apprised of his coming, for as he had the reputation of being very severe, I had always contrived, when he had visited my parents on former occasions, to absent myself from home. He arrived while we were at table, and at the sight of him I became somewhat confused. My mother perceiving this, and fearing that I might find some pretext for

CONVERSION TO CHRIST. n withdrawing supposing also that it would be hazardous to attack my scepticism, which she suspected, in the presence of others asked me at once to accompany M. Bost on his return home. I divined her object, and replied with alacrity that I would do so with pleasure, and so I remained free from attack for the moment. I listened to the conversation, chiefly on religious topics, with perfect indifference, and when the time came for M. Bost to take leave, I set off with him, cheerful in appearance, but in reality with an uneasy mind.

On the way he made several attempts to tell me the truths which my case required, but I contrived to avoid the pointed allusions intended for myself, and to turn them adroitly upon other people. In fact, his task was a difcult one. He could not convict me of any gross sin; and as I had never boasted of my unbelief, he could only suspect me of it. Yet he could not but perceive that I was in a dangerous state of alienation from God. At length I became aware that the faithful man felt ill at ease, for he looked first at me, then upon the ground, in some apparent confusion; for it was not his custom to use so much gentleness and forbearance when he thought himself called upon to speak to sinners.

Now, observing that he was about to make a direct attack upon me, and to say with Nathan the prophet, "Thou art the man," and being unwilling to openly oppose him for fear of his giving an unfavourable report to my parents, I abruptly took leave of him under pretence of an engagement. When I had walked some distance homewards, I looked back, and saw the poor man still standing on the spot where I had left him, and wiping his eyes. At that moment I appeared really vile in my own eyes. I told myself that it was love which had brought this man to our house, and that it was for fear of. wounding my feelings that he had tried so gently to reach my heart and conscience, and now he was reproaching himself with having been unfaithful. I felt that I had dealt hypocritically with him. From that day for-w ard it was in July 1818 I felt less at ease in my state of spiritual deadness.

In the beginning of October that same year, my levity of conversation prompted a companion to make a proposal to me at which I shuddered, and for the first time I saw the danger of playing with sinful imaginings. From that day I could not rest. I laboured hard by day, and, unable to sleep, I spent one night after another in some amusement, usually cards, in order to avoid the melancholy thoughts which pursued and troubled me.

Matters w ent on thus until the 20th of that month, which was a Sunday. I had spent the morning at church, which I still attended regularly for my parents' sake, but had slept the hours of devotion away. The afternoon had been passed in dancing, and the evening was to have been spent in play with some young men of my acquaintance. But when, unobserved by my parents, I contrived to slip away, I was suddenly struck with a sense of the presence of God. I went back again into the house, and took up the Bible with the intention of reading it, which I had not done for several years, unless at the request of my parents. But when I had opened it I had not the courage to proceed, for I felt myself under the wrath of God and unworthy to read His Word. All the sophisms on which I had built my unbelief seemed suddenly swept away, and the Bible once more became to me the true and sure Word of God but, alas! it became so to my condemnation.

For fear lest my parents and sisters might observe my emotion, I simply said that I did not feel well, and with- drew to my room. This was between seven and eight in the evening. Oh! what a terrible, and yet what a blessed nig ht was before me! When alone, I reflected for a moment on my lost condition, and then began to pray in these or similar words: " 0 my Creator! I have been taught from my infancy that Thou hast sent Thine only-begotten Son into the world to save sinners. If it be really so, I beseech Thee to reveal Him unto me, for I am a lost sinner. Have mercy upon me!"

The more I prayed, the deeper became the anguish, the agony of my soul. I felt as if there had been but one step between me and eternal, irremediable death. AVhether I really saw, or only imagined that I saw, three evil spirits standing before me, of a substance like a spider's web, the central one darker than the two others, I cannot tell; but this much is certain, that the Wicked One was exciting me nearly to despair. The agony of my soul was so terrible that I filled my mouth with a handkerchief to prevent my crying aloud while pleading for mercy.

I continued thus praying and crying to God until about three o'clock next morning, when I fancied I saw rays of vivid light coming down from the ceiling of my room and concentrating themselves in an earthen vessel at my right hand. Hereupon the three spirits drev back several paces. I instantly summoned all my courage, and exclaimed in the words of Jacob, "I will not let Thee go except Thou bless me!" At these words the spirits vanished. On a sudden I felt as if the burden of my sins was taken away, and I experienced unutterable delight. I felt the Lord Jesus near me in all the fulness of His love. I felt His assurance, not in words, for I heard no sound, but by a kind of divine power, of my reconciliation with God and of His favour.

Hitherto I had always prayed to God merely as to the Supreme Being, without any distinct mention of the Son and of His work of redemption; but from that moment I was enabled to believe that Jesus was my Saviour, my Lord, and my God. The remaining hours of that night were the most blissful of my life.

Next morning, however, on attempting to rise, I found that I had no strength to do so I was completely exhausted. When, as it grew late, I heard my mother coming to see me, either Satan or my own wicked heart, or else both combined, suggested that I should say nothing to her of what had happened during the night, lest, in case I should not persevere in following the Saviour, she might consider me as a backslider, in greater danger of perdition than before, and so suffer still more bitter sorrow on my account. But God had prepared an antidote to this temptation.

As soon as my mother looked at me, she seemed struck with my appearance. "What is the matter with you? " she asked, with enforced calmness. " Your countenance is altogether changed." And then I related to her faithfully all that had taken place during the night, feeling happy thus to have overcome the first temptation. My mother, for fear, no doubt, of exciting in me feelings of vanity and self-conceit, listened quietly, without betraying any surprise. She went straight to my father, how ever, and recounted the whole matter to him; upon which they both came to the conclusion that, notwithstanding their religious exercises and their well-ordered life, they had not yet experienced the pardon of their sins or the joy of salvation; that, consequently, they were not yet truly converted. My mother sank into deep melancholy. She diligently read her Bible; but her mind being confused about points of doctrinei justification by faith, sanctification, and free salvation, to wit she dared not apply to herself the promises of the Gospel.

Now when this state of mind had continued for about six months, she heard of a young person who was reported to be mad, suffering under the conviction that she was lost without hope of redemption. My mother was filled with deep sympathy, and resolved at once to go and visit the sufferer. On her way she gathered together from memory a good number of Scripture passages adapted to the case in point. Suddenly the thought darted into her heart, "This young girl's state is just like my own. Why should I not apply to myself these same precious promises and declarations of God in behalf of wretched sinners such as I?" With this a flood of light was poured into her soul, so that she not only felt able to receive Christ and all His merits by faith, but also obtained, as by a flash of comprehension, a clear view of the difference between justification and sanctification, such as I never observed in any theologian.

Her first visit to this person did not effect all that she desired, but it broke the spell by which Satan had held her captive, for she could thenceforth pray with some hope of being heard; and in a few days she could rejoice in the Lord her salvation. I believe she afterwards followed Him faithfully to her life's end.

After my mother had left me on that happy morning, I slept for several hours; and when I awoke I still rejoiced, though the vividness of my feelings had greatly subsided. My bodily strength was restored, but I felt my moral weakness very keenly; and I was again assailed by the temptation to conceal the change which had taken place wdthin me, lest a subsequent lapse should expose me to the derision of scoffers. Falling upon my knees, I owned my weakness, and asked for strength to persevere, and boldly to confess the name of my Lord before men.

On rising from prayer I saw through the window a group of my companions. I at once said to myself," Now is the time to make use of the grace and strength for which I have jnst been asking. I must go and speak to them."

Being naturally very shy, I dreaded the idea of expected ridicule; yet I saw my duty clear before me, and there was no time to be lost. I hastened out to them in the full expectation that my words would be received with a roar of laughter, if not with something worse. Lut what was my surprise on perceiving that their behaviour had also altered, and that their habitual levity was replaced by a gravity of manner such as rendered it quite easy for me to address to them a few solemn and affectionate words. I reminded them of the reckless course I had hitherto pursued in their companionship, and told them of the change which God had wrought in my heart. I briefly declared that I was steadfastly purposed from thenceforth to serve the Lord, and that I must therefore bid farewell to their society, unless, indeed, any one of them was minded to walk with me in the narrow way.

A short silence ensued. Then one of the young men, whom we had looked upon as a kind of leader, spoke. " I know that you are right," said he, " but I cannot follow you now." Two years later he forsook his evil courses, and his conversion was so striking that it proved to be the means of an important revival in the neighbourhood.

A few months later I had to pass through another and somewhat similar ordeal.

Having completed my twentieth year, I became liable for the duties of the Lanchvelir, which consisted in performing military exercises for about fifteen Sunday afternoons in the year. On the first Sunday I was cited to appear, with all the other young men of the parish, to be drilled. Athough I was determined not to desecrate the Lord's day by drill, I yet repaired to the appointed spot with a trembling but prayerful heart. It was my intention to protest publicly against this profanation of the sacred day, and to declare that I would take no part in it. I did so, with the full expectation of being ridiculed, most likely insulted; but again my companions seemed solemnly impressed, even the most light-minded among them. The officer now observed that it was the law that every one should be drilled on that day, and that if I absented myself I must pay the prescribed fine. On this I retired, and paid the fine or several successive Sundays. But as each fine exceeded the previous one in amount, the tax told heavily upon my scanty means. I therefore went to the Prefect of the district to ask him to exempt me alike from the duty and the fine. He, of course, tried hard to convince me that I was bound to obey the Government; to which I replied that I was willing to submit in all things not opposed to the law of God. In my efforts to persuade the Prefect of the justice of my arguments on the religious side of the question, I grew bold almost too much so, indeed, for my age and position, when I ventured to add that if the Government persisted in legislating contrary to the Divine law, it would soon fall to pieces; Little thinking that in twelve years' time, 1830-31, that very Government would fall, never to rise again. " Well, you may be right," said the Prefect at length; " and as I have no authority to exempt you, I will pay the fines myself." I thanked him and withdrew, praying that God would bless him and his young family a prayer which I am happy to say was abundantly answered in after years.

The first year of my spiritual life, 18 19, was one of rich blessing and of much joy. I can remember only one instance of departure from the right way. It happened in the week set apart by the villagers for haymaking on a mountain belonging to the community. It was the custom to spend the whole week on the mountain, without coming down to the valley. That year the weather was wet, and the rain poured down for several days without ceasing. JSTobody could go out, and I therefore was almost compelled to pass the days and evenings in large assemblages of worldly and light-minded people. Some of these persons were very witty; and I had not courage, at first, to protest against what was wrong in their conversation, although my conscience reproved me for my silence. By degrees I began to feel interested in their pernicious talk, and neglected the opportunity of saying a word in season for my Lord and Master. On the second day I discovered with uneasiness that I was losing my relish for prayer and Bible-reading. Yet I still neglected to pray. I do not recollect having said or done anything positively wrong; but my heart was already fast straying away from the Good Shepherd.

On the fourth day I received a very kind letter from a lady, in which the following words occurred: " I frequently ask myself what you may be doing during these cold and rainy days; to which I answer that you are doubtless praying or reading your Bible." These words pierced my heart like an arrow. I ran out of the house to seek some corner in which to hide my shame. " Vile hypocrite! " I cried to myself, " while good people are thinking well of you, you are amusing yourself and playing with sin, forgetting Him whom your sins have nailed to the cross!"

I fell upon my knees, confessed my sins, and asked God to forgive me; which He mercifully did, and restored me to liberty of communion with Him. So far I was cured; but my wings had been cut and my strength diminished. My natural shyness, which had been gradually melting away before zeal for my Lord and love for my neighbour, returned, and led me to shun the society of the worldly; but it drove me to Him who was able to give me courage to confess His Name and witness for His truth.

For many months after this I lived in almost uninterrupted communion with the Lord. Whether in the field or at home, by day and night I felt that He was with me. Whereas formerly I hated almost every kind of work, and was most awkward in performing it, I now delighted to labour hard throughout the day, and used to spend half or two-thirds of the night in prayer and praise, counting as lost the time which I must spend in sleep.

I had a great-aunt who had been for many years a member of the Moravian Society, and who was in the habit of lending me many good books, among which were some containing descriptions of the happy state of the brethren, living together in the fear and love of God, and rejoicing in His salvation; as they did, for example, at Herrnhut in the days of Count Zinzendorf. My first idea formed itself into a desire to join the Moravians; but this soon gave way to another and much deeper impression, namely, a profound, overwhelming, abiding sense of commiseration for all men unacquainted with the Lord Jesus, but especially for those of my own parish to whom He was as yet but a name. Oh! how often did I ascend a certain hill, whence I could survey the four villages in the lovely little valley of Grandval which collectively constituted our parish, in order to pray with many tears that God would revive His work among the inhabitants, and, above all, that He would send them a faithful pastor to lead them amid the green pastures of the blessed Gospel, and to the wells of eternal salvation! All of which was to be accomplished by His good pleasure in after years. Ere many years had sped, but five indeed from that time, one careless, faithless shepherd was replaced by another, who laboured there successfully for forty years, to be then succeeded by his son, who was worthy to walk in his father's steps. As a proof of the blessing which attended that good man's ministry, I may mention that for the space of forty years that little parish, numbering less than six hundred souls, all living by the cultivation of their own small patches of land, has, to the best of my belief, never contributed less than fifty pounds a year for missionary works, which sum was divided between the Basle and Paris societies, though of late years a part of it has been sent to me for similar purposes.

Soon after my conversion I began to read the scanty supply of missionary intelligence then published in the Trench language, which greatly enlarged and softened my heart. I began deeply to sympathise with the poor scattered Jews, as well as with the heathen, who were without God and without hope in the world. I prayed constantly and fervently for them, and became conscious of an awakening desire to devote myself to the missionary cause. At first I sought to dismiss the thought from my mind, not only on account of my love for my parents and my wish to succour them in their old age, but also because I considered mvself altogether unfit for the call- ing by reason of my scanty education, my natural shyness, and my awkwardness of speech and manner. Still the idea would again and again occupy my mind, as if it had been a call from God Himself. I earnestly prayed that, if it were His will that I should become a missionary, He would so clearly call me to the work that I should have no doubt remaining on the subject.

One Sunday morning, when there was no service at church, I had been praying most earnestly in a forest for several hours, asking that if it were God's will that I should become a missionary, He would Himself call me through any means He should choose, without my offering myself for the work until I had an inward conviction that my prayer had been accepted. When I returned home I found a lady with my parents who was in correspondence with several members of the missionary institution at Basle, and with whom I had frequently conversed on religious topics. Most unexpectedly she asked me whether I should not like to become a missionary. I was surprised, because I had always avoided speaking to her on that matter, but I simply answered that I was ready, if the Lord should ever call me, provided my parents gave their consent. Hereupon, without asking my sanction, this lady wrote to the committee on my behalf; and about three weeks later I received a letter from Basle stating that I was accepted, and inviting me to hold myself in readiness to enter the institution when the first vacancy should occur.

I had to wait nine months before my summons arrived, and this interval passed over tranquilly, bringing much spiritual happiness in its train. I was sensible of my ignorance on many ordinary subjects of education, so that, besides occupying a part of my leisure with the perusal of the Bible and works of piety, I also read what- ever historical books I could obtain, and studied the French grammar thoroughly.

During this interval I found myself called upon to speak at a communal meeting in defence of certain points of doctrine concerning which I had been called in question. The discussion grew stormy, and the Maire was obliged to interpose. A few days after this circumstance nearly all the fathers of families in the village called upon me and invited me to take charge of the instruction of their children until I should leave for Basle. They stated that the little ones were growing wild and ungovernable, and that they learned nothing under the schoolmaster appointed by Government.

I saw in this call a favourable opportunity of doing, under the blessing of God, the greatest and most lasting good to my native place before quitting it. I at once accepted it, therefore, with my parents' consent; for I was well aware that, although the schoolmaster had ten times more knowledge than myself, he was a drunkard, and could gain neither the affection nor the respect of the children.

I opened the school in the beginning of October, when, to my surprise, all the children, both boys and girls, of the village presented themselves, and continued to attend most regularly, to the number of about forty; so that the Government master was left with three pupils, his two brothers and another boy. He was obliged to resign, for which I pitied him, though he was very bitter against me; but it will not be out of place here to state that he was afterwards converted and became also my warm friend. I hope to meet him in the kingdom of God.

The primary school that is, the school for the mass of the people was still considered as an institution of the

Church, wherefore all that was taught in it, save reading, writing, and arithmetic, related to religion, with the exception of grammar. The Bible was read every day, but only as a tedious exercise in reading. The children were made to learn, besides the Lord's Prayer, the Creed, and the Ten Commandments, as many Psalms, and other passages of Scripture, long forms of prayer, and Catechism, as their respective memories could hold, but without any explanation. All was lifeless mechanism; so that the children never thought about the meaning of what they learned, except those whose parents took care to teach them on a more sensible plan at home. But what was worse was the fact that not only in our own parish, but in general, religion was represented to the children as a gloomy thing, consisting solely in a heap of burdensome duties to be fulfilled under fear of the wrath of God. Wherefore their greatest desire and hope was to be confirmed, considering confirmation as an emancipation at once from school and from religion, I o wonder, then, that all that was expected from young people after their confirmation was that they should go to church once on Sunday, partake once or twice a year of the sacrament of the Lord's Supper, and abstain from gross sins. I knew and deeply felt all this to be ruinous; and I resolved to set my face against the system, relying on Him who said, "Suffer the little children to come unto Me."

I opened the school myself with prayer, instead of calling upon one of the children to repeat a prayer from memory, as had hitherto been the custom. I then addressed my scholars in simple and affectionate words, endeavouring chiefly to impress upon their minds the great truth that God is Love; that He loved them; that the Lord Jesus Christ loved them, and was ready to bless them provided they came to Him; that His service religion, namely is perfect freedom, and that for them it consisted in giving Him their hearts, which He would then fill with joy and peace for ever. I ended by telling them that I had experienced the love of God, and that it was that love which had constrained me to take charge of them until I should be called to go and make known the same love unto the heathen. I asked them whether they were resolved by the grace of God so to behave as to enable me to rule over them by love alone, and was answered with an eager affirmative. I felt that I had their full confidence and love, and the three months which I spent with them were amongst the happiest and most blessed of my life.

I scarcely ever found it necessary to administer the gentlest reproof to any one of them, and once only was I obliged to punish a boy for an act of disobedience, committed out of school, it is true, but positive disobedience notwithstanding. The punishment I inflicted was hazardous, the boy having previously been regarded as unmanageable, and the other children might have made a joke of it. When he entered the room, I took him quietly by the hand and made him sit in my chair, saying softly but solemnly that his wilful disobedience proved that he supposed himself to know better than I did; wherefore it must be right in his eyes for him to be placed in the master's chair. The rough boy was taken by surprise, yet, looking at his school-fellows, he tried to force a smile to his lips. But to my great joy they all remained perfectly serious, and gazed at him with pity. The boy looked down for some time, but whether from shame or from stubbornness, I could not tell. At length, in the midst of the general silence, a child appealed to me for help. I desired him to apply to him who wanted to be master. Of course he did not do so, but the poor culprit's courage broke down, and he burst into tears. I let him weep for some time, until I saw that he was really humbled, and ready to do anything to get out of his unpleasant position. But having never been humbled before, he did not know how to proceed. Perceiving this, I left the room, and made a sign to my mother, who had just entered, to advise him how to behave. When I re-entered the room, he slowly rose from his seat, looked about him trembling, then, coming to me, he fell on his knees, and with sobs sued for pardon. From that time he was one of the meekest lambs of my little flock.

From the very beginning I almost entirely put an end to learning by rote during school-hours; all that had to be done at home. Then I made use of catechising, to make them understand what they had learned by heart. At first it was hard work, as they had never been led to think for themselves; but after a few days their minds began to open, and as soon as possible I made them reproduce in writing all that I had taught them. The first attempts were poor and awkward, but as my pupils were convinced that I loved them, they used every endeavour to win my approbation, and soon began to make rapid progress according to their respective abilities. I say according to their respective abilities, for I have ever observed that to task a child beyond his natural capacity is most injurious; and if persevered in, will make an idiot of a child, who might otherwise have been quite satisfactorily developed.

Towards the end of the three months, when the time of my leaving was at hand, all the parents, seeing the progress of their children and their improved behaviour at home, asked me, some of them with tears, to accept the office of regular schoolmaster, stating that they would take all the steps necessary to have me appointed by the Government. I was so deeply moved that I hesitated for a while, asking myself whether it might not be the will of God that I should accept that office, at least for a season, rather than that of a missionary, for which I felt myself so ill qualified. I again prayed earnestly to God to show me His will so clearly as to preserve me from all false steps. Meanwhile application was made in my favour to the chief pastor and school-superintendent of the district, the same who had baptized me; for without his sanction no master could be appointed. He at once declined to allow me to be elected, on the sole ground, he said, that I was a pietist. Thus my way was once more clear before me, and my soul was at rest.

Xo sooner was this settled than I received an invitation to go at once to Basle, in order to learn German there before entering the Missionary College, where all the lessons were given in that language. It was now the last week of 1819. When I informed the children of my summons to Basle, and told them that I should have to leave next day, there was such a general crying and sobbing that I was myself too much moved to be able to speak further to them then. I invited them to come to me in the evening, when I addressed them at some length, after which I prayed with them, commending them to God and to the Word of His grace. And so we parted with many tears and lamentations. I started next morning before daybreak, and on reaching the outskirts of the villacre I found all these dear children cjathered together to take leave of me once more. We again prayed and wept together.

I have thus dwelt upon that short period of my life.

because it was so richly blessed to me and to the children committed to my charge; wherefore I have often, when in far countries, remembered it with joy and gratitude to God. I may also add, with humble thanks to the Lord, that the greater number of those forty children became by degrees in after years truly converted, as I believe, to God.

CHAPTER 11.

PEEPAEATION IN BASLE, PARIS, AND LONDON FOR MISSIONARY WORK.

(1820-1825.)

A FEW days after my arrival in Basle, I met with an incident which I believe to have been providential, and which has had a great and blessed effect on my after life.

I was requested to accompany a certain M. Zeller to Zoiingen, in the Canton of Argau. This gentleman was then director of all the schools of the district of Zofingen, and professor at the gymnasium of that town; but he was afterwards better known as the founder and inspector of the educational establishment at Beuggen, near Basle.

We arrived at Zofingen late in the evening, and I remained the night at M. Zeller's house. The young children had already gone to bed, but Mme. Zeller brought them all into the room to welcome their father. As my love for children had greatly increased within the last few months, I took them all on my knee, one after another; among others a lively little girl of six years, who was destined to become in due time my companion, the sharer of my joys and trials, and the mother of my ten children.

This visit was the beginning of very friendly relations between M. and Mme. Zeller and myself, though neither they nor I thought of the still nearer relationship which was afterwards to exist. But that friendship and mutual confidence were the cause, humanly speaking, of their intrusting to me without hesitation their beloved daughter when, fourteen years later, I asked her to accompany me to Abyssinia, on whose soil perhaps no European woman had ever till then set her foot. But of this hereafter.

As the study of German was not enough to occupy my time, and as it was considered of great importance that a missionary should understand the art of printing, I was advised to devote as much time as possible to acquiring a competent knowledge of that branch of missionary work. I therefore began at once to work in a printing establishment until a new class of students should be received in the college, and this did not take place till the beginning of the following year.

During the whole course of the year 1820, almost all my days were spent in a somewhat monotonous routiae. Prom five to six o'clock in the morning I had a lesson in Latin from a private teacher, after which I went home, about ten minutes' walk, for breakfast. At seven I went to the printing-office till twelve. From twelve to one I dined and usually took a walk. From one to seven I was again at the office. From seven to eight I had a German lesson and then supper, after which I spent the remainder of the evening in reading and preparing my lessons for the next day.

I spent about nine months in setting the types, which proved very beneficial both for learning German and for acquiring knowledge of divers kinds. It also proved useful to me many years subsequently, when I was appointed to superintend the translating and printing establishment of the Church Missionary Society at Malta.

At first I did not relish the idea of spending so much time in learning this trade; but, convinced that I had been called of God, and thus providentially placed under the direction of the Missionary Committee, I had already made it a rule for my future life to implicitly follow the advice of my superiors in all things not opposed to the Word of God, reserving nothing to myself but the duty of obedience and the privilege of praying that God would direct them according to His holy will. If my compliance on that occasion involved some slight self-denial, it proved to be the means of great blessings, for that year was far from being the least happy and richly blessed of my life. Even in the midst of my work I felt my gracious Saviour ever present with me, and each leisure moment was spent in prayer and intercession. As far as I can recollect, I was almost exempt from temptation that year, probably because my whole time was usefully employed.

Sundays were a real delight to me. At eight o'clock in the morning I used to attend the ministry of the late M. von Brunn, a man full of love to God and man, and much sought after by all those who desired nourishment for their spiritual life. The remainder of the morning I was wont to spend in reading, chiefly the Bible. In the afternoon I attended another service, visited the old and infirm, partly in order to benefit by their Christian experience, and partly to read to them, not forgetting the poor and the sick of my acquaintance. The evenings I passed with the students of the college.

About Easter I paid a visit to my parents; and as there was only one cold and lifeless service at church, I proposed the first Sunday to hold a Bible-meeting in the afternoon at my father's house, to which about twenty persons came. They reported to others what they had heard, and the result was that I was invited to hold similar meetings every evening during the fortnight of my stay. Prom day to-day the number of attendants increased until the house was filled, and notwithstandino-the w eakness of the instrument, a real revival, under God's blessing, took place.

Just at that time, the late Eev. Haldane Stuart was travelling with two ladies through the Mlinsterthal. Heariug of these meetings, he resolved to make a little detour to ascertain the truth of what he had been told. He arrived at my father's house at about half-past ten A. M., and said at once that he could only stay about two hours; but that he should like to address a few words to the persons concerned if they could be brought together for a short time. This was rather a difficult matter, for it was the season of haymaking. It was Monday; a great quantity of hay had been cut, and every day of the previous week had been wet. Sunday had been hot and beautiful, and it was most important to take advantage of the fine Monday in order to bring in as much hay as possible; there was consequently little prospect of bringing many people together in the middle of the day to hear Mr. Stuart. However, my parents at once sent boys in all directions to invite people to come, and in less than an hour my father's house was, full of persons hungering and thirsting after the word of life.

I may here mention that M. Bost having been removed from a neighbouring parish, there was no evangelical pastor for many miles round, and he who had charge of our parish was not only spiritually dead, but also a scandalous drunkard. My mother mentioned these facts to Mr. Stuart before the meeting began.

A hen Mr. Stuart saw above a hundred people col- lected together under such circumstances, he seemed much moved; and after a short jjrayer, he addressed them for about half an hour in very bad French, so that they could not understand half of what he said. Yet, as the words came from a warm heart, their own hearts were touched, and a deep impression was made, which with some lasted to the end of their lives. As soon as he had finished his address, he hastened to the door to shake hands with his hearers as they went out, saying to each of them with great emphasis, "Dieu vous bless." (Blesser in French signifies to ivound.) Of course they did not know what he meant; but they were so sure that he desired for them something good, that they all said " Amen."

When I next met Mr. Stuart, thirty-six years afterwards, he said that he remembered that meeting, and that he felt the influence of the Holy Spirit to be present in that assembly of mostly poor country people.

I should here remark that in his address Mr. Stuart insisted much on the duty and necessity of his audience praying in common to God that He would send them a faithful shepherd. This made such an impression upon them, that from that day forward they not only prayed for such a pastor, but also believed that God would answer their prayer. In less than two years M. Gagnebin was appointed to the parish, the same faithful minister to whom I have already alluded earlier in this narrative, and who laboured so successfully in my native place for so long a term of years.

At the beginning of 1821, I was received as a student at the Missionary College at Basle, with twelve other young men, same from Switzerland, others from different parts of Germany. I had for long anticipated that event with great hope of spiritual enjoyment among dear brethren, and of more rapid increase in the grace and knowledge of our Lord and Saviour, Jesus Christ. But alas! for some time at least, my experience was to belie my bright expectations.

The very first day one of the new students arrived while we were at dinner, dressed in the most fashionable style, and having left his luggage at the posting-office. After dinner I offered to go with him to fetch his baggage, and as I thought that everything connected with missionary work ought to be done as economically as possible (a view which I still hold), instead of hiring a porter, I hoisted his good-sized portmanteau on to my own shoulder, and seeing that he had no inclination to carry anything himself, I took his carpet-bag in my hand. On the way back I observed that he studiously avoided walking by my side, always contriviug to go either before or after me. I could scarcely resist the conviction that he was a proud man, and, as such, unfit to be a missionary; but afraid to judge a brother, I was in great perplexity. However, I resolved to watch him for some days before forming any judgment as to his character. But it required only a few hours to know him thoroughly, and to see clearly that although he had felt powerfully the influence of the grace of God, the old man was still very strong within him, especially in the shape of envy, wrath, and extreme vanity. This little experience, added to the fact that the very next day I witnessed a quarrel between two students, idoth of whom were burning with rage, made me most miserable; so that I felt tempted to leave the college at once. However, a nearer acquaintance with other and pious students reassured me as to my being in the company of true children of God. I was perhaps rash in my judgment of those three candidates, though their subse- quent conduct made the same impression upon men of mucli greater experience than myself. As far as I could subsequently ascertain, they proved but indifferent missionaries. However, they have all preceded me to the tribunal of the Judge of the quick and the dead.

Whether the above experience was the cause, or only the developing agent of a great change in my inner life, I know not. But from that time during the greater part of my stay in college I had to pass through a state of inward darkness and trial such as I had not known before. I am inclined to think that it was my Heavenly Father who in His providence led me through that apparently gloomy w ay, which, in another seose, was light, since it proved to be the means of unveiling to my own eyes the deep corruption of my heart, of which I had no conception before. I had always hitherto retained a lively recollection of the sinfulness of my previous life in unbelief; but since I had tasted that the Lord is gracious, I had been walking in the light of His countenance;

even when I had taken a false step, committed a fault or neglected a duty, and a cloud hid His face from me in consequence, I had only to humble myself, confess my sin, and ask for pardon. I had felt as though treated with the indulgence of a spoiled child, probably because He knew that I had no earthly friend to lean upon. But now that I w as surrounded by dear brethren and faithful, experienced fathers. He doubtless found it necessary to subject me to a severer discipline. For more than two years I had enjoyed an almost uninterrupted sense of His presence; but now all this blessedness seemed to be gone all was changed. I prayed, but it was as if the Lord did not hear me. I no longer had the refreshing sense of the Lord's presence; only from time to time a ray of the light of His countenance pene- trated the gloom in which I was enveloped. I read my Bible, but without being able to taste its sweetness or experience its power. By degrees I fell into a kind of mournful spiritual apathy; in which state, although I studied very hard, I was assailed by manifold temptations, arising rather from within than without, until I abhorred myself as the worst and most corrupt of men, and often exclaimed, " 0 wretched man that I am!"

What puzzled me most was my necessity for struggling against three kinds of inward evils, which seemed to be utterly incompatible with my melancholy state of spiritual depression, namely, an unaccountable ever-flowing levity, of which I had until then felt very little, and which I had always abhorred, even in my unconverted state, in consequence, I believe, of deep and burning impressions made on my mind in my infancy by certain passages of Scripture against uncleanness. I was graciously preserved from yielding to that temptation, but its very presence made me feel vile.

Lioht-mindedness was another of these trials. Beincf naturally of a cheerful dis-position, I had always enjoyed a good joke; but now that I was under a deep sense of sorrow for my depravity, I concluded that it was incumbent upon me to maintain a serious and earnest frame of mind; and I judged it right, no doubt erroneously, to preserve a sombre, mournful aspect, as a means of moving God to be merciful to me. But behold, daily, chiefly at eventide, when I had been secretly confessing my sin and misery, and praying with many tears to be healed of my spiritual diseases, I would return to the room where the students were, resolved to be serious, but generally, at the very first moment, I would observe something at sight of which I felt an almost irresistible impulse to utter some witticism or sarcasm which would excite universal laughter; whereupon I would hasten back to my prayers and lamentations, only to repeat the experience on the next opportunity.

A third evil, by which I was much longer and most bitterly tried, was pride. I well knew that I had nothing to be proud of, for I was poor, weak, and ignorant, and yet I felt the sting of pride within my heart. I was conscious of possessing the power to acquire knowledge of various kinds, and I felt the desire to be, or to appear to be, something in the eyes of men. But " God resisteth the proud and giveth grace to the humble." The words fell like a thunderbolt on my heart; and in answer to my earnest supplications for true humility, a discipline came upon me which at first I did not understand. One humiliation after another fell to my share, of which I will mention but a few.

When, for example, I had fairly begun the study of any branch of knowledge, especially Greek and Hebrew (I never liked Latin), I was anxious to apply all my energy to it, and rose early in order to improve every available moment. But after a few days my eyes, which had always been weak, became inflamed, so that I was hindered from reading, sometimes for days together, whilst in lonoer intervals I was allowed to read and write for but a few hours daily. This, however, obliged me to think more, so that my time was not lost, though my pride was mortified by observing that the progress of weaker brethren was greater than my own.

Again, and this was a still greater mortification, in the quarterly examinations I did the paper work pretty well, but when it came to the oral part I never could succeed. While I thought I could answer every question that was addressed to my class-fellows, I was so nervous and confused when my own turn came, that I could hardly give a siugle reply. This was humbling enough. But when afterwards some of my teachers reproached me with having brought discredit upon them, or when others, like the Principal, the late excellent Herr Blumhardt, endeavoured to comfort and encourage me by saying that they knew my failure to be caused not by my ignorance, but by my bashfulness, my cup of humiliation was only embittered. At last, after many earnest prayers for true humility, I was enabled to perceive that all these successive humiliations were sent to me as an antidote to that very pride against which I had to struggle. I therefore heartily thanked God for them, and suffered no more from humiliation during the remainder of my stay at Basle.

Of my outward life during the two years and a half of my residence in the Missionary College I have but little to say. It was a monotonous routine of hard work every day, from five o'clock in the morning in summer and six in winter until ten at night, except Sundays and a short interval for daily recreation, half of which I spent in visiting the aged, the poor, and the sick. We had instruction in too many branches for us to make great progress in any one. Of Latin I only learned just enough to learn other languages through its medium, as Arabic and Ethiopia I delighted in the study of Hebrew and Greek; and although my knowledge of both was far from complete, yet at the end of my college course I could easily read the Xew Testament in Greek and the Old in Hebrew, with the exception of many passages in the Book of Job and a few in the Psalms and Prophets. I derived great benefit from reading in my leisure hours both Testaments in the originals with the late M. Kugler and Dr. Pfander. I also learned enough English to enable me to converse a little and to read English books.

Besides languages we studied a good deal of exegesis of both Testaments, critical and practical; Church history, dogmatic theology, c., both in the College and the University; together with exercises in the composition and delivery of sermons, and in catechising. Yet when I left the College, it was with a deep sense of my deficiencies, although I felt that my knowledge of the Bible, acquired from my earliest childhood, gave me an advantage over many of my fellow-students.

I always spent the first part of the five weeks' summer vacation with my parents, much enjoying spiritual converse with them, especially with my mother. Her conversation, and almost all the objects around me, by reminding me of my former life in unbelief, revived my sense of the love of God to me before I sought Him. It was, therefore, with a sense of love and thankfulness to Him, accompanied by deep sympathy with and love to those of my former companions who were still strangers to the love of God in Christ, that I gladly embraced the opportunity of holding Bible-meetings every evening. They were numerously attended; and the sight of those who had once been my fellows in unbelief and sin always touched me deeply, and gave me an easiness of utterance in which I was usually very deficient. I have reason to hope that each year some, even of the least promising, were added to the number of those that should be saved.

After spending two or three weeks with my parents, I was wont to take a tour through the country, visiting chiefly those towns and villages where the revival of religion, which had begun some years after the fall of Napoleon I., had flourished and spread. Oh! how delightful was it to come into contact with those people, chiefly the young, who had shortly before been brought over " from darkness unto light, and from the power of

Satan unto God with now and then an old man or woman who had weathered the storm of the French Eevolution and the season of almost universal godless-ness and infidelity, and had remained faithful to God their Saviour! They w ere more or less persecuted, some very severely, chiefly by their near relations and their unbelieving and worldly-minded pastors; but this kept the true disciples more closely together, and was the means of increasing their love to one another.

The aged disciples of the faith, having found it difficult enough to maintain their cause, though very edifying in private conversation and wise in giving advice when asked, were not aggressive, and very few of them ever ventured to address a meeting. Wherefore I was continually requested to hold Bible or prayer meetings. This I willingly did in the villages for the poor and uneducated; but in the towns, among people of a higher and better educated class, I was too timid to open my lips in public, and I several times refused to address religious meetings, though my conscience condemned me for my cowardice and want of faith.

On one occasion, however, I was invited by some noble ladies to visit them; and after I had accepted their invitation they extended it to a large number of their acquaintances and friends. No sooner had I arrived than the house began to fill with people of all classes, and the Bible was placed before me, with the request that I would give a practical exposition of some passage. I was in a measure taken by surprise, and was cowardly enough to decline; whereupon the same request was made to a minister present, who gave a long and dry explanation of the various parts of Solomon's Temple. Whilst he was speaking, and after he had finished, my heart was burning with remorse.

self-reproach, and pity for the poor hungry people who had come for bread and were offered gravel. Ashamed of myself, I went home to ask pardon for my want of courage, or rather my unfaithfulness; after which I made a firm resolution before God never to put myself forward on the one hand, but, on the other, never to refuse to preach the Gospel, in any form, when invited to do so. But oh! how many heart-beatings and agonies has that resolution since cost me!

At Easter of the year 1823 we had a week's holiday, which I spent with my parents, in company with two fellow-students, and greatly enjoyed.

While returning to Basle on foot, a distance of thirty miles, we had to cross a mountain. As we were crossing the plateau, without trees or other shelter, we were surprised by a heavy storm of cold wind and rain mixed with snow. We could not use our umbrellas on account of the gale, and were completely drenched. We had still twelve miles before us, and no means of changing our clothes. The next day we had each of us a most severe cold, attended with fever. My companions remained in bed for three or four days, and recovered fully. But I, who had never known what bodily ailment was, relying on my physical strength, would not acknowledge to myself that I. was ill, but studied as hard as I could for several days. But I was soon made to feel that my health was gone. Pain in the chest, palpitation of the heart, languor, and loss of appetite were the first symptons, and they gradually increased. Yet I kept it all to myself for a while, working as hard as ever, until my outward appearance told my superiors what was going on within, and I was put into the hands of physicians for two or three months. But the symptoms still increased, and at last the committee decided to send me to Geneva to consult the then famous physician, Dr. Butini.

I set off for Geneva in the beginning of July, travelling by short stages, now walking, now riding, and visiting many Christian friends on the way, all of whom showed me such tender affection as frequently to move me to tears.

At Yverdon I visited Pestalozzi's school, but found it a very dreary place, its glory already faded. There were eleven teachers, but they were at war with each other, and good old Pestalozzi was powerless to remedy the evil. Half an hour there was enough to show me that there was no unity in the establishment, and a few years later it fell to pieces. Poor Pestalozzi had built his otherwise excellent system on a wrong foundation, namely, on the supposition that human nature in children is good and only needs a sound development; wherefore it was impossible that in the long-run he could realise his sanguine expectations. Before his death he saw his error, for in 1826 he visited the educational establishment of my future father-in-law, who was teaching on the same system, but building on a very opposite foundation. When the good old man had examined everything during his four days' stay at Beuggen, he exclaimed with tears in his eyes, "This is what I have been seeking all my life long!"

Prom Yverdon I went to Lausanne, where I spent one day, Sunday. I was asked to hold a religious meeting there in the evening, to which I cheerfully consented. At that period there was a general and most bitter opposition in that town to evangelical religion. About twenty persons met together in a retired house for fear of being observed. We were discovered, however, and yet allowed to read and expound the Scriptures and to pray in comparative peace; but on leaving the house, we found a mob waiting for our exit to pelt us with stones. So far as I could learn, no one was seriously injured.

When I arrived at Geneva I was very weak, yet for a few days I was able to pay visits to Christian friends to whom I had letters of introduction. I was everywhere kindly received. Two very pious ladies, no doubt deeming it their duty to inform me in a delicate manner that I had not long to live, put into my hand letters wdiich they had just received from friends whom I had met on my way to Geneva. In one of these letters occurred the following sentence: " We have seen M. Gobat most likely for the last time, as his end appears to be rapidly approaching."

Dr. Butini ordered me to stay in bed, to apply large blisters to my arms and chest, and to take no food but asses' milk, and that in considerable quantities. Upon this regimen I subsisted for nearly three months.

I kept my bed for a month; and being in the house of a friend, I was nursed by his wife with all the tenderness of a mother. I trust that she has been abundantly recompensed of the Lord.

As I had been given to understand that I was hovering between life and death, those four weeks were a time of searching of heart, self-examination, and prayer, but, upon the whole, also of high spiritual enjoyment in the sense of my Saviour's presence. I was also favoured with the visits of many kind friends, among whom were Dr. Gaussen, Celerier, Malan, Empeytaz, Wilson, afterwards Bishop of Calcutta, and Gerard Noel.

That month expired. I was so far recovered that I could leave my bed, and I was advised to go into the country. I accordingly spent two happy months at Bourdigny, about five miles from Geneva, with two

English ladies, Miss Greaves and Miss Milne, afterwards Mrs. P. Gaussen. Their house was the resort of the excellent of the earth. I had the great privilege, the effects of which have been most beneficial to my after life, of enjoying the neighbourhood of Dr. Gaussen, then pastor at Satigny, about a mile from Bourdigny. We met almost daily, and our intimacy grew close and warm, developing into a life-long friendship between his family and my own. Even after his death we were always invited to take up our abode beneath the hospitable roof of his family whenever we were passing through Geneva.

As Miss Greaves' house was the rendezvous of more especially Christian society, so Dr. Gaussen's was the centre around which a circle of the dite, not only as regards religious excellence, but also intellectual culture, used to meet for mutual improvement and edification, to my great mental and spiritual benefit. About twice a week we used to read together the Epistle to the Eomans in the original, when my mind was enriched with many critical and practical views through the comments of Messrs. Gaussen, Gerard Noel, T. Erskine, and others. I did not fully agree with the two latter gentlemen, especially with Mr. Erskine; but as they were thoroughly acquainted with the Greek classics and the Ecclesiastical Fathers, their observations were most interesting and beneficial, especially as Dr. Gaussen always subjected such observations to acute logical criticism. Thus my stay of three months at and near Geneva proved as salutary to my heart and mind as to my enfeebled body.

My complaint,. which at first was complicated, affecting my whole chest and respiration, gradually abated, until there only remained an affection of the heart, or, as my physician said, a disease of the pericardium, for which, he added, he knew no remedy but moderation iu diet and in bodily and mental exertion, together with a mild climate. He therefore urged me to avoid spending the winter in Switzerland, and advised me to go at once to Italy, as the October cold had now set in. But as I had at that time an aversion to Italy, though during my illness I had studied the Italian language, I asked him whether there was any objection to my going to Paris instead, as I was desirous of studying Arabic there under the renowned Baron de Sacy. To my great delight he replied that Paris would do as well as Eome. Having been allowed a moderate diet for the past three weeks, my strength had wonderfully returned, so that towards the end of October I was able to return for a few days to Basle, and start thence for Paris at the beginning of November.

I remained in Paris until the end of October of the following year, 1824. The faithful warnings of my friends at Basle against the moral dangers to which I should be exposed in the French capital rendered me very uneasy in many respects; but after a severe struggle with my own corrupt heart, and a humble confession of my weakness, I dedicated myself, body, soul, and spirit, to the Lord for ever, and He graciously filled my heart once more with peace and joy.

Paris was to me a wilderness, especially at first; but I was abundantly supplied with heavenly manna and the water of life, so that the time spent there was greatly blessed, both to my own soul and, I trust, also not to mine alone. From the earliest days after my arrival, my life and occupations were so uniform, and in some sense monotonous, that I have only a few incidents to relate of that period. My chief occupation was the study of Arabic, of which I knew nothing; and as De

Sacy did not teach the rudiments of that language, I was obliged to take private lessons, which I did daily, except on Sundays, from M. Garcin de Tassi. I rose early in the morning, and worked till late in the evening, partly with the grammar and partly with the dictionary, which just suited the state of my health, as it was a labour of patience and memory, requiring little further exercise of the mind for a good while. My bodily exertion consisted in going to and from my teacher's, some distance from where I lodged, and towards evening taking a walk, generally in the garden of the Luxembourg, close at hand. I had a full hour's walk three times a week to the Bibliotheque Eoyale, where De Sacy gave his lessons; but, except just at first, I scarcely ever saw anything in the streets through which I passed. I was engaged in mental prayer and praise all the time; and if anything ever did strike me, I usually found it was something calculated to awaken my sympathy, and to incite me to pray more earnestly for the people among whom I was moving, and for the conversion of the benighted inhabitants of the great city.

My progress in Arabic was very slow at first. It took me several hours to read and understand a single verse of the Koran. But after having overcome the difficulties of the grammar, I advanced rapidly; so that at the end of eight or nine months I could compete with my fellow-students, who had been studying Arabic for three or four years. I could then read and understand the Koran in the original nearly as well as the Bible in my native tongue; for, supposing that I should be sent to labour among the Moslems, I had made that book my particular study, and committed the greater part of it to memory. De Sacy also did what he could to push me forward. On many occasions, once for three weeks at a time, I was alone in the class; yet he gave me the two full hours which it was his custom to give when twelve or fifteen pupils were present.

Paris w as then an extensive moral wilderness, producing scarcely anything but thorns, thistles, and poisonous herbs of divers kinds. There were, indeed, the learned and pious Herr Stapfer, formerly Swiss envoy to the French court; Professor Kiefer, and an old pastor, Soulier; but all the three were aged, living in retirement, and exercising very little Christian influence around them. There was also the excellent Frederick Monod, who, being the youngest of the four Eeformed pastors, used to preach only four times a year at the Oratoire. As he lived far from me and was scarcely ever at home, it being his duty to visit the hospitals, c., I but seldom had the pleasure of seeing him. The two senior pastors were Eationalists, and the third, M. Juillerat, though he preached the Gospel, did so without life or power. I have frequently heard since that he has much improved. The two Lutheran pastors were orthodox, but without spirituality.

There is still one man to be mentioned, who in many respects was my mentor. He was the prime mover in the different works of evangelisation which have since been established and carried on in Paris. This was the late Ptev. Mark Wilks, an English Independent minister, a man of weak health but of untiring energy. He was rather a poor preacher; his chief power lay in influencing individuals who were themselves men of influence, and in bringing them together to form committees for various good objects, as, for example, the Missionary and other societies.

As Mr. Wilks was my neighbour, I saw him several times every week, and lie committed into my hands sundry works which I, young, timid, and unknown, could never have initiated. The first was holding monthly missionary meetings at the Chapelle de roratoire. This institution began with an attendance of six persons; before I left Paris the re-unions numbered about three hundred.

The next was a weekly Bible-meeting. Mr. Wilks lived in a large house, in which there was a superior boarding-school for English and French girls, in about equal numbers. Now before I went to Paris, he was in the habit of assembling these girls together on Sunday evenings, and reading and expounding the Bible to them. Being but a poor French scholar, he could only do this in English, yet the French girls needed such instruction more than their British companions. Accordingly, soon after my arrival, Mr. Wilks proposed that I should hold these meetings in French on one Sunday, and he in English on the alternate one. This being arranged, he invited strangers to the French meetings. At the first, there was only one lady, Mme. Pelet de la Lozere, besides- the members of the school. The next time she brought the late Baron de Stael and another gentleman with her. The numbers increased from Sunday to Sunday, so that after a few weeks the English readings were given up. Before leaving Paris, I committed the conduct of these classes to the Piev. M. Galland, who had just arrived as first inspector of the French Protestant Missionary Society. Under his successor, M. Grandpierre, those meetings became the nucleus of the congregation of the Chapelle Taitbout still in existence.

About this time I made the acquaintance of a remarkable and learned man, Professor Kostan. He was a native of Marseilles, and had been for many years a zealous Eoman Catholic; so much so, that he had made a pilgrimage to Jerusalem. But his eyes had been so far opened at the Church of the Holy Sepulchre, that lie returned to France convinced that the Church of Eorae, as it then existed, could not be of Divine institution. He had, therefore, begun to study the Bible in the original languages, and, in consequence, had been led to cordially embrace, without knowing it, all the essentials of Protestantism. The little he had heard of so-called Protestant teaching was mere dead Neology; wherefore he had not yet openly left the Church of Eome. He told me that he had been induced to seek my acquaintance by having heard me utter the same truths concerning the person of our Lord Jesus Christ, the Atonement, c., as he had found in the Bible. He had been more especially interested in what he had heard me say concerning the cause of the sufferings and dispersion of the Jews, and their future restoration to the covenant of God and to their own land.

He told me that he knew many Jews in Paris, and we finally agreed to invite as many of them as we could to weekly meetings, and endeavour by means of the Old Scriptures to lead them to Christ. We began at once. On the first occasion we had only about half a dozen. We decided that M. Eostan and I should expound alternately any portion of the Old Testament which the Jews themselves should choose, on condition that they would allow us to speak for an hour, did the subject require it, without interruption; after which they should be free to make any remarks they liked. These meetings continued for several months, and were attended by from thirty to fifty Jews, who all behaved very well One evenin;, when it was M. Eostan's turn to address them, they chose for his text the first cliapter of the Book of Numbers. I could not help strongly suspecting that they had made this selection in order to perplex my friend, as that chapter contains scarcely anything but names and numbers. However, M. Eostan developed it with such pathos, clearness, and power, that many Jewish eyes were wet with tears. In solemn accents he began with the following words, which, after forty-four years, are still fresh in my memory:

"My dear friends of the House of Israel! If the Bible contained only this chapter, it should be enough to convince you that you are fallen from the covenant of God. Look at the good order of your fathers whilst God was with them as their covenanted God. They were indeed one body of many members, and each member knew its proper place, the tribe and family to which it belonged, its privileges, and its duties in the economy of the whole undivided body. ISTotwithstanding their manifold failings, they had the consciousness that God was with them, their Guide and their Protector. Now compare that model state with your present condition. Dispersed among all the nations of the earth, like erring sheep without a shepherd, none of you knowing to what tribe he belongs, cast out of the heritage of your fathers, the securing of which to this people was part of God's covenant with Israel; without Levites, without priests, without sacrifices, almost completely deprived of all the statutes and ordinances which constituted your ancient commonwealth. All this must prove to you that, for the present, God has rejected you from being His people; and as God is a righteous and holy God, it presupposes some crime of which the whole nation is guilty some crime worse than all the sins of your fathers in the wilderness, for which God chastened, but did not reject them; worse than the idolatry and gross immorality of Israel described by the prophets, that were the cause of the Babylonish captivity, which lasted only seventy years; whereas your present captivity has already lasted eighteen centuries. And what can that crime be other than your rejection of Messiah, your lawful King, who had come to save you Jesus of Nazareth, whom you condemned to die upon the accursed tree? Do not say that you are innocent of the deeds of your fathers, for every Israelite who rejects, that is, refuses to believe in, Jesus of Nazareth, and to acknowledge and submit to Him as his Lord and Saviour, identifies himself with those who crucified Him eighteen hundred years ago.

"But it grieves me," added M. Eostan, " to be obliged to remind you of these things, which are only a necessary prelude to the encouraging words which it is also my agreeable duty to address to you. Hear, then, the good tidings of salvation. God draws good out of evil, and the wrath of man was destined to contribute to His praise. When the brethren of Joseph sold him, they committed a great crime; but by the good providence of God it proved the means of saving them, their families, and thousands of other people. So likewise the selling, rejecting, and murder of Jesus the Messiah by your fathers was a horrible crime; but His atoning death has already proved the cause of salvation to millions; and oh! believe it, it will at last prove the source of the salvation and restoration of the whole now captive people of Israel!"

As M. Eostan, soon after my departure from Paris, declared himself publicly to be a Protestant, and went to America, where he was ordained a minister of the Gospel, I very soon lost all traces of those Israelites, who had certainly hearkened attentively to the Gospel for several months.

My private life in Paris was uneventful. I studied hard, especially in endeavouring to acquire a thorough knowledge of the Mohammedan religion as contained in the Koran. After the Bible, I do not remember having ever read any book with more profit than the Koran. I will say nothing of its linguistic charms; but, by the blessinct of God, all its contents had the effect of raisiugf my heart in prayer and thanksgiving. It certainly contains a few sublime passages, alike as to style, form, and moral value; but such are not frequent in that horrible book. It was chiefly the perusal of its masses of nonsense and puerility, its gross immorality, its perversion of the truth, its blasphemies, which moved me to compassion so strong, that often in the midst of my reading I felt constrained to fall on my knees, and, with many tears, to pray for the millions of deluded and perishing Moslems; and this again and again renewed in me the sense of communion with God my Saviour.

At the beginning of the summer vacation I was urgently requested by the late Pastor Colani of Leme in Picardy to visit the numerous congregations gathered chiefly by his faithful labours from the Ptoman Catholic Church in Picardy and Flanders. Formerly, there had been great numbers of Protestants in those parts, who, under severe persecutions, had been tempted to join the Church of Eome. They seemed to have retained some love for Scriptural truth; for when Colani began to go about from place to place preaching the pure Gospel, he found many doors open to him, and people returned to their former faith by hundreds. These formed themselves into congregations, and built a great number of small temples at distances of from ten to thirty miles. It was perhaps the most extensive revival of this century, but it took place without noise and unnecessary excitement.

For several years Colani had been regularly visiting, preaching to, and edifying those dear country people, directing them to search the Scriptures for themselves, and to meet together frequently for that purpose. He also furnished them with a collection of excellent sermons to be publicly read in their churches on the Sundays when he could not be with them.

But at the time of which I speak, the simple people were in great danger of being led astray from the purity of their faith and from their Christian practice. Poor M. Colani had been ill for two years, during which time some Baptists, who seldom attack Eoman Catholics or infidels, had been oinf about amonsj these conojregations of neophytes, troubling them by telling them that they could not be saved except by adult immersion. Yery few had embraced this doctrine, but many were in doubt as to whether, after all, infant baptism by affusion was valid; and contentions had begun in several quarters on this subject. M. Colani suffered terribly to see his worlv thus marred, and invited me to q; o and counteract the incipient dissensions.

I at once decided upon going, and took the diligence the same day for St. Quentin and Leme. But I must have been watched; for that very evening a Baptist preacher took the extra-post, and arrived at Leme before me. It was no time for quarrelling about baptism, nor was I minded to do so, particularly as, from what I had previously heard of liim, I believed him to be a sincere Christian, notwithstanding his opinion on that great doctrine. As he was my superior in age and eloquence, I allowed him the precedence, and decided upon following in his track at an interval of a few days. The next day being Sunday, we both preached at Leme; for M. Colani judged wisely that, by refusing to allow

Liin to preach, he would have given him occasion for doin!: f more mischief.

I remained at Leme for a few days to receive information and advice from the faithful and experienced Colani, after which I began a five weeks' tour, visiting a great number of congregations, large and small, chiefly in the wake of the Baptist preacher. I conducted services, after which many members of the different congregations usually accompanied me to my lodgings, and remained w ith me until midnight conversing on relioiious subjects. They took so deep an interest in the missionary cause that many poor families had given up the use of salt in order to be able to contribute to missionary societies. There was such animation and interest manifested in those free conversational meetincjs, that no weariness was felt; and the next morning those who wished to talk with me more privately on matters re-lathig to their soul would present themselves at my door before sunrise.

The result of my mission to these worthy people was that, with very few exceptions, they resolved to abide by their allegiance to their pastor, Colani, and to follow his advice; so that I was afterwards informed that all was again in order.

After my return to Paris I wrote a report of what I had seen and heard in the North, which Herr Blumhardt published in the Missionary Magazine in 1824. The contents of that letter gladdened the hearts of many believers in Germany, though many thought that I had exaggerated. Among the latter was the late Herr Giitz-laff, missionary to China, who was then living at Eotter-dam. He, like many other Prussians, could not believe that a Frenchman could be a Christian. Therefore, on first reading my report, he pronounced it to be a fabrica- tion; but on a second perusal, he found in it so many marks of truth, that he resolved to go to the various places I had mentioned and see for himself. He accordingly in 1825 visited all the places I had mentioned, and found that, far from my having exaggerated, I had under-stated the facts. He then walked from St. Quen-tin to Paris in order to make my acquaintance; and Avhen told that I was in London, he at once started for England, where we formed a pleasant acquaintance with each other.

During the first few winter months in Paris my health was rather delicate, but without any serious symptoms; but in the spring I had frequent palpitations accompanied by giddiness, which obliged me to lie down at once, no matter where I chanced to be. Whilst moving about in Picardy these attacks became more frequent and more serious, until one day, while walking with a friend, I lost consciousness, and had to be carried to the nearest house, about two miles distant. On the first opportunity I consulted a physician, who bled me, in consequence of which I was free from those alarming symptoms for two months. He advised me to undergo the same treatment whenever the symptoms should return. The first experiment having proved so beneficial, I purchased a lancet, and thenceforth, for the space of nearly ten years, I operated upon myself when necessary; and, with the exception of these attacks, which happened about four or five times in a year, I enjoyed comparatively good health, without any serious illness. The final cure of my heart complaint was in itself a very painful one, being nothing else but a most severe illness, which prostrated me while in Abyssinia, and lasted two years.

Towards the end of October 1824 I left Paris and returned to Basle. While there, I was invited to hold religious meetings for the French-speaking population of that town, they being much more scantily provided with means of grace than their German-speaking neighbours. I gladly accepted the proposition, and began at once. But when, after three or four weeks, these meetings began to be numerously attended, a great outcry arose, as if I were trying to introduce some strange religion. At length, the chief magistrate, himself a man of piety, intimated to me that although he personally approved of my proceedings, he would yet advise me to give them up for the present, on account of the bitter opposition they had excited. After consulting some experienced friends, I adopted his counsel, and reluctantly closed the meetings. However, notliing was lost; for soon after this the newly appointed French pastor, M. Grandpierre, continued the meetings, and conducted them with great success.

I then spent some delightful and profitable weeks with my parents and a few of their chosen friends, after which I was directed by the committee of the Basle Missionary Society to make a tour of five weeks through Switzerland to visit the friends, especially the clerical friends, of the Society. During this journey I had the privilege of visiting many excellent and pious persons, foremost among whom I would name M. Binder of Ziefen, from whose wise and loving dealing with my youth and inexperience I derived much benefit; especially as, finding that the majority of those with whom I met paid deference to me as the learned pupil of the great De Sacy, I was beginning to be aware of an evil tendency to exalt myself in my own eyes. Perhaps M. Binder had observed this, for he took the opportunity, as soon as we were alone, to catechise me on a great number of subjects of which I was ignorant, and upon which I could give no satisfactory answers. I was ashamed and confounded, yet his manner was so gentle and loving that I was able to receive the lesson in all humility. I lost no time in making confession to God of my pride and self-love, and in asking pardon at His gracious hand. Since then, so far as I can remember, I have never again lost the consciousness of my ignorance and manifold shortcomings.

At that time the Missionary Society of Basle had ah eady begun the practice, which was continued for many years afterwards, of sending annually several of tlieir students to England to be employed by the Church Missionary Society, as the latter institution had more money than men, while the former had more men than money for missionary work. It is much to be regretted that the connection between the two Societies has been discontinued, for it contributed much to develop mutual love and sympathy between Christians in England and their brethren on the Continent. The Basle students were then ordained on the Continent, the Church Missionary Society, in imitation of the Propagation Society in its infancy, never requiring the foreign missionaries to be episcopally ordained. It was only after many years, when most of such missionaries labouring in India had, of their own accord, sought episcopal ordination, that the two Societies came to the friendly agreement that the Basle missionaries should, at the outset, be ordained in England, and no longer on the Continent. Whether that first arrangement was right or wrong it is not for me to decide; but I hope the Church Missionary Society will never have cause to repent of its abolition, though, at the jubilee of the Society for the Propagation of the Gospel, the Bishop of Oxford exhorted its members to weep for having formerly employed missionaries who were not episcopally ordained, irrespective of the great success that had attended their ministry.

On my return from my Swiss tour the committee decided to send me to England. As I had not yet been ordained, though licensed to preach, it was arranged that the rite should take place in the United Church of the Grand Duchy of Baden, where the Lutheran and the Eeformed Churches had been united. I was consequently ordained on the 25th of February, without any previous examination, and with so little solemnity, that if I had not been impressed from within, and by the conversation of my companion, the late celebrated Dr. Stier, with a sense of the importance and responsibility of the office, the ceremony itself would certainly have failed to produce such an impression.

It was much against my inclination that I was appointed to go to England; and I was further given to understand that, on account of my knowledge of Arabic and Italian, I was to be subsequently stationed at Malta to help Mr. Jowett in the translation and printing of books and tracts in those and other lanoua es. Like many people on the Continent, I had strong prejudices against the English, owing to the rude and proud behaviour of many would-be English gentlemen. Yet, being convinced that from the first I had been providentially placed under the direction of the Basle Missionary Committee, I had long since resolved to submit myself implicitly to their decrees, believing that God would thus lead me by a better way than I could choose for myself.

Here I may observe, that having acted through life upon this principle of seeking and submitting to the highest guidance, I have never tried to change my position; yet, from my father's house, from the plough, I have been called and led through Basle, England, Malta, and Abyssinia by the Basle and Church Missionary Societies, by the committee of the Malta College, and, lastly, by the late King of Prussia, to my present position as Bishop of the Church of England and Ireland in Jerusalem. Yet, when the time arrived for me to start for England, and I went to take leave of the individual members of the Basle Committee, I opened my mind to the warm-hearted, venerable President of the Society, the late Herr von Brunn, and told him of my misgivings and fears lest I should not be able to work with my English colleagues. I asked him whether, in case I found my apprehensions justified by the event, he saw any objection to my relinquishing my post, instead of remaining to quarrel, and going on my own account to Abyssinia, there to preach the Gospel, while earning my bread by the labour of my hands. He smiled, and only said, "Commit yourself to the Lord, and He will guide you in the right way."

I should mention that a short time previous to this I had been reading the history of the mission of the Jesuits to Abyssinia in the sixteenth century, and the narrative had excited in me the deepest sympathy and compassion for the poor Abyssinians. This sympathy only took deeper root during my five years' sojourn in their country, and ever since that episode it has grown and increased. I have always cherished the conviction that, notwithstanding the errors, superstition, and immorality of the masses, God must still have a people more or less numerous in Abyssinia; otherwise their Church, defaced, it is true, by many errors, yet holding such essential doctrines as that of the Trinity, the Divinity and Incarnation of Christ, and the Atonement, could not have been preserved for twelve hundred years, surrounded as it has been by bigoted Moslems and savage heathens.

When I spoke to Herr von Brunn, I had not the least idea that any missionary society had ever thought of evangelising Abyssinia. What, then, was my agreeable surprise when, a few days later, on my arrival in England, I was asked by the committee of the Church Missionary Society whether I was ready to start for Abyssinia with Herr Kugler. I of course replied with alacrity that I was prepared to go thither. That coincidence confirmed my conviction that the call was from God; and ever after, in the midst of dangers, temptations, and tribulations, the belief has been an unfailing source of comfort to me.

It was towards the end of March when I arrived in London, in company with Herr Lieder. On alighting from the stage-coach, we hired a hackney-carriage and were driven for four hours through the streets of the vast, unknown city before we reached Islington. But when we inquired for the Church Missionary College, no one could tell us where it was. We were therefore in the greatest perplexity, having no other address but that of the College, which, having been but recently opened, was not yet known in the neighbourhood. At last I remembered the name of the Vicar of Islington, the Rev. Dr. Wilson, afterwards Bishop of Calcutta. We drove to his house, and there we found a guide to take us to the College.

We were received with brotherly kindness by the students, but with stiffness by the Principal, the late Eev. K. Pearson, who afterwards proved, however, a warm friend and brother to me. At the very first interview lie requested me to write a sermon on Eom. v. i, which was to be presented to and read by the committee on the second day thereafter. It happened to be a text to which I had already devoted considerable thought, aided by some of the best Endish and German commentators, so that I found the task an easy one; and although my English vas bad enough, the sermon impressed certain members of the committee with a much higher notion of my attainments than I deserved. This caused me some uneasiness, for I was afraid that I should sink in their estimation in proportion to their closer acquaintance with my capabilities.

During the seven months spent in England, I much enjoyed the society of Mr. Pearson and his family, and also that of several of the missionary students, especially Cochrane, afterwards Archdeacon of Eupertsland, and H. AVilliams, subsequently Archdeacon of New Zealand. But my chief associate was the gifted and deeply pious Mr. C. Eriend, who died in India on the very threshold of his missionary career. I have maintained cordial relations wdth his family to this day. I also from time to time spent profitable hours with several Christian families in the neiqhbourhood of the College.

Apart from these associations, my time in London passed in a very monotonous manner, as in a species of solitude. I spent the greater part of my days in my room in study, prayer, and the perusal of edifying books, such as Baxter's " Saint's Best," and Leighton on St. Peter, which latter I enjoyed very much.

It was evident to me that the committee found it difficult to find properly qualified missionary candidates, for several of my fellow-students were very deficient, not only in knowledge, but also in intellectual capacity and true piety, in humility and self-denial, though their conduct w as upright notwithstanding these serious defects.

It was my privilege to frequently see the Secretaries of the Society, Messrs. Pratt and Bickersteth, whose conversation was always edifying and encouraging to me. Under their influence my prejudices against the English soon began to give way.

My prejudice against the form and the length of the services of the Church of England lasted for a longer time, perhaps because I had permission to attend the German services of the late Dr. Steinkopf. Of this privilege I availed myself perhaps too freely.

I had been about two months in England when a trifling incident happened, which for a time strengthened my prejudice. It was my custom, when I did not go to Dr. Steinkopf's church, to attend St. Mary's; and the sermons of the vicar always delighted me. But as the church was always very full, T was often obliged, though not strong in health, to stand during the whole service.! N"ow, having observed that the persons who were best dressed were always the first to be conducted to seats, although not seat-holders, I yielded to the temptation of resorting to an artifice. I happened to possess a large and beautiful ring. One Sunday morning I put it on and repaired to church as usual. I stood for a minute or two with other people of divers classes near the door. Then, taking off my glove, I raised my hand with apparent carelessness to my ear, and immediately I was led to a comfortable seat. I thought of St. James ii. 2, 3; and this revived for a while my fading prejudice against the Engflish Church.

My prejudice, however, was not against her episcopacy or her doctrines, but against the repetitions and the length of her services, together with the dead formalism of many of her members, both lay and clerical, which I had already observed on the Continent.

As it was ae ainst the rule for the En owlish students to attend Dissenting chapels, I never thought of infringing that regulation, though I wished to judge for myself of the services of Dissenters. Mr. Pearson, however, himself advised me on one occasion to attend the service conducted by a pious and experienced Independent. I went, and on entering the chapel was at once conducted to a seat. This made a iavourable impression upon me.

The service began with a hymn, after which a portion of the Word of God was read. Then came what was called prayer, the whole congregation standing for about an hour. The minister was evidently under the impression that his prayer must occupy a certain long space of time. He began tcdhiiig to God, telling Him with many details what He is and what He is not, what He has done and what He has not done, though He might have done it, and so forth. It was all true enough, but not calculated to satisfy the cravings of a hungry soul. The second part of the prayer, though wanting unction, was appropriate, containing confessions, petitions, intercessions, and thanksgivings; but, exhausted by the first part, I did not relish the second, and had no power left to throw my soul into the supplications. I thought I observed the same weariness in my neighbours, who, like myself, had been most attentive to the first part.

From that day I liked the Liturgy of the Church of England; and though the morning service may be too long for children and weak people, it is not tedious to those who have communion with God. I soon learned to thank God even for the repetitions of the Lord's Prayer; for whilst the ofhciating minister is reading it, my mind is often absorbed in one petition to the exclusion of the rest. Then, when it is repeated, I endeavour to realise another petition, and so on; thus it is to me as if in reality it w ere read only once, and in my opinion this is the most beneficial way of using it. It is as if it were read slowly, with a moment's silence after every clause.

As during my seven months' stay in London I had no outward duty imposed upon me except that of occasion- ally holding a German Bible-class for Dr. Steinko Df, and giving Greek lessons to several students with the exegesis of the ISTew Testament, I spent almost all my time in the study of the Hebrew, Arabic, and Ethiopic languages, under the tuition of the late learned Professor Lee. My dear brother and future colleague, Kugler, shared the Hebrew lessons with me. In the two other languages I enjoyed the entire attention of the professor, wherefore I made considerable progress. AVhen, one morning at breakfast, the Ethiopic grammar, with its alphabet of 209 forms of letters, of which I did not know one, was put into my hand, I remembered with shame that when I began the study of Arabic, a year and a half before, it had taken me several days to learn the alphabet, and I at once resolved that it should not be so with the Ethiopic. I therefore repaired to my room, shut the door, and wrote upon it, "I will not open thee until I can read Ethiopic." I had calculated that it would take me the whole day; but, behold! at the end of two hours I could read pretty fluently. But I lost my appetite and had a severe headache for two days afterwards. At an examination about five months later, I could translate the songs of Mary and of Zacharias, with two chapters of Hosea, from the Ethiopic into Latin without the help of any dictionary.

I had almost forgotten to mention that during my stay in London I followed a course of practical or family medicine, given to several missionary students by a warm friend of missions, Mr. Eernandez. I did not much relish that study, yet the little that I learned proved of great utility to me afterwards, especially in Abyssinia.

About the beginning of November I received my commission from the committee, together with fifteen of my fellow-students. Some were told off for India, some for New Zealand, others for Western Africa, my dear Coch- rane for Xortli America (Red Eiver), and five for the Mediterranean (Egypt and Abyssinia).

The instructions, general and particular, were imparted to us at a largje meetiugj at Freemasons' Hall. The scene was a solemn and impressive one. I believe that all of us who were being commissioned deeply felt our weakness, and the weight of the responsibility laid upon us; but the tone of the instructions, the prayers offered up, and the sympathy of those present with the missionaries about to enter on their career, all was calculated to comfort and strengthen us, not on that day only, but for years to come.

The occasion was the more solemn for me, because I had been requested by the committee to speak in answer to the instructions given to us. I was nervous, for it was the first time I had addressed a meetinoj of so hi h and refined a class of persons, and

I was conscious of speaking very bad English. But the sympathy to be observed on many faces before me was so encouraging, that I felt quite at home at the time, whilst the remembrance of it has often sweetened the bitterness of the trials through which Providence has led me for many after years.

CHAPTEE III.

FIRST MISSIONAEY JOUENEY TO PALESTINE AND EGYPT. (1826-1829.)

We were now ready to start for Malta. Kugler and Kruse were to proceed- by tlie direct sea-route, while Miiller and Lieder had permission to return to Switzerland, to take to themselves each a wife. As this involved a journey from Switzerland through France to Marseilles, I was requested to accompany them; for neither of them was acquainted with the French language.

We halted for two days in Paris, and were on the point of leaving that city to continue our journey, when we received a letter from Herr Blumhardt, written in the name of the Missionary Committee at Basle, strongly advising us to go from Paris straight to Marseilles; intimating as his reason for this counsel that the committee were adverse to missionaries cjettino: married. But as we had already paid for our places in the diligence, the letter arrived too late, and we proceeded to Basle.

Almost immediately after our arrival, we were invited to appear before the committee, by whom we were rather coldly received. After a solemn silence of some minutes, the President addressed us in a grave tone, and spoke for about half an hour against marriage in general, and against the marriage of missionaries in particular. As the substance of his speech did not then concern me, I was in a position to criticise it with an impartial mind; and I found in it many good reasons against the marriage of missionaries, at least before they have made a fair trial of their calling. As, however, he omitted to mention the reasons in favour of such marriages, his onesided address failed to convince my two brethren that they were wrong in wishing to be married; and as his arguments against marriage in general seemed to be taken from his own personal domestic experience, their effect was rather that of sympathy with his misfortune than concurrence in his views.

When he had finished his harangue, the good old man turned to me and asked me, in a melancholy tone, what I thought of the matter now; to which I answered, rather lightly, that I was only there as interpreter, and had no wish to marry at present. This reply caused visible surprise to the members of the committee; and I afterwards ascertained that it had been believed among them that I had for a long time past been engaged, while residing at their college and in disobedience to their rules. Their satisfaction was great when I added to my explanation that, even before entering the college, I had resolved not to think of marrying until I had spent a few years in the missionary field.

The sequel to this little episode was that one of my companions, in the face of Pastor Von Brunn's arguments, married shortly afterwards, while the other discovered that the young lady who had encouraged his hopes had no intention of uniting herself with him, and therefore had to remain a bachelor for thirteen years to come.

On the 30th of January 1826 I started from Berne, with Mliller and his young wife and Lieder, for Malta; but it proved to be a long and tedious journey. We travelled first to Lausanne, where, there being no public conveyance from Geneva to Marseilles, we had previously made an agreement with a coachman to take us to Marseilles in twelve days. On reaching the frontier of Savoy, all our books and tracts were taken from us, and we were obliged to send them back to Geneva. Our next difficulty was at Grenoble, where we were arrested on the plea that our passports, vism at Berne, were not in order. We were told that they must be sent to Paris, which would have detained us at least a fortnight at Grenoble under the surveillance of gendarmes. However, we di overed that it was only a trick to extort money from us; for after three days our passports were restored to us, and we were allowed to continue our journey.

At Marseilles we were obliged to wait a long and dreary month before we could find an opportunity of moving towards Malta. At last, finding that there was no hope of any vessel sailing for Malta for a long time, we took passage in a French ship bound for Messina, in hope of finding there an opportunity of getting on to Malta. We had a most wearisome passage, rendered well nigh intolerable by the uncleanness of everything we saw on board. We sailed with a light wind, and in five days reached the neighbourhood of Corsica, when the wind suddenly changed, causing great confusion and sea-sickness on board; and on the following afternoon we landed at Toulon, where we had to spend three long days until the east wind ceased to blow.

Quitting Toulon, we sailed on for five days; but on the morning of the sixth day, the wind being fresh, as English sailors would like to have it, our French sailors took refuge at Gaeta, where we were put in quarantine, and kept in harbour for twelve days, until we passengers sent an express to the King of Naples, who in two days thereafter sent us the gracious permission to continue our voyage. There was evidently foul play, and we suspected that our sailors were engaged in smuggling.

From Gaeta we sailed in three or four days, with good weather, for Messina, where we were again put in quarantine for seven days; after which we much enjoyed a week's liberty in that beautiful spot. We were, however, greatly annoyed by priests following us in the streets and whispering evil suggestions in our ears, and not only in the streets, but in the very cathedral itself. We were more than once tempted to give them a sound thrashing; but, remembering the influence they had over a bigoted, ignorant people, we only reproved them in words, at which they laughed. Oh, how we pitied these deceivers and their miserable dupes of Popery, to whom I could only attempt to speak of better things in broken Italian!

And now, after all these delays, we found the means of starting for Malta in a Maltese esperonade, a small open boat, in which we five passengers, for there was an English gentleman with us, had scarcely space to stretch ourselves. Two days later we touched at Gozo, and soon after arrived at Valetta, forty-nine days after our departure from Marseilles.

On landing at a spot called " Mx Mangiare," we had to answer many questions about ourselves, our native land, the object of our voyage, and so forth. This catechism ended, we were asked to deliver up our passports, which were examined, we thought, rather too leisurely, seeing that we were standing all the time in the hot April sunshine surrounded by a mob of Maltese beggars, who filled our ears with their cries of " Mx Mangiare." The investigation of our passports completed, we were asked whether we knew any one in Yaletta who would be surety for us; for without this precaution we should not be allowed to enter the city.

We mentioned Mr. Jowett, and were requested to send for him, which we hastened to do, and in a shorter time than we had expected, dear Mr. Jowett arrived to our great comfort, not only because his presence was the signal for our release, but chiefly because from the first moment we, or at least I, felt a congeniality of heart and mind with him, which in a few days resulted in an affectionate friendship. This attachment lasted undisturbed until his death, and I trust it will be renewed to endure throughout eternity.

My companions did not remain in Malta, but went on at once to join Kugler and Kruse and his wife at Alexandria. I was detained in the island for four months, correcting Arabic tracts which Mr. Jowett had caused to be translated, and which he intended to have published. It was rather tedious work, but I was abundantly compensated by the pleasure I enjoyed in association with tlie Jowett family, with whom I lived.

At the appointed time, after taking a cordial leave of Mr. Jowett and his family, together with a few other Christian friends, I embarked for Alexandria, where I arrived after a stormy and somewhat eventful voyage, on the 26th of August 1826.

It was my intention to start with my colleague, Herr Kugler, as soon as possible for Abyssinia. Instead of this, we were obliged to remain in Egypt for more than three years (with the exception of a six months' tour in Syria and Palestine), waiting for an opportunity to proceed to our destination. The reason of this trying delay was that the entrance into that country by way of Massowa was universally considered to be absolutely shut against all Europeans. Several great travellers had attempted it in vain.

We had been advised before leaving England to go by way of Nubia, but on arriving in Egypt we heard that the Arabs of Shindy, having murdered Ismael Pasha, son of Mohammed Ali, had taken refuge in the mountains bordering Abyssinia on that side, and would not allow any white man to pass that way. I shall presently state how Providence opened the way before us through inhospitable Massowa.

When I arrived in Egypt, I found that I could not understand the natives, or make myself understood by them. The reason of this lay partly in my defective pronunciation, but chiefly in the fact that I spoke the language of the Koran, which was only understood by a few of the better educated among them. The four brethren who had arrived some months before me were my interpreters, though they had not even begun the study of Arabic before leaving Europe. They had learned it by practice. I was ashamed of myself, but I soon discovered the importance of a thorough grammatical study of good authors. Two months later, when I had acquired the vulgar pronunciation, and measured in some degree the capacity of the people, these brethren wanted me as their interpreter in the more important conversations; and after the space of a year, I could begin to preach every Sunday to from twenty to forty people, almost as easily as in my native tongue.

After spending a few days at Alexandria, I started for Cairo with Kugler and Lieder, and remained there till the end of January 1827. Scarcely anything worthy of notice happened during that time. Seeing that we could not then proceed to Abyssinia, we sought for some person to teach us Amharic, the vernacular language of that country. After much searching we found a young Abyssinian monk, named Girgis, very ill, lying in the dust at the gate of the Armenian convent. We took him into our house, where he soon recovered, gave him new clothes, and made him our almost constant companion.

He knew only a few words of Arabic, but he possessed extraordinary skill in explaining the meaning of words, and in helping us to construe short sentences. We therefore made great progress under his" tuition. Our only books in Amharic were the four Gospels, the Book of the Acts of the Apostles, and the Epistle to the Eomans, which we read with him, and which made a deep impression upon him. After advancing so far as to be able to speak a little, we felt it desirable to have the opportunity of conversing with more than one person. We therefore resolved to visit Palestine, and to spend some time with the thirty or forty Abyssinians residing at Jerusalem.

At the end of January we that is to say, Kugler, I, and our Girgis accompanied by Mr., afterwards Dr., Smith, of the American Mission, and the Eev. Theodor Miiller, started from Cairo through the desert, by way of El-Ariesh, Gaza, and Ascalon, to Jaffa. Nothing worthy of note happened on the journey, which we enjoyed very much, spending our twelve days on camels, and our evenings under our tent in brotherly Christian conversations.

The day after arrival at Jaffa, after visiting its sandy environs, which have since been converted into blooming gardens, we embarked in a small open boat for Beyrout, where Mr. Smith was to be stationed with the other missionaries, Messrs. Bird and Goodell, with whom we spent a delightful fortnight. They could then do very little, for want of access to the people. For a short time previously Assaad Shidiac had been imprisoned for the truth's sake by the cruel Maroiiite Patriarch, under whose Satanic hatred against the Word of God he died a martyr at the convent of Canobin, after suffering every kind of indignity for several years. The people, therefore, were afraid of the approach of the missionaries. It was only when the night was far advanced that some timid Nicodemus would knock at their door, and spend a few hours with them in religious conversation.

Towards the end of February we started for Damascus, leaving Messrs. Smith and Mtiller at Beyrout, and taking with us a converted Armenian bishop named Dionysius. The road was at that time very little frequented, especially in winter. We found the way very rough, and had three days of it before reaching Damascus.

On the eastern descent of Lebanon, as I was riding alone, in advance of our little caravan, down a ravine, I saw the head of an animal lying among the thorns on my left hand, about six yards from me, and about fifteen feet higher than my head. As it was not much larger than the head of a cat, I had no idea of danger, yet I stopped to look at it until my companions came up, not then knowing what I afterwards learned and practised in Abyssinia, namely, that when the human eye has once met the eyes of that animal, it must be fixed until the creature goes away, even though one has to wait thus for hours. However, when that beast saw my companions approaching, it rose quietly to go away; then I saw that I had been in danger, for it was a large leopard. On reaching Khan-el-Merdj, in the valley of Coelo-Syria, that evening, and relating this incident, we were told that a fortnight previously a man had been killed in that same ravine by a leopard. We therefore heartily thanked God for my preservation.

We entered Damascus in brilliant sunshine. In fact, from Cairo to Damascus we had had beautiful weather, with the exception of a slight shower at Beyrout. As a rule, the month of February is very tempestuous in Syria and Palestine. A few hours after our arrival at Damascus, however, the sky grew dark, thunder and lightning began, and continued the whole evening. During the night the latter rain set in, and lasted for a fortnight. This kept us prisoners for the whole time, the streets being impassable on account of the deep mire, so that we were able to see but little of the ancient city and its inhabitants. We lodged with a Greek family, with whom and with whose neighbours we had some conversations on religion.

The plague was at that time raging in Damascus, and one morning whilst I was walking alone through a deserted street I heard the groans of a poor woman who was sitting in a corner apparently suffering excruciating pain, and moving her hand over a great swelling about her left shoulder. I had just turned to go and try to do what I could for her, having altogether forgotten the existence of the plague, when a Moslem came out of a neighbouring house, and I, unwilling to be seen near a solitary Mohammedan woman, went away. Two hours afterwards I heard that she had died of the plague.

As we wished to reach Jerusalem before Easter, we started from Damascus as soon as the weather would allow of our doing so. We travelled in great part along a Eoman road, through an uninhabited country, where we only saw two or three Kurds feeding their sheep, along the base of the Anti-Libanus and Mount Hermon, and crossed the Jordan by the Bridge of the Children of Jacob, half-way between the waters of Merom and the Lake of Tiberias. Thence we went to Safet, in Upper Galilee, where we found the late Mr. Mcolayson, missionary to the Jews, with whom we stayed seven days, the greater part of which we spent in conversation with the numerous German Jews.

We visited the tomb of the Prophet Hosea and other places of note, and every day we went to the top of the half-ruined fort, from which we had the most magnificent view, for nearly the half of Palestine can be seen from that spot. I cannot describe the holy recollections, meditations, and conversations which that splendid scene suggested.

At the house of Nicolayson we found a young Maronite, Joseph, a relative of Assaad Shidiac the martyr, whom the Maronite Patriarch had tried to capture and imprison because he was reading the Bible. Joseph had been obliged to fly, leaving his wife behind. He was cast down because he no longer delighted, as formerly, in reading the Bible, though he felt it to be his duty to continue to read it, notwithstanding the consciousness that it now condemned him. We took him with us to Jerusalem, where for some time he remained oppressed beneath the weight of his sins. One evening, whilst walking with him on the terrace of the house, I related to him the conversion of my mother, and how, whilst intending to comfort another, she had herself found peace by applying to herself the words of Christ, "Come unto Me, all ye that labour and are heavy laden." On hearing this, Joseph abruptly left me and hastened to his room, where he remained shut up for several hours, after which he came to us, Kugler and myself, with a radiant countenance, and said that he had found pardon and peace. He afterwards told me that, although he had read the Gospel of St. Matthew several times through, his attention had never been specially directed to that passage; but that, on hearing those gracious words of Christ, he had felt as if they were ad- dressed to him. He had accordingly hastened to his Lord with the whole burden of his sins, and had at once realised the promise. From that day he was happy, and active in endeavouring to lead others to the source of his happiness. We subsequently took him to Cairo, where he was employed by Herr Muller as the first Protestant schoolmaster. Later on, Dr. Wolff took a fancy to him, had him ordained, and took him to Smyrna and Greece. They ultimately separated, in consequence of some misunderstanding, soon after which poor Joseph died, I hope in the Lord, Whom he had endeavoured to serve.

Messrs. Mcolayson and Muller, who had rejoined us at Safet, accompanied us to Jerusalem. We passed through Nazareth, where we found the people very rude, and thence to Megiddo, having heard tliat the road through! N"ablous was not safe. From Megiddo we crossed through a forest between Mount Carmel and the mountains of Jezreel, to the plain of Sharon, as far as Lydda and Eamlah.

Here we were warned against the old chief, Abu Ghooush, who has given his name to his village, about eight miles west of Jerusalem, and who was then at the height of his lawless power. On approaching the village we saw a horseman with an immense turban, followed by about twenty men, coming through the bushes right in front of our pathway. We at once supposed this personage to be Abu Ghooush. One of our party rode on a little in advance, and when within speaking distance, asked the Sheik if Abu Ghooush was at home. " Why do you ask? " sternly demanded the horseman. " Because we want to lodge with him," was the reply. ITpon this the sternness of the Sheik's features relaxed. "I am Abu Ghooush," he said, in an amicable tone; " you are welcome. Come with me; you have nothing to fear."

He took us to his house, gave us the best room, and at once ordered a grand dinner, which, however, was not ready until late in the evening. While we were waiting and looking out of the window, we saw him in the distance stopping a caravan of pilgrims and levying blackmail plundering them, in fact. But to us he behaved very well, and the next day he accompanied us for some distance on our way, and would accept no present. He also visited us several times at Jerusalem, insisting upon our ao'ain visiting him when we should return through his village. Although scarcely any Europeans journeyed to Jerusalem at that time, he was very anxious to have a good name among them, among the English especially.

We arrived at Jerusalem on the 31 st of March, and took up our abode in the Greek monastery of St. Michael, presided over by a monk called Joel, a man of middle age. As he was far from being indifferent to the Word of God, we had daily conversations on religious topics. He was evidently anxious to know the truth. He and another young monk named Kaisarios were the only two among the many Greek monks who seemed to take any interest in the Word of God. Kaisarios died not long after this. Joel was in process of time made Archimandrite, and has always manifested great attachment to the Protestant missionaries. Indeed, I have been told that but for his sympathy with Protestant truth he would have been made a bishop. His conduct was so modest and exemplary that, although he was not respected by his superiors as he deserved to be, yet he was not much molested. He died a few years ago, in firm reliance upon the merits of Christ. When he felt that death was approaching, he sent for me, and after a short conversation on the state of his soul, he called for two young monks and several other persons. When they were assembled round his bed, he desired them to bear witness that he died in the faith of Christ, Who had died for and redeemed him, miserable sinner though he was. He declared that although his life had been polluted by sin, he yet died without fear, relying upon the merits of his Lord, Jesus Christ.

After making this confession, he sank into a state of exhaustion, from which he rallied for a time, and in the end expired quite suddenly.

We also made the acquaintance of a Greek priest, Butros, who had translated several tracts into Arabic for the late Mr. Jowett, by which he seemed to have been benefited, for he liked to converse on religious matters, and was opposed to many superstitions of his Church without leaning to scepticism, as many Orientals do when they shake off superstition. It might have been said of him that he was "not far from the kingdom of God." He possessed considerable learning, and yet he was poor, despised, and neglected by his superiors and by the monks, very likely because he had a family. Papa Joel and Kaisarios formed an exception to the general rule of unfriendliness towards this poor priest. While we were at Jerusalem he received a sum of money for some translation that he had prepared. The transaction had been effected as secretly as possible, yet the next night an Effendi came to his house with several slaves and demanded that very amount. On the poor priest's refusal to comply, he was pinioned and carried a prisoner to the Effendi's house. The next day an appeal was made to the Governor, and the following evening (it was Eama-dan) that functionary ordered both the Effendi and the priest to be brought before him. We, Kugler and myself, were present, and at first were satisfied with the manner in which the Governor investiirated the affair.

particularly when we heard him sharply rebuking the Effendi, calling him a robber, and finally sending him away in apparent disgrace. When he was gone the Governor turned to the priest, and addressed to him a complimentary harangue, which, however, ended in something like the following words:

"You see what trouble this business has caused us; you must therefore pay the costs of the trial."

And accordingly the unfortunate priest was obliged to pay to the Governor nearly the same sum which the Effendi had demanded. It was supposed that, as in other cases, it was the Governor who had in the first instance instigated the Effendi to the exaction. Let me here observe that the same tyranny and oppression still (1869) characterise the Turkish authorities, though they now exercise these qualities in a more covert and cunning way.

We made it a duty, which proved to be a most painful one, of attending all the services and ceremonies of Holy Week at the Church of the Holy Sepulchre. The Greeks had no preaching. We saw a Greek bishop wash the feet of twelve monks, after which the water was poured into a large cask already nearly full of clean water, that was placed in a large upper room. In a moment the apartment was filled with pilgrims of both sexes, who jostled one another in the endeavour to be the first to dip his or her unclean handkerchief and arakieh (a white cap which they wear under the tarboosh) in order to squeeze out the water thus obtained into small bottles, to be taken home and used as medicine for every kind of malady. At last there remained nothing but a little thick, greenish matter, which could hardly be called fluid; this a number of invalid pilgrims eagerly swallowed for the benefit of their souls and bodies. This ceremony and the holy fire form the chief parts of the Greek services in Holy Week.

On Good Friday evening we attended the Eoman Catholi(chiefly of sermons in divers tongues. There was a sermon i preacher standing opposite to a wooden crucifix four feet I apostrophised, as thouo'h it had been Christ Himself. The declamations against the Jews (who to this day are not all(church). He ended his sermon with these words: " If any afresh this Christ," pointing to the crucifix, "let a thundert Amen." Then they took down the wooden body from the c nails, and carrying it to the so-called stone of unction, laid it down there and anoititu it; upon which a short sermon was preached in Spanish, which I did not understand. Then the body was carried into the small chamber of the so-called Holy Sepulchre, at the door of which another monk preached an Italian sermon with much pathos, the object of which was to depict the atoning sufferings of Mary! The sufferings of Christ were vividly described, but only to show forth the agony of His Mother in witnessing them. I cannot express the anguish which oppressed me while listening to such blasphemies. My only comfort was that few among the many hearers could understand what was said, with the exception of the monks.

We spent the night in the church, vhere several hundred pilgrims were lying pell-mell, men, women, and children, talking and quarrelling till midnight. When in the morning we left the church, dozens of them were crying out in chorus that sundry articles of their property had been stolen.

So LIFE OF SAMUEL GOB AT.

In the afternoon of Easter Eve we went to witness the scene connected with the Greek-zm-holy fire, which I shrink from describing; for, considering the place where it is enacted, the actors believing that it is the Sepulchre of Christ, I cannot conceive a more horrible and scandalous spectacle. To see five or six thousand nominal Christians deluded into the belief that they were honouring the meek Lamb of God by frantic dances half-naked, by howling, pushing, and fighting, is the most melanclioly sight that can be imagined. I could not but weep over those poor, ignorant pilgrims, who were attracted chiefly by the figment of that pretended miraculous light (the Greeks are forbidden to call it fire) to Jerusalem, where their earnings of ten or twenty years are swallowed up by the rich monasteries, to which it is computed that each pilgrim pays on an average about; 20.

The following fact will give an idea of how the money is extorted. One evening a modest-looking young man came to us crying, and asking for bread and shelter for the night from our friend Papa Joel. He related to us his experience of the last twenty-four hours as follows:

"I arrived yesterday evening with a hundred dollars, and was kindly received. I was accommodated with a good supper and a nice room. This morning, after breakfast, I was introduced to the Bishop, who was very affable, and who told me how much fatigue and trouble have to be undergone by himself and the monks whilst praying night and day, not so much for themselves as for their people abroad w ho were occupied in worldly concerns. Then he stated what great expenses they incurred for the church and chapels, for the numerous poor, and, above all, on account of the exactions of the Turks. Upon this he looked at me and said, You are not rich, I suppose,

you will give something to the church. I had already made up my mind
wenty dollars," continued the young man, " but I was moved by the Bishop's
n, and offered to give twenty-five. That is very good said the Bishop, but you
st see how little it will help our poor and numerous community. Can you not give
ifty dollars? I was bashful, and afraid of displeasing him; I therefore consented to
give fifty, whereupon he ordered a monk to go with me to my room to receive the
money. I thought I could still accomplish my pilgrimage with the remaining fifty
dollars. But, this business transacted, I was asked by another monk whether I did not
wish, like other pilgrims, to visit the holy places, chapels, and altars. To this I gladly
assented; and immediately a third monk took me successively to eleven altars. At
each one of them my guide told me that the pilgrims contributed the money necessary
for the maintenance of the sacred places. At first I gave liberally, supposing that there
were but three or four; after which I observed that I had seen enough. He, however,
took advantage of my real want of courage to oppose him, and so constrained me to
visit one holy place after another the w hole day long. On returning to the monastery,
my guide disappeared for a moment, when another monk came and asked me whether
I had given a present to him for his trouble. He advised me to give him two or three
of my few remaining dollars; upon which my guide reappeared to receive two dollars.
I was low-spirited; but I thought that, as I might remain in my room without expense,
I still had enough to enable me to return to my home near Aleppo. But whilst I was
thus musing, another monk came to me with his account for my room, supper, and
breakfast. These were charged at rather a high rate, and I have just discharged the
claim with a heavy heart, and have now only a few piastres left. After having paid,
the monk told me that my well-furnished room was kept for the reception of pilgrims
on their arrival, but only for one night, so that I must look for another lodging. I am
therefore come to you to ask for shelter for one night at least."

Papa Joel received and entertained the young man for several days. Strange to say,
the fanatical youth was not yet cured; for he still believed that the holy fire, being
supernatural, did not burn. We advised him to apply a lighted candle to some part of
his body and test it. He made the trial; for as soon as he had lighted his candle in
the church, he applied it to his beard, half of which was immediately consumed and
the skin of his cheek was singed. When the ceremony was over we asked him if he
still believed that the fire did not burn; to which he replied, "It does not burn." " You
carry the proof of its burning on your face," said we; " why do you not confess it?" To
which he naively replied, "If I said that it burns, I should be excommunicated." This
digression requires neither comment nor apology.

That Holy Week was the most melancholy week of my life; and though I have now
been more than twenty years in Jerusalem, I have never seen or wished to see again
those abominations practised in the Church of the Holy Sepulchre.

We had no wish to profane Easter Day by being present at the ceremonies of that
Church. We therefore remained at home, reading the Bible and conversing on the
passion and resurrection of Christ, and the blessings flowincj therefrom.

But my heart was burning within me. On Monday morning I went to the aged
Bishop of Petra, called the Bishop of the Light, and remonstrated with him most

solemnly, though, I trust, respectfully; and asked him how he could at the day of judgment give an account for thus wilfully and knowingly deceiving thousands of ignorant people. He shrugged his shoulders and asked mildly, "What shall we do? If there were no light, the Turks would murder us." The meaning of which was, "If we have no holy fire, no pilgrims would come, and we should be destitute of the money necessary to satisfy the demands of the Turks."

The practices here described are continued to this day, thou2 h with a little more caution.

During our three months' stay at Jerusalem we tried to preach the Gospel to Jews and nominal Christians, but w e found no entrance among either class, for none dared receive the Bible or the ISTew Testament for fear of the Eabbis and the priests. We therefore spent our time chiefly in pursuing the object for which w e had come to the Holy City, namely, the study of the Amharic language by practice in hearing and speaking, as we had no book but the four Gospels, the Acts, and the Epistle to the Eomans. We passed almost all our time with the thirty and odd Abyssinians, either at their monastery or our house, eating with them or they with us, en-deavourincf, with considerable success, to overcome our disgust at their want of cleanliness. The Abyssinians, like the Coptic monks, think it a merit to be dirty. I once asked the Coptic Patriarch, Botros, why he did not wash his face; to which he replied that it was unlawful for religious people to wash during Lent or on fast-days.

We made good progress in Amharic, so that before leaving Jerusalem we spoke it nearly as fluently as our native language. We held daily religious conversations with the monks and three or four nuns, all living under the same roof; and we had good hope that several of them, notably the intelligent Eeis or Abbot, and a nun, had been really impressed by the Word of the Gospel. But alas! four weeks after our departure, the plague visited Jerusalem and carried off all the Abyssinians, not sparing a single one, either man or woman.

On the 23d of June we left Jerusalem for Jaffa, there to embark for Damietta. On the way I was very low-spirited, as indeed had been the case throughout my travels in Palestine and sojourn at Jerusalem. I was oppressed with grief at sight of the desolation of the land, and the temporal and spiritual misery of its inhabitants, especially the Jews, who then were not permitted even to go to their now well-known place of wailing, to weep over the ruin of their Temple and their nation. To this day I have a vivid recollection of a Jew who, after asking our leave, followed us to that place of wailing; but before reaching it he was seized by some Moselms, who wanted to give him the bastinado for daring to approach the holy place. We could only rescue him by giving a " baksheesh " to the miscreants.

We embarked at Jaffa in an open boat without a cabin for Damietta, which we hoped to reach in one or two days; but the wind being unfavourable, we were carried the first day to Gaza, and the second day back to Jaffa. Next day, the wind having changed, we again embarked late in the afternoon, in the hope of sailing-early in the evening. But one long hour after another passed, and the Eeis, or captain, did not appear. About midnight he came, to be received by a torrent of abuse from some of the passengers for having kept us waiting so long. " My brother was dying of the plague," he quietly answered, " and I could not leave him till I had closed his eyes. He has just died." Some of the Arab passengers, alarmed at this news, would have disembarked; but we reassured tliem, and so we sailed away once more. We sailed to all appearance at random, now right, now left; and after many vicissitudes, including seven days' quarantine at Cyprus and a fast of forty hours, we reached Damietta, whence w e immediately started for Cairo, where we arrived in the middle of August.

Soon after our return to Cairo I was seized with most severe ophthalmia, which threatened to deprive me of my sight. It was so exceedingly painful as to produce delirium of a serious nature. Once, in the middle of the night, when every twinkling of the eyes seemed to be a flash of fire, I fancied there were enemies firing at me. I therefore took my knife in supposed defence of myself, and was on the point of plunging it into my right eye, when a friend who w as near me, hearing my movements, asked me how I felt, which brought me back to rational consciousness just at the right moment.

The regular Egyptian ophthalmia begins with a continuous irritation, as if there were sand under the eyelid, upon which first one eye and then the other becomes bloodshot and dry for about twenty-four hours, after which they suppurate for four or five days. On the seventh day, if no great mistake has been made, that is, if the disease has been left to take its natural course, it is all over. But the eyes being then very tender, the least mistake, especially exposure to the evening air, brings on the malady again for another seven days much more severely and painfully, and so on, sometimes until the eyes are destroyed.

On that first occasion I had three relapses, and it was only on the fourth attack that I discovered exposure to the evening air about sunset to have been the cause of each renewal of the malady. At last I found myself perfectly blind, so that when I looked at the sun it seemed as black as the darkest night. However, by the grace of God, my sight gradually returned, but so slowly that it was six months before I could see as well as of old. I am therefore inclined to think that permanent loss of sight is the effect, not of the ophthalmia itself, but of deleterious remedies.

Having thus described this dreadful disease, let me mention the simple, and, if applied at the proper time, the infallible remedy for it. A short time after my recovery a friend told me that he had just seen a negro curing himself by putting a pinch of snuff into his eyes, by which he had been instantaneously healed. I had another attack of the disease, and made the trial with wonderful success, for in five minutes I was perfectly well. Since that time I have had many opportunities of applying this simple remedy to myself and to others, always with the same result. The way of using it is this: A person must take a pinch of snuff on his thumb and blow it, if possible, into both eyes at once of the patient. The operator must stand a little distance apart, so that the coarser parts of the snuff may fall to the ground. The immediate effect is sudden pain, followed by a discharge of water from the eyes. The cure is then complete. But it is of the utmost importance that it be done the first day, while the eyes are red and dry; after suppuration has begun snuff will not cure, though it will do no harm.

One day while travelling from Massowa to Abyssinia, and resting at noonday in the valley of the Shohos, a Shoho Sheik presented himself with about twenty armed men, looking very wild. Alighting from his mule, he came to me and showed me his eyes, red and dry, just at the right moment. While looking at them I suddenly and adroitly blew a pinch of snuff into both eyes at once. The poor man, with a loud outcry, seized his sword, but as he could not open his eyes for a minute or two, he could do me no harm; but he said something which I did not understand to his men, upon which they all grasped their swords. However, I made a sign to them to wait a moment. In five minutes the Sheik was completely cured, and was so thankful, that instead of levying black-mail, as he had probably intended to do, he obliged me to accept an ox as a token of his gratitude.

It was during the time of my semi-blindness, mentioned above, that the news reached Egypt of the battle of I avarino, in which Ibrahim Pasha had been beaten and the Turkish fleet almost annihilated by the combined squadrons of England, France, and Eussia. So great was the consequent panic among the Europeans, that nearly all of them hastened from Cairo to Alexandria, fearing the vengeance of the Moslems; although the great Pasha, Mohammed Ali, had immediately caused a proclamation to be made that all Europeans should be protected.

I could not move, and should have been left alone, had not a dear brother, Th. Miiller, given up his previous intention of cfoincj to Alexandria in order to remain with me till the supposed danger was over. Kugler had previously gone on business to Alexandria, and also to visit the late Consul-General, Mr. Salt, who was on his dying-bed in a village between Cairo and Alexandria.

As soon as I was sufficiently recovered from the ophthalmia, though I was still so blind as not to be able to discern objects distinctly, I started for Alexandria to consult with my brother Kugler about the advisability of his going to England to make certain arrangements connected with our mission to Abyssinia, in case we should find a way to that sealed land. Shortly before his departure we made a discovery which afterwards proved the means of reopening the door of access to Abyssinia, that land having been closed to Europeans, with the exception of Bruce, ever since the Jesuits had been driven away in the sixteenth century.

This discovery consisted in the fact that we found a poor Abyssinian lying sick in a dark den, almost in despair, his servant being also ill. In his own country he was the governor of a large district, and he had been sent many months before, by the excellent Saba Gadis, ruler of Tigre, as ambassador to Mohammed Ali, who having but a short time previously received and dismissed another ambassador of the same name, supposed this man to be the identical person, returned with a view to extorting more presents. The Pasha consequntly refused to see the new ambassador, vv ho did not dare to return thus rejected to his master. He fell into a state of despondency, which brought on the severe illness from which we found him to be suffering.

As one evil seldom comes alone, the poor fellow having no friends and knowing but a few words of Arabic, he liad been cheated and robbed; so that if he had been willing to venture to return to Abyssinia, he had no means left to do so.

We took him and his servant into our house until he was well again. After which, as I was intimately acquainted with the First Minister of Mohammed Ali, Boghos Bey, with whom I used to spend many evenings in reading the Bible, often till past midnight, we found it easy to introduce the ambassador to the Pasha, who, convinced of his mistake, acceded to all the requests and proposals of the envoy, but detained him for several weeks until his answer to Saba Gadis was ready. In the meantime, our new friend wrote to his master, informinx him of all we had done for him; in answer to which Saba Gadis commanded him to use all his efforts to persuade us to go and see him, in order that he might remunerate us. Thus was Abyssinia unexpectedly opened to us, and we might have started on our way thither about the end of 1828, had Kugler not been in Europe.

I spent the winter of 1827-28 at Alexandria, endeavouring to do something for the neglected, worldly-minded, and, alas! for the most part, infidel Europeans. There was then a Wesleyan missionary at Alexandria, but his work was almost exclusively amongst the English sailors. He certainly held a service at the Consulate every Sunday morning, but it was not very edifying on account of the Consul walking to and fro in his heavy boots all the time.

There were but few English, with some of whom I held Bible-meetings on Sunday afternoons. I also held several services, first in French, then in German. In both languages the first service was pretty well attended. But when the people perceived that I preached Christ crucified, in whom, perhaps, not one of them believed, after a few Sundays my hearers ceased to come.

I was generally oppressed and low-spirited at the sight of the infidelity, worldliness, and immorality with which I was surrounded. Yet there were a few individuals who were seeking the way of salvation. Amongst these were my host, the late Mr. Eobert Tod, and Boghos Bey; also three English ladies, all of them more or less pious. These latter were, however, so different in respect to class, attainments, and dispositions, and they were so much restrained by the influence of their respective husbands, that I could not prevail upon them to unite more closely, so as to form a nucleus around which some less decided persons might be clustered for their good.

During my stay in Alexandria I realised two remarkable experiences in very different spheres of action. The first was as follows: Seeing that I could not collect the people to hear the simple Gospel, I hit on an idea which seemed to be wise, but which proved to be foolishness. I made it publicly known by placards that I intended to deliver a series of lectures or sermons in the French language, on the agreement of true philosophy with Scriptural Christianity. All who were desirous of attending were invited to come.

My first subject was " The Excellency of Human ISTature," and my text was Gen. i. 27. My second theme was " What still Eemains of the Original Excellency of Human Nature;" my third, "The Present Wretched State of Mankind, or the Degeneration of Human Nature;" my fourth, "The Fall of Mankind from God into Bondage under an Evil Power."

I abstained as much as possible from imitating the language of the Bible, making use rather of an argumentative style, and showing that my deductions were in perfect accord with Holy Scripture. I was not satisfied with the assumed garb under which I commended the truth, although my ideas were dominated in my own mind by the Word of God; but I considered this form of presentment necessary in order to attract hearers, and so far I succeeded. I began with forty, and the number increased to two hundred.

When I considered them sufficiently prepared to hear of Christ crucified the history of the Cross in simple Scriptural language I resolved to preach on the next occasion the full Gospel, including all the essential doctrines of Christianity, as far as this can be done within the limits of a sermon. I was intending to recapitulate in a few words the facts of the creation, the Fall, the wretchedness of man, and the danger of his being lost eternally. From these fundamental truths I would have proved our urgent need of a Saviour, none other than our

Lord Jesus Christ, the Son of God, whom the Father, moved by divine love and compassion, has sent into the world to be its Eedeemer by His incarnation, His life on earth. His sufferings, death, and resurrection. I would have concluded by entreating my hearers to receive this their Saviour by faith, and to give Him their hearts.

On the Saturday the French and Austrian Consuls-General sent me word to say that they intended to be present on the morrow, so that I expected a large assemblage. But behold! I was mistaken. Nobody came to hear me except two Protestant gentlemen and one Greek lady. I could not understand why I was thus deserted, till, after waiting about an hour, I heard that the Eoman Catholic priests had that morning excommunicated beforehand all those who should come to hear me. Although nearly all my audience, nominally Eomanists, made an open boast of their infidelity, yet, frightened by the threatened excommunication, not one of them had the courage to come. Oh! how I was humbled for my imagined wisdom! But it was a good lesson, and I resolved never again to preach the Gospel in words that worldly wisdom teacheth.

Another incident of my life at Alexandria, the mention of which may provoke a smile, is the following: One of the three Christian ladies recently referred to in this narrative gave birth to a little son, who for a fortnight cried day and night, and refused to take nourishment. There were only two women to nurse this poor baby by turns, and they were soon perfectly exhausted.

This incident is omitted in the German Life of Bishop Gobat, being probably deemed unsuitable to a published memoir. Yet it so well illustrates the simplicity of mind, tenderness of disposition, and sound common-sense which distinguished Samuel Gobat throughout his whole career, from the plough to the Episcopate, that it is inserted here without apology for the homeliness of its details. Eng. Ed.

The father was utterly helpless. I would most willmgly have offered my services, but, sensible of my awkwardness, I did not dare to do so. However, my host, Mr. Tod, undertook the business; but after the first night he was regularly knocked up. One of the two hired nurses was taken ill, and the other could not watch for two successive nights, besides tending the crying infant all the day long. The mother was quiet enough and resigned, but very weak. The father was tearful and inert. What was to be done? In this extremity I took courage to offer myself for one night to watch and nurse the child, praying fervently that the Lord would give me the necessary skill.

Before taking the little fellow, I had observed that whenever he had ceased crying for half a minute, he turned his little head about before beginning again. I laid myself down on a sofa with the babe by my side, placing his head in the hollow of my left hand. I then ordered a cup of thin arrowroot to be put within my reach, and requested to be left alone alone with God and the child.

Now when he began to move his little head preparatory to crying again, I tried to assist his movements; this kept him quiet, and gave me time to dip my finger in the arrowroot and moisten his mouth. At first he was quite passive, but by degrees he began to suck my finger more and more lustily; and thus he was kept the whole night without uttering a single cry. So still was he, indeed, that about midnight the mother rose, and came trembling to the door, fearing that her child was dead. I motioned to her that all was well, and she withdrew. In the morning, when the baby was restored to her, she had no further difficulty in feeding the child, and from that moment he was as quiet and good as any other infant. Thus I was more successful in nursing than in preaching. However, these two functions must often be exercised together vide 1 Thess. ii. y. I have mentioned this circumstance to show how desirable it is that missionaries should practise themselves a little in nursing young children before going abroad; for I have known some who have lost their babes for want of knowing how to deal with them.

Before taking leave of Alexandria, I must mention another incident of a somewhat ludicrous nature which happened to me there, and which was connected with great subsequent events to be mentioned presently. Having been on one occasion invited to spend an evening with Boghos Bey, who lived at a considerable distance from my quarters, and not feeling quite well, I rode on a poor lame donkey, the only one I could find. It was after midnight when I took leave of my host, and he ordered two of his servants to escort me home with torches, not knowing what kind of an animal I had. So I had to ride my lame donkey through the whole city, at the rate of less than two miles an hour, preceded by the torches, which emitted bright flames and lighted up the whole streets. It was thus that Boghos Bey and the Pasha himself were wont to ride through the town by night. Accordingly, people rose from their beds to see what great personage was passing; and they were not a little amused at seeing a tall man with a long beard seated on a small, lame donkey, which was pushed slowly forward by a donkey-boy. Knowing that nobody recognised me, I mingled my hearty laughter with the merriment that pealed from the windows. My friend Boghos must have heard of it; for ever after that, when I paid him an evening visit, he secretly dismissed my donkey, though it sometimes happened to be a very respectable animal, and lent me his own mule to ride home upon.

On that evening we had been discussing prophecy, and thought to have discovered that the Turkish empire was soon to be destroyed. I looked at these prophecies with a theological eye he from a political point of view; so that, although we seemed to have the same idea, we did not fully understand one another. After leaving Alexandria I thought little more about it, till five years later, on my first return from Abyssinia in 1833, I called upon Boghos Bey. Hearing that I was at the door, he came smiling to meet me, and said at once, "Do you remember that evening when we conversed upon prophecy? A few days afterwards I communicated our views to Mohammed Ali, and read those prophecies with him. The consequence was that he immediately resolved upon attacking the Sublime Porte; and this is the origin of our conquest of Syria." So great a fire may one spark kindle.

It took me about a week to go by the Nile from Alexandria to Cairo, where I arrived in May 1828, and remained until October 1829, with the exception of a short visit to Alexandria for change of air. Throughout this period my health was very indifferent, though I suffered from no especial complaint, save occasional palpitations, the remains of my illness of 1823; but I was growing w eak and losing my energy, which was either the cause or the effect of depression of spirits. I had but little appetite, and perhaps lived too low; my expenses for myself, my Abyssinian guest, and my servant, not exceeding 60 per annum, house-rent included. When, upon the strong recommendation of my physician, I began to take wine regularly, my strength returned in some measure before starting for Abyssinia. But what pained me most was the low state of my spiritual life. I very rarely enjoyed a sense of the presence of the Lord. I had no relish for prayer, and my petitions were cold and lifeless. I Lad a clear consciousness of my lukewarmness, and yet I could find no energy to arouse myself. I was also aware that the physical and moral atmosphere in which I lived had much to do in keeping my spiritual life at a low ebb, and yet this gave me no peace; for my conscience reproached me with many cases of unfaithfulness, of failure in watching and praying, and of conformity to the world, when I ought to have witnessed against its maxims and practices. The contrast between this and my former state of habitual consciousness of being a child of God, of alacrity in confessing the name of Christ my Saviour and in witnessing for His truth, contributed to make me more miserable so long as I remained in Egypt; although the return of my dear brother and colleague, Kugler, revived my drooping spiritual energies a little.

During that time of spiritual gloom I occupied myself with the study of Ethiopic, Amharic, and Arabic, endeavouring to improve all opportunities of perfecting myself in speaking the two last-mentioned languages. Immediately after my return from Alexandria to Cairo, I began to seek out the few German and Erench-speak-ing Protestants, inviting them to attend divine service in either tongue; but as they were all either downright infidels or else perfectly indifferent about God and their own souls, and most of them having already ceased attending public worship in their respective native lands, they came, moved by curiosity only, for a few Sundays, and then ceased their attendance. I also preached sometimes before Lord Prudhoe, the late Duke of ISTor-thumberland, who alw ays invited a number of such of his acquaintances as could understand French to be present; wherefore, the services were performed in that language. My hearers were partly Protestants and partly Eoman Catholics; but I never observed that the Word made any impression, except upon Lord Prudhoe and his friend, Major, afterwards General Felix, whom many years later I met at Geneva as, I believe, a sincere Christian.

I also began an Arabic service, preaching regularly every Sunday for a year and a half. Except the first four or five Sundays, I had always between thirty and fifty hearers of both sexes, among whom were invariably some Mohammedans. Alas! I cannot say that any one was truly converted, though I often observed that the Word made lively impressions on several of them. I attributed the absence of greater success to my own want of si iritual life, which humbled me deeply.

I had also many religious conversations w ith native Christians and Moslems, many of whom seemed, at least for a time, to feel the power of the Word of God; but the Christians were prevented from yielding fully to its influence through fear of their priests, and the Moslems through fear of being put to death if they embraced Christianity. Here I will venture to mention one case, the particulars of which are still fresh in my mind.

I once met a Sheik Ahmed, one of the most learned Sheiks or religious teachers at Cairo, who at once showed himself ready to enter into a religious controversy, expecting to convert me to Islamism. It was well for me that I was so thoroughly acquainted-with the Koran. At first he looked down upon me with an air of commiseration, as he said that all Christians must go to the fire (of hell), citing a passage of the Koran. To this I replied that the Koran says just the contrary, and quoted a long passage from the second Surat, or chapter of that book, where it is written, "Surely the Jew s, the Christians, and the Sabaans, all those who believe in God and do good works, have nothing to fear; on the contrary, their reward is with their Lord gardens in which rivers flow, and in which they shall abide for ever and ever." " Oh," said he, " this passage has been abrogated." (This doctrine of abrogation is a subterfuge under which the Moslems frequently shelter themselves.) "How?" said I; "do you not say that the Koran is the Word of God? Is God like a man, an unrighteous man, who makes a promise and then abrogates it, either because he cannot, or because he w ill not keep it, thus deceivincr His creatures? Such a God cannot be the true God." The poor Sheik grew angry and confused, but he did not yield, and left me with an air of displeasure.

The next day he came again, and at once confessed that our conversation of the preceding day had troubled him, and excited doubt in his mind. But, he added, "If the Koran be not the Word of God the truth where is the truth to be found?" And, resuming the offensive, he continued " You Christians say that the Bible is the Word of God; and yet the Bible says in one place that God is One, and in another place it says that Eisa, Jesus, is the Son of God, and Himself God. Is not that a contradiction?"

"ISTo," said I, "it is not a contradiction, but it is a mystery; a mystery which God has plainly revealed in His Holy Word; and I could prove to you from the Bible that both declarations are true; namely, that God is One, and that in the Godhead there are three Persons of one substance, the Father, the Son Jesus, and the Holy Ghost. But as you do not believe in the Bible, and accuse the Christians and the Jews of having falsified it, my first duty must be to prove to you that such falsification is an impossibility, and that, therefore, the Koran, which affirms such an absurdity, must be false. Let us then, if you please, read the Bible and the Koran together, and compare the one with the other."

The Sheik accepted this invitation, and for more than a month he came twice or three times a week, till by decrees he besjan to confess his doubts about the contents of the Koran, and at the same time to own his sense of his sinfulness and guilt before God. I sought to draw his attention to the work of redemption by the life, sufferings, and death of Christ, which could not avail for us if He were merely a man, even though a holy man and a prophet.

When we had reached this point, for several days he came every day, till at last one morning before sunrise he appeared with tears in his eyes and exclaimed, "I am undone! What must I do to be saved? I could not sleep last night; the burden of my sins weighs too heavily upon me, and I can find no comfort in the Koran."

I preached the Gospel to him as well as I could, with deep emotion and with prayer, and for more than an hour he seemed to drink in every word. On leaving, he promised to come again on the morrow.

I was much encouraged by the hope that for once a learned and influential Moslem was ready to receive and to acknowledge Christ as his Saviour and his God; but I was most painfully disappointed. He never returned to me. For about three months I could discover no trace of him. Then I met him one day in the street. I asked him why he had not called for so long a time; to which he naively replied, "The last time I was with you I felt that if I went to you again I should be convinced of the truths of Christianity, and be consequently obliged to avo'v myself a Christian, for which I should have been killed. I therefore resolved to see you no more until my heart should be hardened against your arguments."

And, indeed, he proved so hardened, that though I saw him several times after that, I could make no impression upon him.

This was the greatest disappointment of my long life.

CHAPTEE IV.

SUCCESSFUL ACTIVITY IN ABYSSINIA. (1829-1832.)

At last, the season of great heat being nearly over, we were able to start from Cairo for Abyssinia.

On the 20th of October 1829, after having made an agreement with the camel-drivers that they should bring us twenty-two camels early next morning, we packed all our things, even our bedding, with a view to starting betimes. But we were doomed to exercise patience such an amount of patience as sometimes causes actual fever to Europeans travelling in the East.

On the 21 st we rose early, and were quite ready by daybreak; but we vainly w aited for a long time in expectation of our camels and their drivers. At length, between ten and eleven o'clock, one driver came with about a dozen camels, saying that the other drivers and their animals would soon arrive. However, they did not present themselves until four o'clock in the afternoon, and then the head-driver was nowhere to be found. In his absence nothing could be done, notwithstanding our remonstrances. Night came on, and the camels had to be driven to feed. Next morning, about nine o'clock, the creatures returned, but two of them were missing, so that a couple of drivers had to go and seek for them in the desert. About noon they were

SUCCESSFUL ACTIVITY IN ABYSSINIA. loi brought back, but then the drivers discovered that they had forgotten to bring the necessary ropes. They must go to the market to purchase them. This took about two hours.

And now they began to distribute the packages and to load the camels, so that at sunset we were ready to start. But we accomplished only about two miles, and spent the first night near the monuments of the Mamelukes before Baab-el-jsTasser. Thus ended the trial of our patience for this time.

On the morning of the 23 d, not very early, our caravan was again set in motion. It consisted of Herr Kugier, a German carpenter whom Kugler had brought from Wtirtemberg, the Abyssinian ambassador, and his servant. I was the oldest of the company; and yet (oh, the patience of God with me!) I am the only survivor. We had four drivers and twenty-two camels, and we carried a goodly number of Amharic and Ethiopic books for distribution in Abyssinia. We made our first halt at Heliopolis, and journeyed from thence for three days until we came to Suez, where we were kept for a fortnight in expectation of a boat to sail for Jidda.

Suez was then a most miserable place, with nothing green in its neighbourhood except a few palm-trees. I believe that it did not contain a single glass window; scarcely anything was to be found in the market besides rice, and the water was brackish, thousjh wholesome.

At last we engaged the cabin of a boat laden with pilgrims going to Mecca; but the cabin was so small that it could only contain two persons, Kugler and myself. It took twenty days, if I mistake not, to sail from Suez to Jidda. At Tor, a small village of the peninsula of Sinai, we took in fresh water, which we much enjoyed for two days; but as the Arabs never cleanse their large vater-jars, by the third day it was already rendered corrupt by the small worms which the rain-water had bred, and which had died and become decomposed. Still we encouraged one another to drink it till we reached Yanibo on the coast of Arabia. There we again found good water, but our dirty Arabs mixed it with what remained from Tor, so that in two days it was worse than the first supply, and at last it became so bad that its putrid smell reached from one end of the boat to the other. We were, nevertheless, obliged to drink it, or else die of thirst, until it was exhausted. Then we were without water for two days, and were still two days' sail from Jidda.

I was ill, but I hardly noticed my own ailments, for the poor women and children pilgrims seemed actually dying of thirst in that sultry atmosphere. Suddenly a small cloud arose. It increased rapidly in bulk, and as we were, as usual, not far from land, our Arab sailors hastened to a creek where they cast anchor. In a few minutes more we were in a storm of wind, thunder, lightning, and pouring rain. We hastened to spread out all that we had ready in the shape of cloths, sheets, and towels to catch the water. Some of the pilgrims had cowhides, on which they slept, and these also were spread out; so we obtained the necessary supplies of water for the two following days.

We arrived at Jidda late in the afternoon of a sultry day, and immediately went to the Governor, who was at the same time English Consul, to whom we had letters of introduction both from the British Consul at Cairo and from the Pasha Mohammed Ali. He received us at first with civility, but when we asked him for a place to live in for a few days, he coldly ordered a servant to conduct us to a square room about twelve feet in diameter, in which there was absolutely nothing but animated dust several inches deep. The living portion of this very scanty furniture speedily began to feed on our nether limbs. We at once perceived that there was no room for our luggage, but before we had time to speak our guide had disappeared, and we had no alternative but to hasten back to the Governor-Consul and ask for a better lodsfinor.

Whilst walking along the streets weary and downcast, and gazed at by the fanatical Moslems, who cast at us their favourite expressions of Xelb and Kdfir, dog and infidel, a kind Armenian merchant, Khawadja Yoosoof, the only Christian resident at Jidda, stopped us, and invited us to take up our abode in his large house. We most thankfully accepted, and lived in great comfort as his guests for the fortnight that we stayed at Jidda. Almost every evening we received the visits of some of the greatest Sheiks of Mecca, to whom we preached the Gospel in the form of conversation, they being much better instructed in history and geography and less bigoted than any of the Sheiks with whom we had met in Egypt and Syria, though they were not free from scepticism.

I may here mention that the Governor-Consul having been detected by us in extortionate and fraudulent transactions, application was made to Bombay for another Consul, and upon our recommendation our good host, Yoosoof, was appointed. He held the office for a number of years, and made the English name to be respected at fanatical Jidda.

We sailed from Jidda to Massowa in an Arab boat, which had much better accommodation than the one in which we travelled from Suez, and it was, moreover, clean. We spent our time on board chiefly in reading and conversing in Amharic with the Abyssinian ambassador, Ali, who w as most willing to make us ac- quainted with the character, views, prejudices, and customs of the Abyssinians. We afterwards found his information most valuable.

I was unwell all the time till we reached Massowa, a little before Christmas. Our faithful Ali being known at Massowa as an officer of Saba Gadis, the ruler of Tigre and Lasta, who had much influence there, we were well received by the Governor, and consequently by all in. authority. This was contrary to their usual behaviour towards the few Europeans who had previously visited the place and asked in vain for permission to proceed to Abyssinia. The Governor allotted to us the best house on the island, and issued orders that no one was to molest us. Immediately after our arrival, Ali sent messengers to Saba Gadis to inform him of the fact.

In the meantime I was seized with severe dysentery, and for some days my life was despaired of; the more so that we had recently read in Bruce's Travels that Massowa was called in his time " the grave of Europeans." However, by the goodness of God, I recovered in time to start when all else was ready.

Before leaving Massowa we witnessed a very touching scene. A lady of rank in Germany had given money to Herr Kugler to redeem an Abyssinian female slave, either in Egypt or Arabia; and through the help of our friend Yoosoof at Jidda we had discovered and purchased one who, a few months previously, had been caught with her little boy, and with him sold into slavery. The boy could not be traced, but we had brought the woman, deeply mourning the loss of her son, to Massowa, with the intention of restoring her to her family in the neighbouring district of Hamassion. We had, therefore, requested several persons to give

Tis notice if they sliould see any Christian from that district.

One day a man brought us the news that three men from Hamassion were coming. All our people went to the door to see them. The poor woman, having already learnt the practice of Arab women, covered her face so as to see without being seen. On perceiving the three men, she was seized with hysterics and sank into a corner. As we could not speak to her, she knowing only the Tigre language, with which we were unacquainted, we had not intimated to her our purpose of restoring her to her husband, whom she had just recognised as one of the three who had passed our door. Fearinsr lest, if she told us that she had seen her husband, we might not allow her to see him again, she said nothing until she could speak privately with Ali, and beg him to intercede for her. Her intention was not, indeed, to ask us to let her go free, for although we had already told her, through Ali, that she was so, she did not believe it. Her request was that, as her husband was not rich, we would undersell her to him.

The worthy Ali, before mentioning the case to us, sent for her husband, who came while he was explaining the matter to us in her presence. The poor man was very shy, and when he had looked at his wife for a moment to assure himself that his eyes did not deceive him, he began to tremble, not daring to approach her. Her eyes were fixed upon the ground. When Ali told them in our name that the woman w as free, the husband remained motionless for a moment, evidently doubting whether he had heard aright, till one of us took him by the hand to lead him to his wife, who was also motionless. They just looked straight at one another, and then falling into each other's arms, they wept for joy long and loudly. All present wept with them. Then they left, after asking God's blessing upon us.

A few days after this incident an answer arrived from Saba Gadis, inviting us to go to him without delay. The message was brought by a high ofhcer, accompanied by about forty soldiers, who also bore an order to the Governor of Massowa to have all our luggage carried through the district of the wild Shoho to the foot of the high mountain Shumfeito, farther than which the camels could not go. Saba Gadis had likewise sent us mules to ride.

Acting on All's advice, we delivered all our effects into the hands of the second officer of Saba Gadis, who promised to restore the whole to us in good condition at Adigrad, the residence of Saba Gadis.

We started for Adigrad at the end of March, and arrived there on the 14th of February. It proved to be a very pleasant tour, as we were exempted from all care about luggage, and only rode for five or six hours a day, so as never to get fatigued. We only regretted not being able to speak of the one thing needful to the people travelling with us.

Arrived at the foot of the Shumfeito, near the Taranta of Bruce, our camel-drivers left us to return to Arkiko, near Massowa. Next morning the men of Halai, the first village of Abyssinia, came down early, and, with the soldiers whom Saba Gadis had sent, hoisted our luggage upon their shoulders and began to ascend the high and steep mountain. A little before sunset we all arrived safely at Halai.

It was a solemn moment for my colleague and myself when for the first time we saw stretched around and beneath us the vast expanse of land, the field which we had been sent to cultivate. We deeply felt our insufti- ciency, and prayed that the Lord would give us light, strength, and wisdom to testify to the Gospel of the grace of God in that benighted region, and that He would accompany the words of our testimony with the influence of the Holy Spirit, to the salvation of many souls.

We spent two days at Halai, and as it contained a few individuals who spoke Amharic, we conversed with them on divers topics. Having heard the roaring of lions at Shumfeito, we took occasion to ask about wild beasts, and how we ought to act if we encountered any. The following rules were imparted to us unanimously by those whem we questioned:

Never turn your back to a hyena; that animal never attacks a man from the front. When you see a leopard, never cease fixing him with your eyes until he quits his ground; he only attacks those who, having seen him, turn their eyes away from him.

When you meet a lion, keep your self-possession; he only attacks those who fear or threaten him.

The people repeated these maxims in a kind of rhyme, as if they were well-known proverbs. I had previously heard something similar from some negroes in Egypt. They added with respect to the lion, that being proud, he must be treated with indifference, as if he were unworthy of notice.

The very next day I had an opportunity of testing the value of these sayings. After leaving Halai, and while travelling through a wild district, I diverged from the path with a view to shooting some guinea-fowls or partridges for our dinner. After a while I thought I heard a partridge behind a large bush. I crept cautiously towards it, in order to get as near as possible to my game; but when I was about six paces from the spot, a lion slowly emerged, and nonchalantly stretched himself, as if he did not see me. 1 imitated his indifference, and continued to walk very slowly towards the bush, looking to the right and left as if I did not observe him, yet keeping the corner of my eye upon him, and holding my gun in readiness to discharge it into his mouth if he should come towards me. Otherwise, having only small shot, I did not dare to fire at him. However, after stretching himself, he went quietly away.

After quitting Halai, we journeyed for four days through the now well-known district of Senafeh to Behaat, the district of our friend Ali, and for his sake we rested for one day at his house. It was thronged the whole day with people bringing presents of sheep and honey to welcome him on his return home. We amused ourselves with his lovely children.

From Behaat we travelled for two days to Adigrad, where we found all our luggage safely bestowed in the best house of the place, which Saba Gadis had had as well prepared as was possible in poor Abyssinia.

That prince received us with open arms, as if we had been his brothers, and as lon as he lived he was most kind to us, because, as he more than once said, we had come to teach the Gospel in his country.

Having some Shoho blood in his veins, Saba Gadis had been very wild, daring, and sometimes cruel, in his youth, when hunted by the jealous, though otherwise mild and moderate, Eas Walda Selasse, after whose death Saba Gadis had waded through streams of blood to the throne of Tigre. But he was now mild, charitable, and benevolent. He had felt the sting of sin with excruciating remorse long before our arrival, and had tried in many ways to atone for his sins. He was punctual in fulfilling what he understood to be his religious duties, and by being just yet mild in his rule, so that he was highly esteemed and beloved, not only by the people of Tigre, but throughout Abyssinia. He had dismissed with rich presents all his wives save one; he had been diligent in almsgiving, rising frequently at night to carry i7icognuo succour to widows and orphans.

All this had prepared him for receiving the good tidings of the Gospel. Unhappily we had no language in common, as he knew only the Tigre and Shoho dialects, of which we were ignorant. We were therefore obliged to converse through the medium of an interpreter, which is always a drawback in preaching the Gospel; and yet he seemed from the beginning to receive the Word with joy. My dear brother Kugler remained with him for nearly eight months, and made great progress in the study of the Tigre language, so that he could at last speak freely with him, and unfold the precious truths of the Gospel. The effect of this was, as we are thankful to believe, that before his death, which took place in less than a year after our arrival in Abyssinia, he was a truly converted man.

Before reaching Adigrad we had resolved that I should undertake, without delay, a tour into the interior, for the purpose of disseminating the portion of the Holy Scriptures printed in Amharic, consisting of the four Gospels, the Book of the Acts of the Apostles, and the Epistle to the Ptomans. But when we mentioned this project to Saba Gadis, he would not hear of it at first, saying that there were too many dangers, against which he could afford us no protection, though he must consider himself answerable for our safety. Bat during the ten days which I spent at Adigrad there arrived a high officer of Eas Marujeh as ambassador to Saba Gadis, accompanied by about a hundred soldiers. This gave us the opportunity of reiterating our request that one of us should be permitted to start for the interior under the safe escort of that officer, Belata Darcopti. Saba Gadis finally consented, commending me most warmly to the officer's care. He also gave me one of his own officers to accompany and take care of me, at least as far as Gondar, and there to commit me into faithful hands. He was evidently most anxious for my safety, and made me promise to return to him as soon as I could.

Having made the necessary preparations for the journey, and agreed with ten men, besides two servants, to carry the books for distribution, I started for Gondar on the 25th of February, accompanied for a little while by my two brethren, Kiigler and Aichinger. On that day I began my "Journal of a Three Years' Eesidence in Abyssinia," published in 1833 by the Church Missionary Society. The object of that journal was to give to the Committee of that Society a clear sketch of the religious views and morality of the Abyssinians, in order that the Society might judge how far it was their duty to continue and enlarge their mission to Abyssinia, or whether it would be desirable to withdraw it. I shall, therefore, in the present pages avoid as much as possible entering into these details, and simply record some incidents of my long life, and my experiences of the dealings of my gracious and merciful God and Saviour with me. His unworthy servant. I will just quote the first few words of that diary, written in the evening of the first day of my journey:

"I never experienced a deeper sense of desolation and weakness than at the moment of taking leave of my two missionary friends, Kugler and Aichinger. As I rode slowly on, I confessed my sins to God, implored His guidance, and entreated Him to go with me, and pre- serve me from the dangers of the way, especially from sin, and to bless my journey to the salvation of some souls."

Throughout the whole of that month, we made our halt for the night between two and three o'clock in the afternoon. The reason for choosing that hour was, that it was the season of Lent, when all Abyssinians fast; at least, with very few exceptions. They are so strict, that they do not even drink a drop of water before three o'clock P. M. As Belata Darcopti, though very strict in fasting, had a good appetite, he liked to have his dinner ready punctually at that hour of the day. After dinner it was my custom to gather together all who wished to hear the Gospel, and to read to them for about two hours. Before long the whole company of my fellow-travellers formed my attentive audience.

Having been repeatedly warned by the late Mr. Salt, then Consul-General in Egypt, against the prejudices and errors of the Abyssinians, as, for example, the merit of fasting, the worship and invocation of saints, especially the Virgin Mary, and of angels, the Archangel Michael in particular, I abstained at first, in these readings, from making any other comment than a simple, practical explanation of what I read, in the hope that, in proportion as they became acquainted with the truth, they would discard their errors.! N"ot that a mere intellectual assent to the truth often avails to root out old errors from the heart, as I had often had occasion to experience. My hearers soon began to question me, however, asking why I did not fast, why I did not kiss holy pictures, or pray to the Virgin. This gave me the opportunity of directing their attention to the love of God, the work of redemption by the Lord Jesus Christ; the justification of guilty and sinful man by the free grace of God through faith in the merits and the person of Christ, and by degrees I discovered that I could speak on all religious subjects as freely as I could have done in England.

On one occasion, I had been reading the fifteenth chapter of St. Luke, and was deeply affected by the fact of my being surrounded by so many erring sheep and prodigal sons. This led me to recapitulate the whole chapter in a simple practical way; and when I had finished, I observed that many of those rough soldiers had tears in their eyes. One near me said, "I am the prodigal son;" to which several added, "And so am I." Oh! how earnestly did I pray that the Holy Spirit might deepen that impression! But here I must say that in general the Abyssinians are easily impressed; being ignorant and light-minded, however, such impressions seldom last long.

On another occasion I met with a very touching incident. We had encamped near a large village on the top of a mountain, and I was surrounded, as usual, after our frugal meal, with a great number of the inhabitants, young and old, to whom I read and expounded the Gospel, according to my custom. The next morning, feeling the need of solitude, I had withdrawn to pray and write a little in a neighbouring thicket. On returning to the camp, I found that the whole company had left, my own people supposing that I had gone on in advance, as I had several times done before.

While descending the hill and passing through a dark forest, I all at once heard a noise behind me; and on looking back, beheld from fifteen to twenty black boys running after me. The idea struck me that, supposing a Hack man to be found alone by so many white boys in some European forest, he would have nothing very pleasant to expect. Nor were my anticipations agreeable at that moment; but I had no choice, and so was obliged to continue my way. The boys overtook and passed me. Having done so, they all stopped with one accord, turned round, and falling on their faces, asked me to bless and pray for them. I acceded to their request with deep emotion. I never again passed through that forest, but may I not hope to meet some of those boys among the blessed of the Father at the right hand of Him who died for them as well as for me?

The day before reaching Gondar, I had been riding and walking for hours under a hot sun, with no food but a little barley-bread and garlic. (I was obliged to eat the latter in self-defence, as my travelling companions made such plentiful use of the highly odorous vegetable.) I had suffered much from thirst all the afternoon, being feverish and tired, so that I could hardly sit upright on my mule. When we arrived at our halting-place for the night on a wide plain in the neighbourhood of Tshambelga, I was completely exhausted, and could neither stand, sit, nor eat, though I had partaken of no food since the morning. I was in a burning fever, which within an hour or two brought on delirium. A thunderstorm broke, and I thought I was in the midst of a battle. At last a pouring tropical rain began to fall, which so far restored me to consciousness as to make me feel most miserable.

I was lying upon a carpet under the open sky. I desired my servant to cover me with a mattress, and stretching myself on the grassy ground, I once more fell into a kind of delirious slumber, which lasted for about two hours. I was startled and again aroused to consciousness by water trickling into my ear. My head was aching severely, I was in a burning heat, and the rain was pouring still. Looking around, I saw my companions squatting, almost one upon another, under some cowhides. There were two houses upon an eminence not far off, but no other shelter for miles. I told my servant to go and ask if I could be taken in at either of them, promising to pay well; but after a little while, which seemed long to me, he returned with the news that I could not be received at any price. I then asked my man to place a stone under my head to prevent the water running into my ear; and in a kind of despair, yet committing myself into the hands of my Saviour, I fell asleep, and slept until sunrise in about three inches of water. When I awoke, my fever was gone, and I felt so well that I at once mounted my mule and rode about thirty miles that day, till I reached Gondar at sunset, hungry and thirsty, but in excellent health, on the 30th of March 1830.

Gondar had been much reduced since Bruce's day, sixty years previous, when it contained sixty thousand inhabitants. It now numbered barely twenty thousand; but it was still the capital of Abyssinia, with its poor old kinf livinoj in a hut beneath the shadow of the ancient palace, without a court, and destitute of the least influence. It, however, continued to be the centre of ecclesiastical authority, and the headquarters of the Etchega, the head of all the monks, and, in the absence of a bishop in the land, the chief of the whole Abyssinian Church. Being a sacred asylum, it formed the refuge of many members of the ruling families now in disgrace, but who might in a few months to come occupy the most powerful positions in the land. I therefore at once felt the necessity of my weighing all my acts and all my words, and prayed that I might have vouchsafed to me the wisdom of the serpent and the harmlessness of the dove.

This was the more essential because, although I only proclaimed myself to be a simple minister of Christ, people would insist upon making a great man of me, on account of the honour paid me by Saba Gadis, the most powerful among the chiefs. It thus became necessary, after waiting upon the Etchega, to make the acquaintance of all the refugees of rank. This was a most delicate affair; for it would have been imprudent, on the one hand, to make them my friends, and so expose myself to the suspicion of their enemies then in power, or, on the other hand, to allow them to become my enemies, which, in case of their being restored to power, w ould have laid me open to their revenge. In order to remain neutral until I should become better acquainted with their characters and circumstances, I began to speak to them through an interpreter, who, in all indifferent and temporal matters, translated correctly. But when religious topics were in question, and I happened to say anything opposed to Abyssinian prejudices, I could not make him repeat it, though he knew that I understood him. I was soon obliged to silence him, and to speak for myself in Amharic. This proved to me how useless it must be to try to preach the Gospel through the medium of unconverted interpreters.

My books had all been seized at the custom-house, and heavy duty was demanded. I had no mind to pay this, and so establish a precedent. I therefore appealed to the Etchega for help, and thereby unexpected benefit sprang from what I at first regarded as a difficulty. The Etchega, having no idea of any but religious books, considered the action of the custom-house as an interference with his authority, and ordered my property to be delivered to me at once. He was at the same time flattered by my having asked his assistance, and thus gave me a fair opportunity of presenting him with a copy of my books (the Amharic editions of the Gospels, the Acts, and the Epistle to the Eomans). He had never seen them before, and accepted them readily. A few days later he told me that he had read them, and that they were very good. In the meantime I had offered copies of the same portions of Scripture which, for convenience, I will call collectively the Gospel to several persons, who had refused to accept them lest they might contain errors. As soon, therefore, as the Etchega had expressed his approval, I gave him six copies, with the request that lie would distribute them among the heads of the most celebrated churches, coupled with a recommendation from himself. He at once complied; and from that day forward my house was beset with people, first from the neighbourhood, and, by degrees, from all parts of the country, who came to ask for copies of the Gospel, and to hold religious conversations with me, chiefly on subjects then agitating their Church. After a few weeks my house was daily filled with people of all classes, and among them were always some of the best educated, who came to consult me. Their inquiries most frequently related to a controversy concerning the unction of Christ, which had been a subject of dissension in the Abyssinian Church for the past three hundred years or more, and which still divides it into two parties. The extremes of these parties are, on the one hand, the ultra-Mono-physites, who pretend that Christ, being God, was from all eternity united with the Holy Spirit, had never been anointed by Him, and had never received Him. They further hold that, although Christ became incarnate, He became so by His own power, and He so completely absorbed human nature into the Divine, that the human ceased to exist. The practical consequence of this is that the example of Christ is nothing to mankind, as He was not a real man.

The other extreme is nearer the truth with respect to the doctrine of the two natures in Christ, though the form is evaded, the language having no term to express the word nature in the sense of the orthodox Church. This party admits that Christ was very God and very man, and they call themselves the party of the Three Births, i. e., they say that Christ was born in eternity from the Father, and that in due time He was born of the Virgin Mary by the influence of the Holy Ghost; thirdly, that he was born of the Holy Spirit at His baptism in Jordan.

Some of them connect the unction vide Acts x.) with His conception, and some with His baptism. The chief error of this system consists in calling the unction of Christ, or His reception of the Holy Ghost, "Christ's second birth through baptism."

I need not say how trying it was to me to be daily discussing these interminable, and in themselves unprofitable, points of dissension; and yet I was persuaded that both wisdom and charity required it of me. However, it gave me daily opportunities of protesting against many current errors, and of preaching Christ crucified; of presenting Him to these poor people in His various offices as Prophet, Priest, and King, and as " The Lamb of God which taketh away the sin of the world."

All this went on while my house was filling. When it was full, I contrived to bring the conversation to. a close. I then was in the habit of reading a portion of the Word of God. and of addressing the people for a short time, exhorting them to search the Scriptures, to repent, and to believe; upon which I dismissed them in order to make room for those who were standing waiting at the door. Tliis went on several months daily, from sunrise to nightfall, so that I had no time to take any refreshment until nearly eight o'clock in the evening. New hearers continually came from all parts of the country, so that the Gospel was preached to many thousands, and it seemed to produce, in numerous cases, a deep impression before my audience turned homewards ag ain.

I may here observe that the Abyssinians do not believe in the doctrine of the immaculate conception of the Virgin Mary, but they hold that before the conception she was made clean and free from all sin.

One of the most delicate questions in a country like Abyssinia is that relating to the priesthood, the priests exercising great influence over the people. Many of them were opposed to the Gospel being read in the vernacular, and they were almost my sole opponents from the bei innins, until a circumstance soon to be mentioned completely shut their mouths.

I had determined at the outset to speak as little, against the priests as possible until I had become personally acquainted with a good number of them. I met with many, though a decided minority, who were most pious, conscientious, upright, and self-denying, for whom I could feel cordial respect, notwithstanding their ignorance of the way of salvation. This fact proved very useful; for in testifying against the errors, the corruption, and the immorality of the great mass of the priesthood, I was able to bear witness to these laudable exceptions of priests fearing God, and seeking to do good to their people according to their knowledge.! N"ow, as my experience on this point was that of the generality of the people, they always acquiesced in what I said, except some of the priests themselves, and their opposition was frequently the result of ignorance rather than of malice.

Of this I can recall a striking example. I was once speaking to about two dozen persons concerning the way of salvation, when a respectable-looking young priest several times interposed remarks which seemed to militate against what I was saying, "My friend," said I, "let us not quarrel: rather read a chapter of the Gospel for the benefit of these ignorant people." With this, I put a copy of the Amharic Gospel into his hand.

On opening it, he remarked that he could not read Amharic, but that he understood Geez (Ethiopic).

Upon this I gave him an Ethiopic Psalter and repeated my request.

He, knowing the Psalms by heart, began to read as fast as his tongue could articulate.

"This is not the way to read the Word of God," said I; " here, translate the 19th Psalm for the benefit of the assembly."

He then began fluently to talk in Amharic, as if he had been translating,

"Stop," cried I, " that is not the meaning. Translate this first line."

He was mute for a moment, and then said with great simplicity, "I do not understand the meaning."

I turned to the small congregation. "Behold, my dear friends," said I, " in what danger you are of perishing in your ignorance, by intrusting your souls to the guidance of ignorant priests. Our Lord says that if the blind lead the blind, they shall both fall into the ditch." Then turning to the priest, I solemnly addressed him thus:

"How dare you take upon yourself the care of immortal souls, and, through your ignorance, expose them to the risk of eternal perdition? How will you be able to give an account to God at the day of judgment?"

"Be so good as to teach me," was his naive reply.

I gave him the Gospel, and asked a friend to teach him Amharic. When, about two months later, I saw him again, he had not only learned to read fluently, but had also made himself perfectly acquainted, if not with the letter, at least with the substance of the four Gospels and the Acts of the Apostles, and he asked the interpretation of several passages in the Epistle to the Eomans.

I made the acquaintance of a goodly number of Abys-sinians, both priests and laymen, who were well acquainted, not only with the Bible, but with the writings of the Eastern fathers of the first four centuries, as well as with the chief questions which disturbed the Church during the third and fourth centuries. I found many acute and subtle reasoners, who delighted in metaphysical niceties rather than in practical investigations. They frequently put questions to me, to which I was obliged to answer," I do not know." But this humble confession, which no Abyssinian servant ever makes, proved to be very much in my favour; for the hearers concluded that when I did positively affirm anything, it must be true; the more so because I always endeavoured to prove my assertions by passages from the Bible. This again commended me alike to the learned and unlearned; ior, with all their faults, that which has ever given me hope for the Abyssinians is the fact that they hold the Word of God in the highest esteem.

Being of a retiring disposition, I never sought popularity, yet, after a few months' residence at Gondar, my name was known all over Abyssinia, and people came from every province to see and hear me; many with the object of obtaining a copy of the Gospel. By degrees, people of all classes began to speak of getting me appointed Bishop of Abyssinia, instead of sending for an ignorant and passionate Coptic bishop like the last, who, in a fit of wrath, killed a boy.

One day I paid a visit to the Etchega and found him in conversation with several of the most influential priests and Debteras (learned laymen), with all of whom I was on friendly terms. They had just been speaking of the necessity of appointing a bishop. Hitherto there had been a general division of opinion as to whether they should have a Copt, as heretofore, or an Armenian. As soon as I was seated, they proposed that I should be chosen, observing that the large majority of the people would gladly receive me.

Here the Etchega began to speak in Ethiopic.

"I have seen much of this man, and have great confidence in him; but remember that our forefathers had the same confidence in the Frengees."

Nrot willing to hear what was not intended for me, I interrupted him by saying that I knew the history of the Jesuits in Abyssinia. He was evidently surprised at my knowing Ethiopic, their ecclesiastical language, with which by far the greater number even of the priests are unacquainted; but I could see that my interposition had made a favourable impression. We then spoke of the troubles which the Jesuits had caused in Abyssinia in the sixteenth century, and I gave a sketch of the Church of Eome and of the reformation in Europe about the same time. Erom that time I began on all suitable occasions to speak of the necessity of reforming the Abyssinian Church.

I must confess that I often met with much opposition, or at least contradiction, in the discharge of my missionary duties, and, as I afterwards discovered, sometimes with no other object on the part of my opponents than to exhaust my patience and excite my anger.

Some person having once observed in my absence that I was different from all the white men he had ever seen, whether Copts, Greeks, or Armenians, who always lost their temper when contradicted, several of the most learned men of Gondar agreed together that they would try to arouse my impatience and wrath by putting intricate questions and violently opposing all that I should say. This they did for some days, either two by two or all together, in the presence of many other persons.

This really afflicted me deeply; the more so as I had had, until then, a good opinion of them all, as not being far from the kingdom of God. But my sorrow on their account, instead of movinc me to angler, excited me to earnest prayer. They must have become aware of this, for after a few days they came in a body to ask my pardon, confessing the unworthy motive of their conduct, and owning their conviction that I soudit their real G Ood, even their salvation.

As to the actual fruits of my work in Abyssinia, I cannot say much; all will be revealed hereafter. All that I can say is, that many Abyssinians changed many of their views for the better, and that I observed numerous individuals on whom the truths of the Gospel had made a deep impression, but I knew only four or five whom I could consider as truly converted.

I found such medical skill as I possessed a powerful auxiliary in gaining the attention and respect of the people. One of the most noted of my patients was the brother of the most distinguished lady of Abyssinia, Oizoro Tekleet, who by her influence virtually governed

Gondar and its neighbourhood. I received a pressing invitation from this lady to visit her relative, who was said to be possessed by an evil spirit. For three months past she had appointed all the priests of Gondar to watch him and pray for him. There were always about a dozen of them in his room, but he had not improved, being still as furious as ever.

I had no wish to undertake such a task, but I could not refuse without giving offence. As it was on Sunday morning that the lady's request arrived, I sent her word that I did not pay visits on the Lord's Day, but, if it pleased God, I would go on the morrow. It would not have been against my conscience to visit a sick person or a madman on Sunday, but I wanted to gain time to inquire into the case and to ascertain some particulars respecting the habits of the madman. I learned that he was a great eater and drinker and very stout. I felt sure that my grandfather, a very skilful surgeon, would have bled him, and I decided to adopt that mode of treatment; not, however, without first obtaining his consent. I had heard that he was so fierce as to have killed one of his sisters not long before; they had supposed him to be a little better, and had set his right arm at liberty.

When I entered his room on Monday morning, he cast a savage look at me. " Come, Gebts," he cried (Gebts means any white person), " let me see whether you are a liar like these priests, who say that I am possessed of a devil. What do you say?"

"You must not be angry with them," I mildly replied; " they see that your eyes are red, and therefore they think that you are possessed; but if you will allow me to bleed you, your eyes will become white again, and they will perceive that you are not possessed."

He was delighted, and begged that his arm, which was chained to his leg, might be set free. I resolved to let the blood flow until he should faint, hoping thereby to produce a crisis; but this did not happen until he had lost between five and six pounds of blood. I then ordered the attendants to lay him on his bed, and promised to return after two days.

When I entered his room on the third day, he smiled gently at me, and said, "Come near; you are my only friend. But you did not tell me that I was deranged." (He did not use the expression possessed.) " I was so, and I am not yet fully cured; you must bleed me again."

That was just what I wished to do, that he might be fairly enfeebled. I again took sufficient blood to make him faint (I made him stand, that the desired effect might be produced with a less copious loss of blood), and said I would return on the third day. On my next visit I found him perfectly sensible in fact, cured; so that I did not hesitate to order the chains to be removed from his arms and legs. This cure gave me a great name, so that no priest dared to say anything against me, because the people would retort that I had cast out an evil spirit which had defied all the priests of Gondar.

But this celebrity was also the cause of much trouble to me; for from that time all those who were ailing thought that I could cure them. And, indeed, my success far exceeded my expectations; but my stock of medicine was soon exhausted, and there remained nothing but the lancet, which, however, did wonders, even when I did not expect any good result. I was so much urged to use it, that my great care was not to do harm with it. In the case of an old man of eighty, and in that of a young man between five-and-twenty and thirty years of age, the one utterly powerless to walk, the other suffering from palsy to such a degree that he could neither move a limb nor articulate a sound, the use of my lancet produced such amazing results, that I could only attribute the cures to the blessing of God and the faith of the patients and their friends.

I did not fare so well when I myself fell ill, a few days later. I had for some time previously been holding intercourse with Falashas, the black Jews of Abyssinia, visiting them in their villages, and receiving visits from them. Now all the Talashas were considered by the Abyssinian Christians as Booda, that is, sorcerers or witches, endowed with the faculty of transforming themselves into animals of different kinds, especially into hyenas. What is worse, they are believed to have the power to eat by slow degrees the inward parts of man and animals until death ensues, if the ravages be not checked.

Among my numerous Falasha visitors was an elderly, strongly- built, intelligent, and resolute woman named Mareet, whom I was inclined to call a mother in Israel, though she opposed all my arguments in favour of Christianity with reasonings partly, I believe, of her own invention. This woman was well known, and considered by the Christians as the queen of the Boodas, and when they saw her approaching my house, they all used to run away. I had often endeavoured to cure them of this absurd and dangerous superstition, now in solemn earnest, now in simple jest; but all to no purpose.

A peculiarity of the hyena is that it emits a double sound or voice, the most frequent one resembling the roar of a lion, while the other is exactly like the laughter of a woman. One evening this loud, sudden laughter was heard in the street, quite near to my house. It was clearly the voice of a hyena; but I called aloud " Mareet! " as if it had been my friend transformed into a wild beast.

I meant it as a joke, but ten or twelve persons present took it in earnest and were frightened.

The next day I had a severe attack of illness, and in a few minutes the rumour went all over Gondar that I had fallen under the nefarious power of poor Mareet, and that she was already gnawing at my vitals. Immediately the house was filled by sympathising people, each of whom had some Booda story to relate, with the view of proving that I was under the malign influence. Whatever was said to the contrary was considered as a proof of the truth of their assertion. Likewise every one had a remedy to propose; and some of these suggestions were so ridiculous, that, notwithstanding my depression and acute pain, I could not help laughing; which again was taken as proof of my being a prey to the Booda. Amulets were the most popular specific, which, after much consultation, they agreed to apply to different parts of my suffering body. But as I had often protested against the use of amulets, on account of the purchase of them being the ruin of many poor families, I positively declared that I would not allow one to be brought near my bed; this declaration was, however, deemed the expression of the very Booda, speaking through my lips. Upon this several of the bystanders drew near to hang the amulets on my arms and neck; my efforts to push them away were of no avail. Some of them were moved to tears of pity, and said that my life was so precious that it would be a crime to let it be destroyed by the Booda when it was in their power to save it. With this, and encouraging one another, they seized my hands and feet in order to hang heavy amulets upon them.

I had a strong servant, who had already given up many superstitions, but who till then had done nothing to help me, evidently from fear of being brought into contact with the Boodas, for he was otherwise a man of great courage. I told him in the most peremptory tone that if he allowed the people to touch me with a single amulet, I would dismiss him that very day. Upon this, being greatly attached to me, he successfully resisted my would-be benefactors, and ordered them to leave the room for a while.

I had been inwardly praying for them all the time, and I could scarcely refrain from tears of pity, being convinced that they were actuated solely by love for me and by a sense of duty.

After a while they re-entered my room, and offered to apply other remedies, to which I consented, rather than exhaust my strength in disputes, only declining to swallow any remedy which was strange to me.

They accordingly covered my bed and filled my mouth, nose, and ears with various kinds of herbs. It was now evening, and I made that a pretext for begging these oppressively kind people to leave me to rest. So they left me, after expressing all the good wishes they could think of. When alone with my servant, I ordered him to let no one come near me next day, save one or two discreet friends whom I named, in order that these few might assure all inquirers that the Booda had not yet consumed me. The next day I suffered much less, and in a short time I was able to resume my work.

When I started from Adigrat for the interior, I had taken with me twelve men to carry my books for distribution, intending to dismiss them soon after my arrival at Gondar. But just before reaching Gondar I met Oubea, the ruler of Samene, with his army, returning from a marauding expedition in some province belonging to Eas Marieh, who was pursuing him. closely w th a larger army. All the passes between Gondar and Tigre were occupied, and the way effectually blocked against all travellers for the space of three months. "When Oubea at last surrendered, the rainy season had set in and the rivers were swollen, so that nobody thought of travelling. Thus I was obliged to keep my twelve bearers and my servant all the time of my absence from Tigre, at a season of quasi-famine. I had only taken with me enough money for the maintenance of myself and my servant during the three or four months of my intended absence; therefore, when I found myself shut up in Gondar with thirteen persons to support, I economised as much as possible; and yet before three months were over all my money was gone. It was a trying moment when I sent my last dollar to the market; for there were still four or five months to be provided for ere I could start for, or receive any remittance from, Tigre.

I felt this predicament the more strongly because, when a child, I had once seen my father shed tears because he had no means at hand to pay a pressing debt. I had there and then made a solemn vow never to incur any debt without making sure of being able to repay it within a few days, and this vow I have, with God's help, kept to this day.

I had also frequently and publicly reproved the Abyssinians for their begging propensities, and exhorted them to pray to God, in faith, for their daily bread, assuring them that if they believed, God would grant their requests. Of course they did not believe me, but I was bound to act in accordance with my own teaching. But what was to be done? I asked God's help and guidance, and waited. Soon after this, I heard accidentally that there was an abundance of game a few miles distant from Gondar. The next day I took my old gun and several of my men, and went towards the hills where the game was said to exist. I shot a gazelle and some partridges, and instructed my men as to what they were to do when I was not with them. From that day I was free from care for several months.

I had no need to go myself to the hunt. About half my men went daily, except on Sundays, to the hills, and never returned empty. Sometimes they broucrht as much as two laroje gazelles and a number of guinea-fowls, so that I could exchange half my meat for bread, vegetables, and other necessaries. Our supplies were so plentiful that I was enabled to feed several poor people every day, as w ell as beggars, whom I reproved while I helped them. I learned to make tolerably good gunpowder, so that I felt quite independent.

At the beginning of October, the rainy season being over and the river Tacazze fordable, the time for my leaving Gondar for Tigre had arrived. As soon as it became known that I was about to leave, people of all classes came flocking to my house in such numbers that both house and court were filled from morning till night. Avoiding as much as possible all controversy, I insisted upon the necessity of individual conversion and faith in the Lord Jesus Christ; and 1 laid great stress upon the need for reformation of their Church as the only means of raising the people from their degraded state. In consequence of this last recommendation, some of the most influential men, both lay and clerical, convened a large meeting to consider what could be done to restore the country to peace and happiness, and to inquire how far Great Britain might be disposed to help them. They all admitted the necessity of reforming their Church as the first step towards reforming the nation; but they

"were not all agreed as to the extent of the requisite reform. Knowing that they were not prepared to make essential changes in the more difficult and weighty points of doctrine, I suggested preliminary steps; for example, the establishment of superior schools or colleges for the training of a new class of clergy, as I considered the ignorance and corruption of the priests to be at the root of all the evils under which the country had gone to ruin. I also proposed that thenceforth no man should be ordained who was not thoroughly acquainted with the whole of the New Testament and part of the Old. To this they all assented, but observed that they could not do it effectually without help from abroad; upon which I replied that, if they were in earnest, my friends in England would gladly send them teachers and otherwise help them.

I next proposed that, in place of sending but a few boys to the monasteries to learn to read in a dead language, they should establish schools everywhere, in order that their children of both sexes might learn to read the Word of God in their own vernacular; and I promised that England should supply them with books, especially Bibles. At this they were all as delighted as if the proposal were already realised.

I further laid before them the proposal to have several learned and godly native bishops, instead of having but one, often ignorant, Coptic bishop, and that they should have less pomp and power than that enjoyed by the present prelate. To this they all agreed. But when I added that the bishops and clergy should be free to marry, there was a division; though a small majority agreed with me.

The removal of pictures from the churches was my next proposition (they have no carved or molten images).

To my great surprise I found that the greater part of the assembly were of my opinion on the subject, though it provoked a long discussion. Some asserted that the pictures were merely reminders of the virtues of the saints and holy personages whom they represented, and not objects of worship; while others admitted that, although the better instructed view them in this light, yet the mass of the people do worship them, and thus incur the sin of idolatry; for which guilt they own that the more enlightened portion of the community were answerable.

After this I mooted the abolition of the invocation of the Virgin Mary, of the Archangel Michael, of angels and of saints, pointing out that there is but one Mediator between God and man, the Man Christ Jesus.

Here a small majority was against me, but I was again astonished to find that a considerable minority was with me; and this I attributed, as in the former case, also to the effect of my previous teaching.

We touched upon many other points of doctrine and practice, and all went on peaceably, without any angry feelincr.

At the conclusion of the conference they thus addressed me: " You are now leavin us with a full knowledge of our wretched state and the ruined condition of our country, from which we have no means of raising ourselves. Commend us to the English people, that they may have compassion on us and come to our assistance."

I took an affectionate leave of them, and prepared to start the next day.

It was my intention soon to return to Gondar, there to settle, perhaps with my dear brother Kugler, or else with some other missionary whom the Church Missionary Society might send to our aid; but this w as not to be.

When I reflect upon my stay and work at Gondar, the most active part of my missionary life, and the wide door which Providence had opened to the preaching of the Gospel there, I am confounded. Is it in any way my fault? I have enough to reproach myself with and to humble me when I recall my failures in faith, love, and. self-denial; when I look back upon my self-complacency when I met with success, and my despondency when I met with none; when I think of instances of my neglect, of coldness in prayer. And yet I have the witness within myself that I endeavoured to preach and testify to the Gospel of the grace of God, the word of reconciliation by Jesus Christ. Or was it the result of some mysterious judgment of God that the opened door should be shut unto this day against the Gospel of peace? I do not know. But since that time I have ever prayed for the salvation, the peace, of Abyssinia.

Many years later I made another effort to introduce the Gospel into that country, and not altogether without success.

A few days before starting from Gondar, Saba Gadis sent me a sum of money, for which I was exceedingly thankful; for although I bad not actually borrowed money, I had incurred obligations to several persons, and the idea of leaving without paying what I considered as debts had previously oppressed me. One good old man, for example, hearing that I was short of money, just before my last few dollars were gone, had sent me twenty dollars as a gift, while others had sent me more or less valuable presents. I therefore looked upon it as a gracious providence that I was thus enabled to pay all my debts; and although, after doing so, but one dollar remained in my possession, my confidence in God had been so much strengthened that I could in this state of poverty cheerfully begin a journey of thirteen days with fourteen persons for whom I must provide.

For several weeks before my leaving Gondar I had observed a young man named Gabrow, who came daily to spend hours at the door of my room, paying the greatest attention to all that was said, but without speaking a word himself. When he heard me rebuking the people for begging, and telling them to pray to God, who would give them all things needful, he afterwards confessed to saying within himself that it was all very well for a rich man like me to talk so, but he would like to see whether, if I were destitute like many of the poor people around me, I would act as I preached. However, when he heard that I was about to leave Gondar, he came to me trembling, and asked me to take him into my service, not for wages, but on condition that I should teach him. I accepted his offer, as he seemed very intelligent, and hoped that he would not only be benefited himself, but become the means of blessingj to others.

On the evening before our departure he came to me to suggest that, as we were about to travel for many days through a country devastated by war, where there was neither food to be bought nor game to be shot, it would be well to lay in a stock of provisions before beginning the journey. His surprise was great when I told him that I had nothing but a little flour, which I had bought with my last dollar.

We travelled the same way as that by which we had come six months before; but it was now, in consequence of the war, little more than a desolate wilderness. When in the vicinity of the high, bare rocks of Silky, my provision of flour being all but exhausted, I saw about a dozen rock-goats, as large as a good-sized stag. It is a rare animal, even in Abyssinia, and when full grown has black horns, four or live inches in diameter at the roots, and from eight to nine feet long, nearly in the shape of a semicircle, the points passing between its hind-legs. If I could have killed one, we should have had food for our whole party for a couple of days. But having been hunted by the soldiers, they had grown very shy. My hunt, by no means devoid of danger among crags and precipices, ended unsuccessfully, and I returned to the camp tired and hungry enough to relish my share of unleavened cake, the last remnant of our provision. This was a crisis in which Gabrow secretly watched to see whether I should verify my words to the beggars, and whether God would really send me bread in answer to my prayers.

Next morning, having still a small cup of butter, we melted it, and every one of the party received a small spoonful of it for his breakfast. About mid-day, when we made our halt, I sent one of my men, according to the custom of the country, to salute an influential lady who lived about six miles out of our line of march, and to whom I had once sent a copy of the Gospel at her own request. My servant had not been gone more than a quarter of an hour when we came to a man sitting by the roadside with a large basket of loaves and a jar of beer, which he asked me to accept, with, a message from that very lady to the effect that, having been informed that I was to pass that way on that particular day, and knowing that no food was to be had on the journey, she had therefore sent me the bread and beer. I accepted it thankfully, and it proved sufficient to satisfy my whole party, with half-a-dozen poor people in addition, who had followed us for safety's sake.

The next day we started at daybreak, and travelled the w hole day through the valley of Telenit without food until sunset, when we found a spring of clear water in a forest. I told my people that we would stay there for the night, and ask God to bless the water to the satisfying of both hunger and thirst, which recommendation they took in good part. I may here mention that I have often travelled for a whole day, once for two days and a half, without tasting any food; and yet I have never suffered from hunger, but very often from thirst.

AYe had set up our encampment hardly ten minutes when we saw two horsemen coming towards us. They alighted a little way from us in token of friendship, and approaching, told us that their master, the Governor of the district, having heard that a white man who had distributed the Gospel at Gondar was to pass that way, had sent them to look for him and bring him to their master. They offered me a horse to ride, and though the distance was five miles, and I and my people were very tired, we at once arose and went. When we arrived, we found that our host was ill in bed; but he had caused an ox to be killed and a sumptuous supper to be prepared, with plenty of wine and beer, so that some of my young men drank too much.

On the morrow, while my people were getting ready to start again, the Governor sent for me to go and see him. I found him ill and low-spirited, and in great care about his soul. I unfolded to him the treasures of the grace and love of God, as revealed in the life, the teachings, the sufferings, and the atoning death of Christ, and exhorted him to repentance and faith. After spending about an hour with him, I left him greatly comforted. A few months after this I learned that Oubea had had his feet and hands cut off, and that he had survived but a few hours.

My people had started in advance of me, except Gabrow, who was to show me the way. Shall I confess that, when I found myself on the verge of the valley of the Tacazze, about 4000 feet deep, a howling wilderness inhabited only by wild beasts and poisonous reptiles, a doubt mingled with my accustomed prayer for 'daily bread"? "Can God furnish a table in the wilderness? " The experience of the two preceding days and my own conscience rebuked me, and asking pardon for my want of faith, I began the steep descent, which took me four or five hours. On arriving at the bottom of the valley, I found that our host had secretly sent out two servants before daybreak with meat, bread, and wine, to await us near the river. There was enough not only for that day, but for the next also.

The river was still much swollen and full of alligators. Our meal was seasoned by many a story of men having fallen a prey to those creatures; but all agreed that the monster never attacks his victims where they are wont to cross, but waits a little farther down to catch such men and animals as are carried away by the current.

The heat was so intense in the lower part of the valley that my sealing-wax, packed away in the very centre of my little portmanteau, was completely melted.

A question arose as to how we should cross the river, and it was arranc ed that the tallest and stronc est should carry the shortest and weakest. I alone proved to be a coward, for I had courage neither to carry nor be carried; and so I contrived to ford the current by taking a heavy stone on my shoulder, to prevent my being lifted off my feet by the volume of water and borne down the stream to the crocodiles. We encamped that night in a lovely grassy spot, and rested in peace, notwithstanding the roaring of lions and hyenas which were prowling in the neighbourhood.

Soon after this we emerged from the wilderness into a well-cultivated country, through which I had passed eight months before, and the people, knowing that I was in favour with their great ruler, Saba Gadis, invited me daily, during the last few days, to lodge in their villages. All my-wants were supplied without my having to ask for anything. On the last evening, at Axum, they made a kind of feast for me, which gave me an opportunity of speaking to the assembled people about the one thing needful.

Wlien I arrived the next day at Adowa, I heard that Saba Gadis was there with his army, and that he had just sat down to dine with about a hundred of his chief oficers. Before I had time to inform him of my arrival, he sent an officer to invite me to dine with him. I went direct to the diuing-hall, and found it no easy matter to make my way through the crowd of officers and servants to my princely entertainer. When I reached him, I took his hand to kiss it in sign of submission, but he would not suffer me to do so until he had kissed mine. He then made me sit beside him on his throne or bedstead, by way of commending me to his subjects. Thus from the depth of poverty I was exalted to sit with the prince of the people. The next day he started on his march against Mareyeh and Oubea, who were conjointly preparing to invade Tigre, and I saw him no more. That same evening I had the great pleasure of welcoming my dear brother and colleague. Christian Kugler, who arrived from Adigrad.

The short time, less than a month and a half, which I was permitted to spend with Kugler at Adowa was a period of spiritual refreshment, but also of trial. As almost all the men had followed Saba Gadis to the war, and the rest were ignorant of Amharic, while I was unacquainted with the Tigre dialect, I could do but little missionary work, except in the way of conversation with a few lay and clerical individuals. Gabrow also took occasion to open his heart to me, and this was the beginning of what I believe to be his sincere conversion. During the year following he witnessed powerfully for the truth of the Gospel. At last his elder brother took him by force to Amhara, and I never had any trustworthy tidings of him after. But I hope to meet him again in a better land.

I suffered much from my eyes at this period, but I enjoyed, nevertheless, many blessed hours of conversation with my colleague, he relating his experience with the humble and teachable Saba Gadis during my absence at Gondar, and I recounting my experiences of the last eight months, and making plans for the future, which, however, were not to be realised. He practised medicine with much success, which gave him many opportunities of preaching the Gospel in private houses, as he had learned the language while I was at Gondar.

One day, December loth, being both of us not well, we took a ride on the banks of a rivulet which in some places was very deep. In one of these watery hollows we saw what we in the distance took for a crocodile.

"Which of us will go and kill that monster?" I exclaimed.

"I will go," returned Kugler, with some hesitation, not at all natural to him.

On drawing near, he thought the animal was a hippopotamus, and fired on it; but the gun burst, and inflicted several wounds on his left arm, of which he at first made light. But a few days later the danger fully appeared, as I find from my Journal of December 23 d.

"To-day Kugler sustained a great loss of blood from the largest of his wounds, upon which fever set in. I am struck with his daily references to his approaching dissolution. More than a month ago, indeed, when I myself was ill and he quite well, he said to me with much solemnity, If I should soon be called hence, of which I have a strong presentiment, write to all my friends, telling them that I love them, and that if I have offended any among them, I ask their pardon."

I will not enter here into the details of the anxiety, anguish, and consolation of the ensuing days, as they are described in my published Journal; but the following extracts I cannot refrain from giving:

"Dece77iher 2gth. Yesterday evening the pains of my dear brother were so excruciating that a heart-rending cry escaped his lips; but immediately after he said, It is the will of the Lord that I should suffer; I will therefore bear it patiently. At the same moment he fainted, but soon recovered.

"In the meantime a good number of people had assembled in the room, to whom he spoke most earnestly for a good while in their Tigre dialect; and, to my consternation, he ended by saying, I am on the point of leaving this world. When the people were gone, he remarked to me, I had almost forgotten my suffering while speaking, but now it is so terrible that it seems to consume all my bones. Yet he passed a fairly good night.

"Dccemher 2,0th. It is with the deepest sorrow that I describe the event of last evening. Yet the Lord has hitherto sustained me, and I trust He will further help me. Yesterday evening, while we were quietly speaking of the furtherance of the kingdom of God, a torrent of blood burst from my dear brother's wound, and he sank exhausted into my arms. "When he could again speak, his first words were, I am dying. I should have liked to live longer to preach the Gospel to these poor people.

but the Lord's will be done. Upon this he prayed, Lord Jesus! bless and be gracious unto me. Take me to Thyself.

"When his voice began to falter he said to me, I can no longer speak; but tell these people (present) that Jesus is my portion, and that they must not weep for me when I am dead. Then to me, Speak to me of the Saviour. I could not yet believe that he was dying; my heart was so full that I could with difficulty utter the words, Be of good cheer; the Lord will be with you in life and in death. ' I know it, he responded in a firm tone; He has never forsaken me, and with these words he fell quietly asleep in Jesus.

"As soon as I said, He is gone, the numerous men and women present began to lament as if each one had lost an only son. I let them weep and cry for a little while, and then. I addressed a few words to them in Amharic on I Thess. iv. i 3, to which they hearkened with great attention. A Mohammedan present said, I have witnessed the last moments of many dying persons; four have died in my arms. But I have never before seen how faith can be victorious over death.

"I had much difficulty at first with the priests, who objected to any one being buried in the churchyard who had not confessed to or received absolution from them before his death, but when they were told that Kugler was a holy man,. they yielded the point, on condition that they should say a mass for his soul, to which I positively objected. But I should never have finished with them if it had not been for a young prince of the ancient royal family, Tecla Georgis, with whom I was daily reading the Word of God, who took the matter into his hands with great decision, so that at last all went on well in accordance with my wishes.

'January Jtli, 1831. The man whom I had sent to Saba Gadis. to inform him of Kugler's death came back and told me that when Saba Gadis heard the sad news, he covered his face and wept loud, and called for several of his highest officers to come and weep with him; but soon after he bethought himself and said, I had forgotten in what circumstances we are. It is better that I weep alone secretly; for if my enemies were informed that we are weeping together, they might suppose that we are mourning for some high officer, and refuse to make peace. He then covered his face, and for. two hours he did not say one word to any one. He then inquired about the burial of Kugler, whom he called his friend, his brother; and when he heard that the priests had made difficulties, he got very angry and threatened to punish them severely."

A few days after these events, the young prince, who visited me almost every day, met his confessor at my house; and I believe it was on account of this latter circumstance that he at once began to put questions to me as to how sinners can be justified before God, about saving faith, prayer to the saints, and so forth. With respect to the last point he said, "Your faith is better than ours; you pray direct to God, and you are sure that He hears you; while we pray to the saints without being sure that they hear us. We worship them without knowing whether we are doing right or wrong."

Here his confessor interrupted him, saying, "We worship neither the saints nor their pictures."

"I beg your pardon," replied the prince; " we do worship them."

"I do not worship them," cried the priest with impatience.

"Then why do you teach me to worship them?" retorted the prince.

The priest was somewhat confused.

' I will not worship them any more," he conceded; " I will only worship God and the Virgin Mary."

"If you do not worship the saints," said the prince, " why should you worship the Virgin Mary? Was she not also a mortal like as we are?"

The poor priest could not answer him.

My time at Adowa passed very tediously. Every day I heard new and contradictory tidings of the two armies on both sides of the Tacazze, who remained inactive for three months.

At last Eas Mareyeh and Oubea crossed the Tacazze, and a great and bloody battle was fought, in wliich Eas Mareyeh was killed, but his troops were victorious. Saba Gadis was taken prisoner; and as he was an inde-)endent prince, he expected, according to precedent, to be treated as such. But the numerous sanguinary Gallas of Mareyeh's army imperiously demanded that he should be killed in atonement for the death of their chief; and Oubea was suspected of willingly yielding to their clamour, in the hope of bringing the whole country under his own rule, as he was decidedly the most powerful of Mareyeh's officers, and had for several years ruled independently over Samene and Walkait. Tor two months Oubea ravaged a great part of Tigre, whilst the sons of Saba Gadis, who had been almost adored by the people, were collecting an army in the neighbourhood of the Shoho country towards the Eed Sea. They succeeded so far that Oubea was driven back across the Tacazze; but they fell into strife among themselves about the succession, and finally Oubea defeated them, and ruled in Tigre for several years.

When the news reached Adowa that the army of Tigre had been beaten, the wildest confusion prevailed. Then came the news that hostile soldiers were at hand, plundering and marauding. All the inhabitants fled, except a few old women who remained behind, screaming on the terraces of the houses. I was at first undecided whether to fly or to trust to Oubea's protection, my name being so well known in all the country. But at that critical moment the thought struck me that the marauders would arrive long before any one in authority to whom I could appeal would reach the spot. I therefore resolved to seek a place of safety, together with my disciples, six young men whom I was instructing.

I hastily removed my books and all my little property into the nearest church, which was considered to be a safe asylum (though it was shortly after burnt down by accident, and all was destroyed), and fled, taking with me only the barest necessaries.

As I was very weak, I rode on my mule the whole day, except when, from time to time, I lent it to one or other of the party who was nearly fainting from fatigue. We went on as fast as we could, as every now and then we were overtaken by horsemen bringing the tidings that marauding parties were close upon our rear, nor stopped until it was quite dark, when we laid ourselves down upon the grass. We were so tired that we had not energy enough to kill a sheep we had brought with us, or indeed to eat anything. Of course, we dared not kindle a fire. When we awoke in the morning, we found that a hyena had eaten our sheep, and we were therefore obliged to start fasting, as we had done the day before.

We marched the whole day with nothing to eat, as prudence led us to avoid human habitations, but met with several rivulets of good water, which seemed to feed as well as to quench our thirst.

On the third morning we met Walda Michael, one of the sons of Saba Gadis, who told me of his father's death, and made me promise to be his friend for his father's sake; he was the eldest son, and expected to succeed. Meanwhile his people were engaged in killing an ox, of which he gave me a large portion, sufficient for myself and my young men. I enjoyed it much in its natural warmth, having already accustomed my palate to the taste of raw meat. After advising me whither to go for safety, Walda Michael departed, leaving me one of his men to accompany and protect me. Being now out of danger, we rested for the remainder of that day. At night we had a terrible thunder-storm, with much rain, quite out of season. But I was already an Abyssinian in my apparel and furniture, and instead of a mattress I had a large tanned cowhide, which served the further purpose of protecting me against the weather in case of need. I dug a ditch round about my resting-place on the grass, arranged my cowhide, remained perfectly dry, and slept soundly all night.

In two more days we reached Behaat, near Senafeh, where I had a faithful Moslem friend, who begged me to instruct his son, a boy of nine years, who some years afterwards was baptized by the Eev. C. Isenberg, and who subsequently became famous in King Theodore's reiofn under the name of Samuel.

I remained about three months at Behaat, till that place became too hot for me, a number of wild Shohos having agreed to attack and spoil my house. By the advice of Walda Michael I took refuge at Adigrad, from which I was several times forced to fly for the same reason as I had fled from Behaat, and finally found an asylum at the almost inaccessible monastery of Debra Damo. I spent one year and nine months in this part of the country, which was still claimed, though only half protected, by the sons of Saba Gadis.

Those were long months, during which I could do very little, chiefly because I did not know the language of the people; and though by degrees I learned a little of it, it was not enough to enable me to make any impression on the indifferent, ignorant people.

My principal occupation was teaching my six pupils, without any book but my j)olyglot Bible. I was obliged to teach general history, church history, geography, c., from memory. I had also frequent opportunities, botli at Adigrad and Debra Damo, of preaching the Gospel in Amharic to individual priests and laymen who visited these localities, and in one case, at least, not without success, as I shall relate hereafter.

I was seldom well, and suffered much from my eyes. Nevertheless, I was generally in good spirits, being encouraged by the love and obedience of my pupils, though I cannot say that more than two of them were really converted wlien I left them.

After the first year, my position became critical from another point. I had only as much money left as I thought would suffice for returning to Egypt, and I had no means of obtaining any. While at Behaat and Adigrad I had adopted an expedient by which I was enabled to support myself and my family of ten persons for several months. After teaching my young men in the morning, I used to take them in the afternoon to the uncultivated parts of the neighbourhood to seek for a root, the bark of which is essential to the preparation of good hydromel, or honey-wine. It was easy to exchange this root for wheat and other necessaries, sometimes even for money.

But when at last I was obliged to remove to Debra Damo, this source of income ceased, and I was obliged to encroach upon my travelling money. However, I contrived to live entirely upon barley and water with my young men, who were all satisfied to share my fare for about one dollar per month.

When I was at Adigrad I had an old woman to cook, and a younger one to grind the corn, fetch wood, and carry water. The wood had to be brought from a forest at a considerable distance. None but women will perform labours of this kind in Abyssinia, unless on a journey. One day we had no wood in the house, and the younger woman was not well. I therefore told my young men to go and fetch some fuel from the forest; they shrugged their shoulders.

"We are not afraid of the work," said they, " but it is a shame for men to carry wood."

As I well knew that prejudices cannot be eradicated by mere force of authority, I did not insist, but withdrew, and went to the forest myself secretly and alone. After a while they observed that I had disappeared, and began to inquire after me. They were told that I had been seen going towards the forest. They all ran off in pursuit of me, and when they found me, I had already collected a bundle of wood, which each one wanted to carry home.

"No," said I mildly, "let me carry it, since it is a shame for you to do it; I do not want to put you to shame."

However, they implored me so earnestly that I was obliged to yield; and though it was beginning to get dark, each of them gathered a load, and insisted on carrying a good-sized log.

A few days afterwards, when only one day's supply was left, I rose early in the morning and directed my steps to the forest; but they were on the watch, and came running after me, begging me not to trouble myself, and saying cheerfully that they would bring enough wood. I said jestingly that I would go with them and bear their shame while they bore my wood. From that day forward I never had to remind them; they themselves took care to keep the household well supplied.

ISTow these young men were better behaved and better instructed than any others in that district, and were highly respected. A number of the men of Adigrad met together in consequence of these incidents, and after some consultation came to the conclusion, that if such learned people were not ashamed to carry wood, neither should they themselves be ashamed to do the same. Before three months were over there was no more sendino-of wives and daughters to the forest, at the risk of being stolen and enslaved by Shohos, as had frequently been the case; and the men congratulated themselves upon their own change of domestic discipline.

It now only remains for me to describe Debra Damo. It is an isolated, perpendicular rock, on the top of a hill. There is only one spot where a particular path might be cut in it. The inmates of the monastery are drawn up and let down by a rope a height of sixty feet; and I confess that it was not without some misgivings that I confided my more than usual weight to that rope grasped by the monks, especially the first time.

The story received by the Abyssinians relates that Frumentius, the Apostle of Abyssinia in the fourth century, wishing to establish a monastery on Debra Damo, and finding no means of ascending the rock, asked God to help him. He had no sooner finished his prayer than he beheld an immense serpent, which at once threw its head on to the top of the rock. Frumentius hastened to take hold of its tail, by which he was drawn to the summit; hence he is called Aragavee, the Ascender.

The monastery consists of about forty houses or huts, each one inhabited by three monks. The oldest of the three professes to be engaged exclusively in spiritual things, the second has the care of the temporal concerns, and the third is the servant of the two first. It is asserted, and probably with truth, that no female has ever been on the rock.

The top of the rock is a plateau about half a mile long and a quarter of a mile broad. I used to walk the length of it almost daily to amuse myself with the games and grimaces of a herd of monkeys, about a hundred in number, w iich rested every day at the same hour for about forty minutes on a grassy spot under the rock. They used to come in the following order: Five or six of the strongest males walked in front, four or five on the right and on the left, while the younger ones and the females carryiug their nurslings occupied the centre of the procession.

Just under the place where I stood there was a large flat rock even with the ground, upon which the mothers deposited their young ones; and, although in perpetual motion, the little creatures never transgressed the boundaries assigned to them, though their parents were a short distance from them. As soon as the females had deposited the young ones, the males took up their position in every direction, and beckoned to their mates to come to them, a signal which was instantly obeyed. They then walked in pairs about twenty paces farther and sat down. The females occupied the whole time in divesting their consorts of their parasites. The males w ould gently pat the females on the shoulders from time to time.

Monogamy seemed to prevail; yet a few males had each two female companions, which both went to them at the first beckoding. The. male then gave a slight tap on the head of the one which was to follow him, when the other looked down and remained motionless, evidently much displeased. But there were some males which had no helpmate, and these, seeing the neglected females, used to go and sit at a distance of four or five paces from them, looking at, but never touching, them. After a while the bisramist would remember his nedected wife, and go slowly creeping towards her. Perceiving his rival, he would run at him; but the latter was so fully upon his guard that I never saw one caught. Then the husband would return to his poor, innocent mate, and give her a sound thrashing, but only with his hand, never biting her.

When the recreation-time had expired, the males resumed their former positions, and the females took up their little ones, and they marched off in the same order as before. I observed that if the march happened to be through rugged and rocky parts, most of the males carried the little ones.

Most of the monks were hostile to me, and manifested this feeling by avoiding me. Only a very few had the courage to dispute with or to oppose me, while three or four were really my friends, especially my aged host, so mild, humble, and pious I might almost say holy evidently loving God and His Word, with its essential truths, so sincerely, that I considered him as a dear brother in Christ.

There was another monk, whom, though ignorant, I sincerely loved and respected on account of his humility, benevolence towards all men, and his faithfulness in proportion to his scanty knowledge of the truth. He related to me the following fact: " I was in easy circumstances at Axum, enjoying a most happy life with my faithful wife, when, a few years ago, I became very ill. I was considered to be dying; but my wife said to me, I cannot see you die before my eyes; I will die for you. So saying, she took a chicken, walked three times round my bed, and killed the bird in my presence. She fell ill that same day, and the next day she died, and I began to recover. I vowed that I would never look at another woman."

I have myself witnessed a similar case, except that it was a healthy young man devoting himself for his apparently dying master; and instead of killing a chicken, he broke an egg, and died two days later, while his master got well. The young man was my servant, and he did it for my unworthy self. How to explain such facts I know not; but they prove at least that Abyssinians are capable of devotion and self-sacrifice. It was therefore not difficult for my ignorant friend to believe in and to rely on the atoning sacrifice of our Lord Jesus Christ.

About three weeks before my leaving Debra Damo I received a visit from Walda Selassia, the most learned Abyssinian I have ever known. He had travelled a distance of more than three hundred miles to see me, and he introduced himself by saying that he had heard of what I had been preaching at Gondar, and his mind had become troubled and his views unsettled upon many points. He liad therefore resolved to come and consult with me.

He began at once by asking what were my views upon some of the religious and metaphysical questions which were continually under discussion among the learned. As I had done at Gondar, I just answered his questions, and then tried to lead the conversation to more practical subjects, but lie contradicted all that 1 said. He came and spent with me several hours of every day, to my great annoyance, for he persisted in opposing all that I said, although I saw that more than once my words had made a deep impression upon him.

At length, on hearing that the sons of Saba Gadis had surrendered to Oubea, and that consequently the war and anarchy were at an end, I perceived that the time for my departure had arrived, and prepared to start at once. I took leave of Debra Damo on the 27th of November, and many of the monks accompanied me to the spot whence I was let down from the rock; several descended after me. On parting from them, I again gently exhorted them to give their hearts unreservedly to our Lord Jesus Christ, and to trust in His grace for everything.

Suddenly Walda Selassia burst into tears, and in the presence of all the monks he thus addressed me: " Now that you are leaving, I ask your forgiveness for all the trouble I have caused you. I had heard of you at Gondar after you had left there, and I resolved to come here to see you, and to hear by what proofs you maintain your doctrine in opposition to ours. I resisted you with all my might, several times even when convinced of the truth of your words; but it was for the sake of obtaining stronger proofs of your doctrine. Now that we are about to part, perhaps for life, I ought to be frank and candid with you. You have opened my eyes; I will treasure up your instructions in my heart, and will publicly avow myself your disciple. You are my father."

On saying these words he again wept bitterly, and I left him leaning against a rock bathed in tears.

It seems that after some years this x oor man became troubled in his mind; for, nearly ten years later, he went to Jerusalem in search of me, and being told that the year previous I had been on the Lebanon and at Damascus, he went thither, and made out by means of the little Arabic he had learned that the " Inglees " lived in India, He accordingly started for India, but not finding me there, he returned to Abyssinia. After that I could obtain no tidings of him for nearly twenty years, when, in 1861, I saw the Eev. Mr. Stern on his return from his first visit to Abyssinia. He told me that he had met with the same Walda Selassia at Gondar, and that he was the only really converted Abyssinian he had known.

On leaving Debra Damo I w ent to Behaat, where Oubea w as encamped with his army. When I approached his tent, the guard frowned at me and made no haste to introduce me. The prince at first received me with civility; but after a little while he put on a fierce expression of countenance, and demanded in harsh tones, "Why did you not come to me when I twice sent to Debra Damo to invite you? " " Because," I answered, " you were then the enemy of these my friends" (two sons of Saba Gadis then present); " but now that you are reconciled, I am glad to see your face again." Oubea turned to his officers. " This is the only man in Abyssinia who speaks the truth," he observed. After this he was very kind, and gave me opportunities of speaking a word in season.

Wlien I took leave he gave me thirty dollars towards my travelling expenses. I proceeded through Senafeh, Adee Kie, c., to Halai, where I found one of the Sheiks of the Shohos, whom I had formerly seen almost starving in the stocks at Massowa, and to whom I had given a dollar. He at once offered to be my guide and protector through the wild country of the Shohos, though he was himself afraid of meeting? with members of a neidibour-ing tribe at war with his own. He led me and my two lads, Hadara and Keedan, through thorny bypaths, and after passing the more open country around Hamhamo at nightfall, he led us into the bushes, where we dared not kindle a fire for fear of beiog discovered by the enemies of our guide. Having travelled since before daybreak, we were exceedingly tired, and lying down, we at once fell asleep. After a while I was roused by the roaring of a hyena at a distance of about ten yards; and when I prepared to rise and drive it away, I heard a leopard on the other side. Having been told that the leopard never attacks men unless they have seen it, I again lay down and covered my head. When I awoke early in the morning, I heard no more of the hyena, but the leopard was still in the same place; and when we rose and continued our journey, it followed us at a distance of fifty yards for two hours, until daybreak. However, I learned afterwards that there had been no real danger; for the leopard and the hyena hate and fear one another to such a degree, that they Vvdll stand on opposite sides of a carcase for two or three days, neither having the courage to attack it for fear of the other.

On the following day I reached Massowa, where there was only one boat ready to sail in two or three days for Jidda, the little cabin of which had already been secured by the Governor of Massowa for himself and his harem.

Whilst waiting for the sailing of the boat, I had a controversy with a number of Mohammedans. One of them made an assertion which led me to tell him that he was an unbeliever, when I ought to have used the word gjiairmoomin; but not having spoken Arabic for three years, I called him by mistake a kaafir, " infidel," a word which no Christian dare apply to a Moslem under pain of death. No sooner had the word passed my lips than they all cried, "He is worthy of death! " And laying hold of me, they dragged me along the street to throw me into the sea. Now, among the insults which they were heaping upon me, one said that I and all other Christians would be cast into hell-fire. Makinor a strong effort, I forced them to stand still, and looking steadfastly at them, I asked whether this was their belief. Several of them replied in tlie affirmative. I then said that I had been mistaken in calling one of them haafir, but that now I had a right to call them all hofaar, because they did not believe the Koran; and I quoted that passage from the second Surat of which I had made use when disputing with the Sheik at Cairo. " Surely the Jews, the Christians, and the Sabeans, all those who believe in God and do good works, have nothing to fear, for their reward is with their Lord," c. Upon this they grew calm for a moment, till one said that such was not the meaning, and another declared that the passage had been abrogated. They resumed their hold upon me and were dragging me onward, when a learned Sheik, revered as a saint, was observed coming towards us. Fearing lest they might put into his mouth what they wished him to say, I called to him by his name and title from a distance, and asked him whether the passage had been abrogated. " No, God forbid," he answered. I inquired its meaning, and he replied with a smile, "It means that you may be saved." Hereupon they all dispersed, and let me go my way. Thus the Lord delivered me out of their hands.

We embarked for Jidda, and found the boat laden with ghee or butter, contained in large jars, and a large number of negro and Abyssinian pilgrims. Each passenger had his place measured, about five feet and a half long by two feet broad, over the tops of the jars, or rather between them; and in this rather disagreeable position we had to abide twenty-one days, exposed to the burning sun. The excessive crowding, contact with my neighbours, and the invasions of their minute and all too numerous attendants effectually banished rest. Moreover, in addition to the usual hatred felt by the natives of Massowa and Arabia for all Christians, the sailors had an especial grudge against me on account of the controversy mentioned above. They therefore not only abused me in words, but, when going to and fro among the people stretched between the jars, they contrived to jump upon me, often inflicting great pain.

Yet with all this I was in good spirits. I felt myself, as it were, secure in the arms of my Saviour, and could sincerely pray for the benighted people around me; and besides this, I felt heartily thankful to God when I remembered that three years previous, while sailing in the opposite direction, I was suffering from severe illness, whereas now I was in perfect health.

At last, on the 2d of January 1833, I landed at Jidda, where I met with the officers of a surveying ship, who had just been surveying the neighbourhood of Massowa, and who, on hearing that I was there, had gone to Massowa itself on purpose to take me to Jidda, but found that I had left two days before. They had made the voyage in four days. They were all very kind to me, especially the first lieutenant, Mr. Powell.

On arriving at Jidda, I was hospitably received, with my two young Abyssinians, by my former host, Moallem Yoosoof, now British Consul. He had already made the English to be respected by the following bold act.

A few weeks before my arrival an English ship had been wrecked near Suakim, and the people of the place, with the Governor at their head, had plundered its contents and its debris. On hearing this, the Consul had obliged the Governor of Jidda to bring over his subaltern, the Governor of Suakini, to Jidda, to have him bastinadoed, and then led bound through the streets by a man crying, "This is the punishment due to those who injure the English!" And, indeed, I found the people more civil than they had been three years previously.

I took advantage of my month's stay at Jidda to converse almost every evening on religious subjects with several Sheiks of Mecca, whom I found less bigoted and much better instructed, particularly in ancient and modern history, than any I had met with in Egypt and Syria; they were also more anxious to inquire and to learn. When, too, in the course of controversy, I felt it my duty to speak against the nonsense, the errors, and the immorality of the Koran and Mohammed, they never lost their temper. I fancied that one of them had a leaning to Christianity; but he never came alone, and was therefore not at liberty to express himself openly.

I had also much encouraging conversation with my two Abyssinians, until I was obliged to leave them behind when I embarked for Suez en route to Cairo, which I reached on the 16th of February. They were to follow me in a native boat; and the time of waiting, and the tedious voyage of over forty days to Suez, was much blessed to their souls. The following fact may serve as a proof of the reality of their conversion. When I quitted Cairo for Europe, I left them with the late Herr Isenberg, partly as his servants, and partly as his instructors in the Amharic language. One day they met in the street a man who had once sold them into slavery. Their former enemy was now in the deepest destitution. Instead of having him punished, as it was in their power to have done, they not only forgave him, but for a whole year maintained him out of their scanty wages, until he died, a deeply penitent and believing man.

Hadara himself died in 1838, the most consistent, sincere, humble, and zealous Christian I have ever known.

CHAPTER V.

KETUKN TO EUROPE MARRIAGE SECOND MISSIONARY TOUR IN ABYSSINIA SERIOUS ILLNESS.

(1834-1837.)

About the end of April I left Egypt for England by way of Alexandria, Trieste, Venice, Milan, the St. Gothard, and Switzerland. I spent one day at Berne with my wise and experienced sister, and one at Cremine, where I addressed a large meeting in presence of my dear parents, to whom I owed so much. Thence I went to Basle, where I also spent a happy day, and finally arrived in England early in July, to be most kindly received by the Committee of the Church Missionary Society.

I remained only about two months in England, living the greater part of the time with the late Baptist isToel at Walthamstow, where, after many years of comparative solitude, I again enjoyed the delights and blessings of Christian family life, as well as the stimulating conversation and beneficial counsels of Mr. and Mrs. Noel. I frequently accompanied Mr. Noel to town in the morning to confer with the Secretaries of the Church Missionary Society, and to visit my friends, especially Dr. Steinkopf, returning in the afternoon to Walthamstow. This was indeed a period of rest and refreshment for both body and soul.

It must have been a great disappointment to the

Committee of the Church Missionary Society to find that they could make no use of me to visit their auxiliary Societies and stir up a missionary spirit in the country; but during the last eight years I had almost forgotten the little English I had formerly learned. It was only towards the end of my stay that I was invited to attend a missionary meeting at the house of the late Samuel Hoare at Hampstead. But when I arrived, I found that I was to be the only speaker, under the presidency of the local clergyman. This perplexed me very much. Instead, therefore, of trying to make a speech, I proposed at the opening of the meeting that the clergyman should put questions to me, and I would answer as well as I could in my broken English. This was done for a little while, but perceiving that the worthy man was at a loss to put proper questions, on the one hand, and observing, on the other, that I was understood, I spoke unquestioned for about an hour. I was comforted by being told afterwards that the meeting had been a success, and the collection a very good one.

This experience encouraged me so much, that when, two or three days later, Mr. Baptist Noel invited me to address a missionary meeting at his chapel in Bedford Eow, I accepted the invitation, and succeeded better than I had expected. I even venture to believe that the bread then cast upon the waters was found after many days; for thirty-four years later, in 1867, I was sitting at table and looking at a gentleman opposite to to me whom I did not know. He presently addressed me, and proceeded to relate that he happened one day in 1833 to be in the company of some light-minded young men like himself, when one of the party observed that a missiojiary from Abyssinia was about to address a meeting at Baptist Noel's chapel, and proposed that they should all go and hear what he had to say. " We went," continued my interlocutor, " and this proved the first step of my conversion to God." This gentleman was Lord C.

Having now attained all the objects of my visit to Enofland save one, of which more hereafter, the Com-mittee having agreed to all my proposals and allowed me an extra credit for the sum of; 5oo in case I should require it, it was now time to start for the Continent again with a view to returning to Abyssinia. It only remained for me to receive the instruction of the Committee for my further missionary operations.

The day and hour w ere fixed, and I went at the appointed time to the Church Missionary House in Salisbury Square, where were assembled many friends of the Society. After a short prayer, the (on that occasion) too humble Edward Bickersteth, who had been appointed to deliver the instruction, rose. "My dear friends," he simply said, "I feel altogether unfit and unworthy to give an instruction to our brother Gobat, and am conscious that we all need his instruction. I will now request him to impart it to us before he takes his leave."

I was thunderstruck by this unexpected turn of affairs; but crying inwardly to God for help, I began to address my superiors, the Committee and the meeting, scarcely knowing what I was to say. I never knew, in fact, what I did say; I only remember thanking God afterwards for not permitting me to be confounded. Thus I left England with the blessing and good wishes of many dear friends.

I alluded just now to one object which I had not attained in England. I had not found a help-meet, not only for myself, but for Abyssinia. As already stated, when I entered upon the missionary career, I had re- solved not to think of marrying before I had spent at least two years in the mission-field. Consequently, having been detained by the will of Providence eight years, instead of two, between Egypt and Abyssinia, I did not know one person upon whom I could set my affections. In fact, for several years I had been often on the point of determining never to marry. But after I had passed my thirtieth year, I was, as it were, haunted by the idea that I might die childless. From that time I had cherished the anticipation of marrying whenever Providence should give me the opportunity of doing so; and even before my arrival in England I had asked and obtained the consent of the Committee.

But after these preliminaries, my case was most delicate and difficult, on account of my being, in a sense, wedded to Abyssinia. For myself I wanted a person of good education and refined feelings; whilst for Abyssinia I desired one who would be able to accommodate herself to the rough Abyssinian life. I knew, or at least I supposed, that these two sets of qualities rarely meet in one and the same person, although, as followers of Christ, all Christians ought to possess them.

I had no choice but to commit my case unto the Lord, who had hitherto so mercifully guided my steps. After beseeching Him to lead me the right way, I resolved, first, not to rely on my own judgment alone without the advice of some competent person; secondly, not to ask the advice or help of anybody; and, thirdly, to weigh together as much as possible the advice which any experienced Christian might be led to offer me unasked.

Now, although I always avoided mentioning the subject, almost all my friends had taken it for granted that I wished to be married, and they did not fail to advise me;

but they failed to place themselves fully in my posi- tion. One suggested a friend of his or hers on account of her experience; but she was too old to change all her habits. Another had been brought up too delicately; another was strong and healthy, but her education had been neglected. Another possessed the requisite qualities, but she happened just then to be ailing. Several months passed without my having made any progress, when several very good friends agreed to recommend what they called a very pretty and pious girl of twenty, who had more than once expressed her wish to become a missionary. I had known her parents many years previously.

I accordingly went to call on the family, and was most kindly received. Soon after luncheon I was left alone with this charming young lady, when I made a point of speaking of Abyssinian life, and of showing its darker side. She twice interrupted me by saying naively, "That is just what would please and attract me."

This was indeed charming, and greatly enhanced her personal attractions. I was inclined to think that I had now attained my object; the more so, because, during the course of the conversation, she had said that she was in the habit of going out at four o'clock to visit the sick and the poor of the neighbourhood.

But what was my consternation when, at four o'clock, I saw a sumptuous coach and two beautiful horses stop at the door to carry the young lady to her sick and poor! " This," I said to myself, " will not do for Abyssinia;" and I took the earliest opportunity of leaving the house.

From that time my marriage became, apparently, of secondary importance; for the Committee of the Basle Missionary Society requested me to visit their auxiliary branches, and to address meetings in many of the most important localities, such as Basle, Zurich, Berne, Neu- chatel, c., where, until then, but little interest in Christian missions had been apparent. But seeing that everywhere the name of Abyssinia, and the numerous facts and anecdotes with which I contrived to season my addresses, were attracting many hearers, and occasionally gaining the goodwill of the authorities, who till then had been opposed to missionary work, the same Committee invited me to make a tour in Wiirtemberg, wdiere they had by far the greater number of friends and supporters. I cheerfully consented, I trust with a hearty desire to advance the cause of Christian missions, but also, I confess, in the hope of meeting with a companion suitable for myself, and for my dear Abyssinia; for I expected to come in contact with many disciples of Christ in richly-blessed Wurtemberg, I resolved to start for Basle in the last week of the year 1833. The day before that fixed for my journey, I was conversing with a valued friend about the route w hich I was to take, and he advised me to go through Strasburg, where there was a pious family, among the three daughters of which I might find the person suitable for me. I had almost resolved to follow this advice, when my friend's wife, a most pious, wise, and prudent lady, who had know n me intimately for many years, came forward and spoke to me as follows: " I have twice helped to promote marriages, both of which have proved unhappy; wherefore I had resolved never again to interfere. But now my conscience forbids me to be silent, for I am convinced that Fraulein Marie, the second daughter of Herr Zeller of Beuggen, is exactly the person most suitable for you and for Abyssinia."

On hearing the name of Fraulein Marie Zeller, I could not help smiling, for in my mind she was still the little girl who had sat on my knee at Zofingen fourteen years before. Yet, trusting in the wisdom and good sense of my adviser, and, above all, perfectly confident in the uprightness of Herr Zeller, I was sure that out of the treasure of his experience and profound knowledge of human nature he would give me the best possible advice. I changed my plan, and decided upon going direct to Beuggen the next day. I had been on very friendly terms with them for years, yet I doubted whether Herr Zeller and his dear wife would consent to send their beloved daughter to barbarous Abyssinia, though I was sure that, if they believed it to be the will of God, they would make any sacrifice.

The next day I started for Beuggen alone. I was in a very solemn mood, and prayed most earnestly that God would graciously direct the whole matter in such a way that I might have the most perfect assurance that I was doing His will before taking the most important step of my life. I even ventured to ask for a sign that He approved my object; and the sign I fixed upon in my own mind was that Herr Zeller should begin to speak to me of marriage. I did not know then, what he told me afterwards, that, having several daughters, he had previously resolved never to mention the subject of matrimony to unmarried missionaries.

I spent the first evening at Beuggen in friendly conversation with Herr and Frau Zeller. The next day I was requested to hold a missionary meeting, and in my address I made a point of describing, as far as time would permit, the dangers and difficulties of missionary life and work in Abyssinia. There were about half-a-dozen young girls in Herr Zeller's institution, whom I watched the whole day long as narrowly as I could without myself attracting observation. But I saw only one whose appearance and behaviour told me that I could be happy with her, but I did not know her name. Tlie

day thus passed without my ascertaining which was Marie, and I was to start early the next morning for Schaffhausen.

After supper I happened to mention to Herr Zeller a plan which I had for Abyssinia, when he unexpectedly remarked, "But for this you ought to be married to a lady of mature age and experience." I wondered at his observation, remembering my prayer of the previous day; but I only replied that experience is not to be measured by years.

At that moment Frau Zeller came in, and we continued the conversation until it was nearly time to separate. All the while I was tempted to ask which of the girls was Marie; but I could not bring myself to utter the question, partly through shyness and partly on principle. I prayed, nay, I cried inwardly, to the Lord, asking Him to remove my doubts, and to let me know before I started whether the young person who had touched my heart was the one whom He had appointed to be my companion for life. Suddenly Frau Zeller opened the door and called for Ifarie, who came in quite innocently; and behold, it was she whom I had admired, not for her beauty, but for her frank and ingenuous expression and her unaffected manners. I could not speak then, though my heart was filled with thankfulness to God.

I started at two o'clock next morning. It was very cold, but I was scarcely conscious of it, being lost in prayer and communion with God. At last I felt perfectly convinced that Marie Zeller was the person He had chosen and prepared to be the sharer of all my concerns.

At mid-day I stopped at Waldshut to take some refreshment, and just as I was entering the inn a carriage drove up from the opposite direction, and out came my old and most intimate college friend, Count Zaremba, who had been labouring as a missionary at Shusha, on the frontier of Persia. We embraced each other and dined together.

During dinner I opened my whole case to him, and asked him, as he was going to Beuggen, to be my Eliazar with Herr and Frau Zeller and their daughter, to which he very readily consented. He performed the duty so well, that seven days later I received the news that the parents had given their consent, though the daughter had asked for a few days for deliberation. Six days after this I received full permission to call her mine.

During my tour I addressed many numerously attended meetings, four in particular, where the attendance in each case numbered at least two thousand. At Kirchheim I spent an evening with the pious Duchess Louis of Wiirtem-berg, who shed many tears when I related some of my past troubles. She gave me letters of introduction to her two daughters, the Queen of Wtirtemberg and the Margravine of Baden, whom I saw a few days later, and who continued warm friends of Christian missions until their death.

Our missionary meetings were conducted in a more solemn manner than is usually the case in England, and they were generally held in the churches, though there had formerly been a Government prohibition preventing the churches being used for this purpose. I obtained a concession on this point in my favour, and since that time all the churches in Wiirtemberg have ever been open for missionary meetings. The effect of this has been that the little kingdom of Wiirtemberg, though not rich, has, up to the present time, contributed more in proportion of men, money, and I believe of prayers also, than any other country in the world.

I quitted Wiirtemberg on the 13 th of February, and returned to Beuggen to improve the acquaintance of my future wife. Our first meeting was very solemn and rather stiff, for we had never exchanged one word before. Yet we both had the assurance that we were in God's way, and in a few days we felt that we were one in love and could pray together without constraint.- We wished to be married directly after Easter, but our respective Governments required so many formalities, that it was not until the 23d of May that we were united in my native parish. I spent the intervening three months partly with my parents, partly at Basle, and partly at Beugjqen.

And now the time had arrived for starting again for Abyssinia. On June the 7th we left Beuggen, after a solemn service, and not without many tears on the part of my wife and her family. After visiting many Christian friends on the way, foremost among whom were my dear parents, we reached Marseilles on the 29th of June, where I preached several times, and embarked in a sailing vessel on the 14th of July for Alexandria. We were accompanied by Fraulein Gering, who had travelled with us from Basle to be married to my future colleague, Herr Isenberg, which event took place on the fourth of that month.

After about a week at Alexandria we all journeyed together to Cairo, where we remained about three months, waiting for the arrival of a parcel of books for distribution in Abyssinia. I employed the time chiefly in teaching my young wife Amharic, which study we had already begun on the voyage from Marseilles, and we afterwards continued it on the Eed Sea, with such success, that by the time we reached Abyssinia she could speak it fluently. In expectation that thenceforth I should have but little time for reading, I made it a duty to read solid books as much as my weak eyes would permit, and wheu they were tired, my dear wife read for us both.

We arrived at Suez on the 25 th of October. Our party consisted of the Isenbergs, the two young Abys-sinians, two Germans, and ourselves; and our cortege included thirty-eight camels, and two donkeys for the ladies to ride upon. Our luggage consisted of a little furniture, for we expected to spend our lives in Abyssinia, personal effects, provisions, and sixteen camel-loads of Amharic books, amongst which were two thousand Bibles, New Testaments, and separate portions of Scripture. As we were all in good health and excellent spirits, we enjoyed the pure air of the desert exceedingly.

At Suez we embarked in an Arab boat full of pilgrims, in which, however, we bad a pretty little cabin for ourselves, and arrived at Jidda in the middle of November. Here the two ladies were obliged to adopt the Arab costume, closely veiling themselves to the eyes.

We were very kindly received by my old friend Consul Yoosoof, who gave us rooms at the top of his house with a terrace, where we could take the fresh air after the great heat of the day.

We were detained twenty-five long days at Jidda by stormy south winds, which terminated with a thunderstorm, such as I have never witnessed even in tropical and mountainous Abyssinia. It lasted from one o'clock P. M. till four the next morning; the thunder rolling, and lightning flashing among the mountains, and the rain falling in torrents. When night came on, the scene was superlatively grand and solemn, and for several consecutive hours the whole atmosphere was like a sea of dazzling light, with hardly any intermission between the flashes. When bedtime came, the rain was already falling through the roof, and we had to fold up our bed- ding and sit upon it under an umbrella for several hours.

As far as Jidda, our travelling by land and water had been prosperous and cheering; indeed, it had been one long honeymoon. But now began a series of trials and sufferings, the remembrance of some of which still makes me shudder.

After spending a few days at Jidda I began to be aware of some internal disorder, but as the pain at first was not excessive, I did not make much of it. Yet I consulted a clever German physician, an old friend, who happened to be at Jidda just then, and he attributed my ailment to a cause which was soon afterwards completely removed without producing any amelioration in my condition.

On the 9th of December we embarked for Massowa, where we arrived on the 20th. I suffered much on the voyage, which was very distressing to my poor wife. From divers untoward circumstances we were obliged to spend eleven weeks at Massowa, and during the whole time I was very ill, sometimes suffering excruciating pain, though with intervals of occasional ease. By degrees my illness took the form of chronic dysentery, sometimes so violent, with choking oppression on the chest, that those around me, as well as I myself, thought that I was on the point of dying.

As the way opened for our starting for Abyssinia, the question was whether I should proceed or go back. We had very little hope of my recovery, and no medical assistance beyond the homoeopathy of which Herr Isenberg was enamoured, and of which medicine he administered to me a great quantity of various kinds without the least effect.

I could not bear the idea of turning back, and in this I admired the behaviour of my sympathising wife, who never tried to influence me in that direction, but continually prayed for my recovery with a confidence which was only shaken when I seemed to be actually dying. I reflected that there was as much likelihood of my dying if I tried to return as if I tried to proceed to Abyssinia; while I thought there might be some hope of my recovery if I could reach the high land and pure, cool air of that country. Above all, I was anxious to introduce my colleague to some of my Abyssinian friends, that he might continue the work which was so promising when I lefc Gondar four years before; after that I could be content to lay down my head in death.

As w e continued to travel my health seemed somewhat to improve, and seeing the rest of the company well and cheerful, and observing the lively interest taken by my wdfe in the strange birds, plants, and other objects so new to her, I almost enjoyed some parts of the journey.

I must here mention an incident which may interest the disciples of Mr. Darwin.

One of our party happened to kill a monkey; whereupon the wild Shohos, who were accompanying us and driving a herd of oxen to carry our luggage up the steep Shumfeito, moved towards us in a body, declaring with menaces that they must avenge their brother. Of course it was a jest; but the Shohos have their own philosophy, and really believe that monkeys are degenerate men. Whether they get this from the Koran, which mentions something of the kind, or whether they hold a theory of evolution, I do not know.

When we reached the foot of the Shumfeito I felt very comfortable, and cherished hopes of a speedy recovery; but there I experienced a relapse which lasted for the next twenty months. As I w as the only man of the company who could speak to the Shohos, partly in. Amharic and partly in Arabic, I had to make all the arrangements for the transport of our things to the top of the mountain. We had to employ forty of their oxen to carry several camel-loads. Most of our property had been left at Massowa. The demands of the Shohos were so exorbitant that I had to bargain with them from morning till night for two whole days before a fair price was agreed upon. I was often tempted to give up the argument much sooner; but I well knew that the terms then fixed would become a precedent for the future, and so I persevered. But when the bargain was concluded I was thoroughly exhausted, and suffered considerable pain, which did not again leave me for more than a year and a half.

We stayed at Halai two days, then proceeded to Behaat, where I suffered much, morally and physically, from the tantalisincj behaviour of the Governor of the district. I was obliged to send a message to Oubea, who was at a distance, asking him to help us to reach Adowa; and he at once gave orders to one of his superior officers to take us to Adowa under his protection. We travelled through rocks and thorns, and arrived on the fourth day at a small village called Ebn Harmas (Stone of the Elephants), on the border of a wilderness much frequented by those animals, as well as by lions and other formidable beasts. Here Oubea's officer left us, explaining that there were rebels, i. e., robbers, before us, and that therefore he could not take us farther on account of our luggage. As, however, it was very necessary that Erau Isenberg should reach some more settled place, he yielded to our entreaty, and sent her and her husband forward with a small escort; but my wife and I were obliged to remain quietly where we were for the next three weeks.

The simple folk of the village, who had never before seen a European, were very kind; but we found it difficult to procure the necessaries of life. Yet, after a few days' rest, I began to feel better, so that I was able, with my wife's assistance, to walk a little each day. It was a time of great spiritual blessing to us both. We were in good spirits, and very thankful to God for His having so far preserved my wife in good health, notwithstanding the roughness of the way, the coarse and scanty food, and above all, her mental sufferings on my account. Until then we had scarcely ever been alone since we were married. If we neither knew nor loved each other when we were engaged to be made one flesh, we were now the more thaukful and happy to feel and confess that we were not only one flesh, but one in heart, in reciprocal love and respect, the Lord being with us.

But the improvement in my health did not continue, and I was very unwell when we reached Adowa, May II, 1835, after ten weeks of painful travelling from Massowa.

My plan had been to go directly to Gondar; but my strength was exhausted, and I was glad to have a comparatively good house, with one room for my dear wife and myself, and there to rest until it should please God to strengthen me for proceeding farther.

I had hoped to get better at Adowa, but God had willed it otherwise, for during the very first week all the symptoms of my illness returned, with great and continuous pain. I also experienced a great disappointment; for my friend, Habeta Salasseh, on hearing that I had reached Massowa, had come with other friends from Gondar, about two hundred miles, to meet and escort me; but my weakness and acute sufferings hardly allowed me to say a few words to them. However, a few days later, hearing that Oubea and his army had pitched their tents about fifteen miles from Adowa, and knowing that, according to Abyssinian usage, in order not to lose his favour, one of us should go and salute him and place ourselves under his protection, I asked Isenberg to go, but he refused, on the ground that he was still ignorant of the language. One day, therefore, feeling a little better, I started to pay my respects to him; but on the way I was seized with almost intolerable pain and oppression, so that, on reaching the camp, I was obliged to lie down under my little tent for two full days unable to move, or even to speak more than one word at a time. I suffered mentally, also, for I had left my wife in the midst of a severe fit of illness, and led her to hope that I should return the same day.

When able to enter the tent of Oubea, he received me most kindly, showed much sympathy with my sufferings, and ordered a supply of provisions to be given us sufficient to last for a long while.

On leaving his tent, I mounted my mule to return to Adowa, and was again detained on the way by excruciating sufferings. It was night when I reached home, and was glad to find my wife better than I had expected, though still far from well. We fell on each other's necks and wept like little children for a long while. We had been married just one year.

From that day I was confined to my bed for nine long months, and for the most part restricted to one position. I became so reduced that I could clasp my arm with my thumb and middle finger from wrist to shoulder, excepting the elbow, and my lower limbs were in proportion. But although my bones almost protruded from the skin, there were no abrasions, for the cuticle got thick and tough, like that of the sole of a man who always walks barefoot. I do not think that, throughout the whole of those nine months, I enjoyed natural sleep more than ten times, and when I did fall into a delirious doze, it never lasted for more than a quarter of an hour at a time. Even thus I was disturbed by troublesome dreams.

Formerly, when I had heard of men weeping, or when I read of the Psalmist washing his bed with his tears, I thought it merely a form of speech for expressing deep sorrow; but I now learned that a man of mature age may have his heart so softened as to enable him to shed an abundance of tears. My tears were, however, far oftener those of joy than of sorrow, either when I reflected on the love of God, or contemplated all that my poor wife was doing for me. Then if, after a long and sleepless night, I heard an anxious, affectionate inquiry addressed by some person from without, tears of gratitude would gush from my eyes at the simple idea that I was not forgotten in my misery.

I must confess with shame that I was sometimes selfish and exacting, and perhaps increased the burthen of my devoted wife by refusing to receive either food or drink from any hand but hers a not uncommon feature in the idiosyncrasies of illness.

My malady continued to increase in intensity until it assumed almost all the symptoms of cholera. My hands and feet frequently became as cold as ice, and none of the usual remedies would restore natural warmth. At last we accidentally hit on a very simple one. On one of the first occasions of the kind, feeling cramps in my icy feet, I desired my servants to rub them as hard as they could with their hands. After about an hour of this treatment the warmth came back and the cramps ceased. This remedy proved efficacious in my most virulent attacks; and I have often thought since that it might save many lives in times of cholera.

In the midst of my illness, on the 2d of August, my wife gave birth to our eldest child, a little daughter. We were painfully circumstanced, for we had no one at hand to help us. It is true that Frau Isenberg was near; but although she had undergone a similar experience but two months before, her infant died on the day of its birth, and she was therefore ignorant of what was required in such cases. I heard the earliest cry of my first-born with deep emotion, and breathed a word of thanksgiving to God; yet the idea of soon leaving my child alone with her mother in a country like Abyssinia drew tears from my eyes. I was the more grieved because I was too weak to take the babe into my arms. But God dealt very graciously with us, and I was much comforted by observing the deep interest which our dear Abyssinians took in both mother and daughter, especially a young prince, Georgis, of the ancient royal family, who stood sponsor at the baptism.

The time of my illness brought another and a heavier trial than any I have yet described. This was a deep religious depression which fell upon me and plunged my soul in gloom. The whole of my past life, with all its sins, negligence, and unfaithfulnesses, seemed to rise up in judgment against me and to condemn me. The mercy of God was as if obscured. I realised that I was altogether corrupt; "from the sole of the foot even unto the head, there was no soundness in me." In my dire extremity I could only cast myself as lost and undone at the feet of Him who " came to seek and to save that which was lost" by giving Himself a ransom for all. There I found, not for the first time, but in greater power, pardon, joy, and peace unspeakable in the sense of the love of God. From that time I could look at the grave, which in hours of half delirium I continually saw open before me, without dismay. Nay, I could not only endure my sufferings with resignation, but frequently, even in seasons of the most intense pain, I felfc constrained to say, "Oh, my God and Saviour! if it be for my own and my brethren's greater good or for Thy glory, increase my sufferings. I am ready to bear all."

Of course, I had gloomy hours after this; but I had always liberty to cast myself and all my cares upon God, and He always " restored unto me the joy of His salvation."

Towards the end of those nine months, in March 1836, I had some respite in my illness. Its symptoms did not cease, but they became comparatively bearable. I gained a little strength, so that I even hazarded an occasional short ride, and I much enjoyed the sight of all that surrounded me. But it did me no other good, for I always felt worse afterwards. It was then that I could take my child in my arms for the first time and rejoice in being a father.

This amelioration in my condition was brought about, humanly speaking, by the following remedy, at which the reader may smile or shudder.

After having exhausted all the means at our disposal without sensible benefit, I was told that an old man who had come to Adowa had said that he would cure me if I w ould try his remedy. A drowning man will catch at a straw, and I allowed the stranger to prescribe for me. His recipe was as follows: Take three pounds of milk, three pounds of butter, two pounds of honey, one pound of garlic, and (I believe) three ounces of spices of divers kinds. Boil the whole together for some time, then divide it into three doses, the doses to be taken on three successive days.

I resolved to try the remedy, and though I could not take nearly the whole of a dose at one time, I made it my sole food, with the exception of a little bread, for ten days; even then I could not finish it. From that time I began to improve, though I still had great sufferings before me for several months.

In the May of that year cholera raged at Adowa, and for about three weeks the daily number of deaths averaged from thirty-six to forty in a population of about three thousand. My wife caught the disease, but by taking at once the remedy which had proved beneficial in many cases when promptly applied, namely, camphor dissolved in spirits of wine, she soon recovered. About a month later, when it was supposed that the scourge had completely disappeared, she was suddenly seized with a most severe attack. It began about eleven o'clock at night, and when I saw her at daybreak, she looked almost like a corpse. Her face was livid, her eyes without the least brilliancy, and she had already lost the power of speech and movement. It was one of the most painful moments of my life. Neither of us could stir or speak audibly, and we lay alternately looking at our child in a cradle between us, at each other, and then up to heaven, meaning by this sign to encourage each other to look up to God for help and comfort. This lasted about an hour; for we were alone in a hut which had only one room, and neither of us had strength to rise and open the door to call for help.

At length a female servant came in, and when she saw in what state we were, she ran to call Isenberg, who came at once with Dr. Wolff, who had just arrived. When the former saw my wife, he at once concluded that it was too late to try homoeopathy. But Dr. Wolff said that when he was in India in time of cholera, he heard that many people had been cured by the application of very hot iron.

For want of any other remedy, and thinking it might prove beneficial, I ordered a piece of iron to be heated and wrapped in a quantity of cloths. When it was brought in, Dr. Wolff insisted on applying it himself. Now the good Doctor was excessively awkward, and let the almost red-hot iron fall on the bare skin of the patient. I heard it burning the skin, and my wife uttered a piercing cry. A profuse perspiration followed, and the cholera was broken; so that, humanly speaking, I attribute my wife's recovery to Dr. Wolff's awkwardness. However, it took several weeks to heal the burn, and for many years my wife suffered from the effects of the terrible malady.

We had frequently consulted about the advisability of our leaving Abyssinia; but at first, hoping that I should recover, I was opposed to the measure, and afterwards because I thought I could not bear the fatigue, and in case of my dying on the way, my wife and child would be obliged to travel without proper protection through the country of the Shohos, one of whose trades it was to steal young women and children and sell them as slaves. But when Dr. Wolff, seeing that he could not penetrate farther into the interior, had resolved to return to Mas-sowa, I made up my mind to return with him. As I was too weak to ride, I had a kind of litter made that I might be carried by men.

After commending ourselves to the protection and help of our gracious and merciful God, we started from Adowa on the 1st of September 1836.

The road being very rough and uneven, and my bearers being unaccustomed to the work, I suffered very much all the way to Halai. On the day before we reached Halai, while resting at mid-day, I was so exhausted by terrible pain that it seemed impossible that I could sur- vive the steep and long descent of the Shumfeito the next day. I therefore dictated something like my last will to my weeping wife. I cannot describe the hundredth part of what she suffered at that moment, and indeed almost uninterruptedly for a year and a half, in that strange land, almost without comfort, save what she received from God in answer to her prayers, and that which she derived from the enjoyment of nursing her lovely baby.

We rested one day at Halai, and then came the question as to how I was to descend the Shumfeito. The way down that mountain was so steep and narrow, often between rocks and precipices, and with many steps three feet or more in depth, that it was from the first taken for granted that I could not be carried by men. My walking down was out of the question. Dr. Wolff seriously proposed that I should be packed in a cowhide with plenty of straw round me, and dragged down; but that would not do. The only question remaining was whether I could venture to ride down, which, it was said, no one had ever done. I decided to try this method, and when I was fastened upon my mule I felt perfectly calm, and resigned to whatever might happen.

I made the start in good spirits, and soon perceived that my mule was used to rough ways; for whenever there was a deep step, the thing I had most feared, she bent her knees, so as to come down almost insensibly, without any shock; and this encouraged me greatly. And oh! with what surprise and thanksgiving to God did I observe that, after having descended less than 2000 feet, my sufferings, instead of increasing, were diminishing. This improvement continued till I reached the bottom of the mountain, when I stretched myself under a high rock, almost free from pain, though very tired.

But it was hard work for my poor wife to walk down that high and rugged mountain; and her fatigue was much increased by the very kindness of good Dr. Wolff. Seeing how tired she was, he insisted upon giving her his arm; but in his mental abstraction he contrived always to walk in the very narrow path himself, while she had to struggle through thorns and shifting stones. However, on reaching the resting-place, she almost forgot her fatigue when she saw how comfortable I was.

The next night I slept soundly for two hours, and on the next and following days I was able to ride a little; and so we arrived at Massowa.

At Jidda Dr. Wolff left us. During the three days of our stay there all my sufferings returned, so that we hastened to leave it. We embarked in an empty boat with a low cabin; and when at daybreak the boat began to move seawards, I fell into a sound sleep. When I awoke, my first words were, "Thank God, I am cured!" I felt such a change in my whole body that it seemed as if I had never been ill; and the alteration was so real, that by the time we reached Cosseir (in twenty-eight days), I had recovered so much flesh that I was as stout as I had been when we started for Abyssinia two years previously. Yet our food was such that I am sure the description of it would not excite the appetite of the least fastidious of my fellow-men.

Our voyage was not accomplished without some very real dangers, owing to the bad seamanship of our sailors; but we arrived in safety at Cosseir, after many hindrances and delays.

Cosseir was then a most miserable place; yet, as we were accustomed to frugality, we found the only procurable provisions, rice, onions, and coarse biscuits, sufficient for our needs. But as for moving through the IX PERIL BY WATER. Pore iso.

desert, we found absolutely nothing but the bare-backed camels, except a very rough machine called sjmcjcdaf, consisting of two most primitive cases placed pannier-wise on the animals. These might have answered if we had had plenty of cushions, but we had none. Yet we tried it for a couple of hours, feeling as if all our bones were breaking. We found it impossible to continue this mode of locomotion. We tried to walk in the sand, but as both my wife and myself were still very weak, we could only accomplish a few paces.

And now what was to be done? We had not found a single saddle; but we had two portmanteaux, and happily a small mattress. We placed the portmanteaux on a camel, and spread the mattress upon them. Upon this hard seat Madame Gobat had to sit bolt upright for six long days, exposed to a hot sun, without bonnet or umbrella, all having been torn to pieces by the Abyssinian thorns. This w as within two months of the birth of our second child. She had not even the comfort of carrying our little daughter; for the latter had fallen ill on the very first day of our journey, and could not bear the movement of the camel. We had three servants with us, but two of them were also ill, and had enough to do to keep themselves on their camels. In this emergency our dear Hadara, whom I intended to place in a college in Switzerland, carried the child on foot through the greater part of the desert.

Ophthalmia was the ailment which first attacked our little girl; but this soon developed into inflammation of the brain, and every step of the way became more trying and painful, especially to her mother, who could not bear to hear her groans, and yet could not endure the little sufferer to be far from her. The trials of the whole party were much increased by the scarcity of water, which the wastefulness of the Arabs reduced to a still smaller quantity. Before long we found ourselves absolutely without it.

One part of this journey in particular I can scarcely look back upon without shuddering and tears. We were still a long day's journey from the valley of the Nile, where water was to be found. Our strength was exhausted, and we were all more or less unwell. I begged that one of our Arabs would go and fetch us water, but they all refused, although I offered to pay almost any amount; and so we were obliged to start early in the morning. Our child had grown worse in the night, and seemed to suffer great pain; her groans and cries pierced the heart of her mother, who was frequently obliged to take her in her arms and soothe her, though she herself was quite exhausted.

Already in the forenoon my wife asked me to allow her to alight and rest, but I, myself very tired, tried to encourage her by reminding her that we had no water, and that if we rested we should not be able to reach water that day. But about noon, when the sun was burning and the child crying, Madame Gobat was utterly cast down, and said in a decided, almost desperate tone, "Now we must rest; I can bear it no longer." It nearly broke my heart; but I was sure, from former experience, that if we rested in that state of discouragement and excessive fatigue, without a drop of water to reanimate us, we should have preferred to die on the spot rather than remount our camels in time to reach the well. I therefore hardened myself to the utmost of my power and replied firmly, "No, we must go on; " but I turned aside to hide my abundant tears.

Oh, it was a hard task for me to be obliged to be so harsh to her who had so patiently and faithfully nursed me through the first two years of our married life. My dear wife, who could not see my heart, thought me very inhuman, and grew angry; it was hardly in human nature to feel otherwise. But the excitement of angry feeling gave her strength, and she said to herself, "Very well, I will go on till I drop dead." And so she continued, her inward emotion making her almost forgetful of fatigue.

I had not the courage to go near her; but oh I how earnestly did I pray for more than an hour! At length we reached an elevation whence we could see the whole green breadth of Egypt stretched beneath our eyes, and water not far off, the remains of the last inundation. I now ventured to ride near my wife, whom I found bathed in tears of repentance for having allowed herself to give way to anger; though she was not yet convinced that it was my duty under the circumstances to speak with an accent of authority, which, though it sounded harsh, was really the expression of my deepest sympathy. I do not think that she ever was convinced that I was in the right, but we amicably agreed to differ in our respective views of the case.

A little before sunset we reached the longed-for well of pure water, where we hoped to rest that night in the shadow of an old wall. As we had only one short day's ride to the Nile over cultivated land, we thought that the worst was over; but it was not so.

The night was very cold, and our coverings very inadequate; moreover, the malady of our child reached the climax of its intensity. From the beginning of the night until daybreak she uttered piercing shrieks without respite. At daybreak the screams ceased and the child fell asleep; but consciousness had fled, only to return for a moment next day, to revive in us a fading hope.

On arriving at Kena, on the Nile, we hastened to engage a boat to take us to Cairo, where we hoped to find medical aid; but it was two days before the boat was ready. We then sailed day and night for eight days, during which time the child was unconscious, sleeping most of the time, till it pleased God to take her early on the eighth morning, three hours before we reached Old Cairo.

I hastened to the town to procure a teskery (permission) from the Consul, and found that almost every European, at least all of my acquaintance, had either died of the plague or fled the country. There remained only Herr Lieder of the Church Missionary Society. I went to his house, but he was not at home, and nobody could tell me where he was. I had to wait for two hours in great agony of mind, mourning for my first-born and grieving for my wife's sorrow.

At last Herr Lieder came, went with me to the Consul, and thence to a carpenter's to have a coffin made at once. This done, we proceeded to Old Cairo, and hastened to bury in the Coptic burial-ground the remains of the child, which her mother had held upon her lap during the whole of that solitary day. It was a most trying time for us; but, blessed be God, it was the term of our prolonged and unusual troubles. It was night when we arrived at Cairo, where we were quartered in the comfortable furnished house of our old and intimate friend, the Eev. Theodor Mtiller, now vicar of a parish in Somersetshire.

The period which followed was a season of rest and of many spiritual and temporal enjoyments. Our health was comparatively good, though we still felt, and have for many years, the effects of our sufferings in Abyssinia. We were in strong hopes that a year or two in Europe would restore us so far as to enable us to return to our field of labour in Abyssinia; but that anticipation was never to be realised.

On the 3 I st of December my wife gave birth to a strong and healthy boy, whom we called Benoni, in remembrance of our past sorrows. We had no female assistance except that of a young Abyssinian girl, who had no idea how to handle a new-born babe. A German physician was present at the crisis, and helped me to perform the baby's first toilette; but after that the entire duties of a nurse devolved upon me alone. To my wife there was something laughable in the sight of her tall, long-bearded husband, in ample Arabian costume, pacing the large room, and singing, badly enough, to the infant in his arms; but to me it was delightful.

On the 13th of February 1837 we left Cairo and travelled by boat to Alexandria, where we stayed two days. As I had no desire to appear in Europe with a long beard and in Oriental attire, I withdrew on the second day to a private room to shave and assume a European dress; but when I returned to the apartment in which my wife was sitting, she took me for an impertinent intruder, nor did she recognise me till I burst into laughter at her perplexity.

We sailed for Malta in the " Blazer," the first steam vessel, I believe, which ever went so far as Alexandria; and although we met a tremendous gale, we arrived safely in five days, and once more set foot on European soil.

CHAPTEE VI.

A YEAR OF WAITING MISSIONAEY WORK IN SWITZERLAND;

AMONG THE DRUSES; IN ITALY; AND AT MALTA. (1838-1845.)

We arrived at my home on the iith of May. Great was the joy and thanksgiving at my father's house, for many reports of my death had reached my family. For a long time my mother would not credit them, saying, that when she prayed for me she had a conviction that she was praying for some one still living in this world. But at last the rumour of my death was so positive that her confidence was shaken, and she began to mourn for me, though not as those who have no hope.

Now there was a certain devout, sober-minded, elderly Christian friend, who was in the habit of traversing a distance of six miles at least once a week to spend an evening with my parents. This man occasionally had, when he prayed, the gift of seeing things and events at a distance, both as to space and time. One evening my mother told him that she was at last forced to believe the news of my death, as tidings had ceased to reach her from Abyssinia. " Do not believe the report," was her friend's reply, " neither mourn for your son, for he is alive, and you will see him." "How do you know?" asked my mother. I was praying for him the other day was the answer, " when I suddenly saw him and his wife alighting at your door with their little boy " (the boy was not yet born at that time) " and I have not the least doubt that the thing will happen as I have seen it." " This time," returned my mother, "I cannot believe you; for they have a little girl, but no boy." Upon which he repeated with unmoved assurance, "You will see your son and his wife with their little boy."

This conversation was often repeated between my mother and her friend, but the former could not be convinced. However, when we alighted and presented our little son to my parents, they exclaimed with astonishment, "The vision of the Maire de Eoche is verified!" and they mingled thanksgivings to God with their joyful greetings.

From Cremine we went to Beuggen to visit my wife's parents. We made it our resting-place for a season on account of its convenient proximity to Basle. Before our arrival at Beuggen, I had received a most kind letter from Mr. Coates, Secretary of the Church Missionary Society, advising me to consult the best physicians, and to follow their advice without regard to expense. We accordingly consulted a man of high reputation. Dr. Sttickelberg, who recommended the water of Kreuznach, in those days but little known, the healing qualities of the water having been but recently discovered. We there spent three months, from June to September, very agreeably, and were benefited, but not wholly cured. We returned to Basle by way of Frankfort and Wlirtem-berg; and at Frankfort I received the news of the death of my mother, at the age of sixty-seven. I was the more deeply affected by this event because I had spent only a few days with her after our return from Abys- siiiia; but on her own account I could rejoice and thank God for having taken her to Himself from a world in which slie had lonc felt herself a strancfer. She died of a most painful illness, which she suffered patiently, saying frequently, "I cannot think of or feel anything but excruciating pain; but I know in whom I have believed, and I am safe in His hand until He takes me to Himself for ever."

For my father, then over seventy years of age, I felt very deep sorrow, remembering that of late years he had grown more and more dependent on the sound judgment and resolute character of my mother, both with respect to things temporal and things spiritual. Though I knew that my brother would take the most tender care of him, I hastened home as quickly as circumstances would permit. I found him in profound grief, but thankful to God for having delivered my mother from her sufferings and taken her to rest. Durincj the ensuin? winter, 1837-38, I frequently visited my father, but spent the chief part of my time at Beuggen, refreshing my memory by reading nearly the whole of the Bible through in the original, and conversing much with my learned and experienced father-in-law.

In the spring of 1838 the Committee of the Church Missionary Society invited my wife and myself to go to England for further medical advice, and we spent the entire summer in London, greatly enjoying the society of many old and new friends, but not benefiting by the medical treatment which we underwent. My wife fell ill, and remained so for a long time, while I was never well. If I exerted myself I at once became ill, and when I rested I reproached myself with being a useless burthen to the Society. This produced a depressing effect on my mind, especially as it convinced me more and more that I could never return to Abyssinia, where my heart still tarried.

In the winter of 1838 39, my third child, Hannali, now married to Herr Zeller, missionary at Nazareth, was born at Beuggen. This, for the most part, uneventful time was spent by me in preaching, giving missionary addresses, and in writincj a short sframmar of vubar Arabic, with an appendix of three short dialogues, containing about two thousand of the most common words.

In December 18 3 8 I had the great sorrow of witnessing the death of our dear Hadara, who had bidden fair to become a most useful missionary. If he had been the only fruit of my work in Abyssinia, I should still be thankful to have been employed as an instrument to lead him to the Saviour of sinners.

In the autumn of 1839, after another visit to Kreuz-nach, the Committee of the Church Missionary Society sent me to Malta to assist their missionary, Herr Schlienz, with the revision of the Arabic Bible.

Soon after our arrival there, the health of my coadjutor gave way, and he left Malta never to return thither. I was then put in charge of the large translating and printing establishment of the Church Missionary Society, and I did not find the work above my strength.

I remember one circumstance in connection with my work at Malta which would have convinced me, had I not already been convinced, of the Divine inspiration of the whole Bible.

Whilst translating " Keith on the Fulfilment of Prophecy," the two chief translators, Phares Shidiak of Mount Lebanon, and the Eev. Mr. Badger, both very good Arabic scholars, were puzzled continually, not knowing bow to render the imagery in which the meaning was clothed in the English original, because that imagery consisted chiefly, or at least in great part, of terms derived from divers kinds of mechanism, the works of men, of which the uncivilised Arabs have no idea, and therefore possess no words to express them, especially when employed in a non-natural or immaterial sense. But the imagery of the Bible is nearly all taken from nature, the work of God, and thus intelligible to all, and can consequently be translated into all human languages. However, the pains taken in the translation of the work has rendered it acceptable to the best-educated Moslems; for of all the works published in modern times by the missionaries, "Keith on Prophecy " is to this day the most highly appreciated among them. My chief part in that translation, as in other ones, was to see that the meaning was correct.

The summer of 1840 was a very trying season for us, owing to the prolonged and dangerous illness of my wife. It was in that year that our fourth child and second son was born, but he only survived thirteen months.

In 1841 the Committee of the Church Missionary Society requested me to visit the Druses, chiefly on Mount Lebanon, to inquire whether it would be practicable to begin the work of a Christian mission among that strange and interesting people, or at least to establish schools for their children, in which the Bible might be freely taught. I started early in July and returned towards the end of September. As it was so difficult to find means of distributing Arabic books and tracts, of which we had a great quantity at Malta, I took eight boxes full of them. I travelled with two EDglishmen as far as Bey rout, where we met with a very interesting clergyman, Mr. Eowland, who had just come from Damascus. He was enthusiastic as to the civility and kindness he had met with on the part of the Greek clergy; and related that, having given an Arabic copy of the Book of Common Prayer to the most learned priest of Damascus, named Yoosoof, the right hand of the Patriarch, the priest had coupled the expression of his warm thanks with an earnest aspiration for a reunion between the Greek and English Churches.

Of course all this passed through the mouth of a dragoman. This report determined me to accept the invitation of my two travelling companions to accompany them to Damascus, and thither I went. On the very first day I distributed a goodly number of Bibles and other books; but they were all brought back to me the next day, because the Patriarch had excommunicated all who should accept any of my books. That dignitary had also forbidden his people to visit me, with the exception of one priest, who was esteemed a master of controversy.

In a discussion which we had about the adoration of saints and angels, I cited, among others, the example of St. Peter and Cornelius (Acts x.), and of the angel with St. John (Eev. xix. and xxii.), to prove the unlawfulness of such adoration. To both cases he answered that the respective parties were equal in degree, and therefore needed not to worship each other; that is to say, Cornelius occupied the same grade in the Emperor's service as St. Peter occupied in that of Christ; and the degree of the angel was the same in heaven as that of St. John upon earth. He added that the case is altogether different with those who occupy a lower position in relation to those of a superior degree.

The conduct of the Greek Patriarch had not been such as to encourage me to pay him a visit, as I had intended to do; but meeting his chief priest, Yoosoof, above referred to, in the street, I accosted him. But he addressed me very rudely. " What do you mean," he demanded, " with all your books? We do not want them. A few days ago one of your priests made me a present of your Prayer-Book. Did he suppose that I would make any use of it? We have plenty of better books."

I was about to reply, but he abruptly went on his way, as if afraid to be seen talking to me.

The next day I was seized with a severe attack of my old malady, which I knew to be most dangerous at Damascus at that season of the year. I at once resolved to leave the next morning, which intention I stated in the presence of my host and of several members of the Greek Church. In less than two hours I received a most kind message from the Patriarch, inviting me to pay him a visit that same afternoon, mentioning that he and his clergy, whom he would call together, wished very much to make my acquaintance.

I went at the given hour, and found the Patriarch surrounded by about a dozen priests, all of whom showed me the greatest kindness, as to a representative of the Church of England. (I was not at that time formally a member of that Church, though I took a hearty part in all her services, because they are Scriptural.) The Patriarch extolled the English Church, and expressed his regret, in common with his clergy, that the English and Greek Churches were not re-united, adding that the Pope of Eome was the only hindrance to this measure. Upon this they all joined in abusing the Church of Eome. Finally, they all expressed their regret that I was leaving so soon. How far that expression of regret was sincere it is not for me to judge; but I should have been better pleased if they had asked for some copies of the Word of God, of which they, especially the Patriarch, were very ignorant.

The day after my return to Beyrout I started for the district of the Druses, and spent about a month among them, going from one place to another at intervals of a few days. Besides visiting their families, I attended several large meetings of their chiefs.

At that time they were expecting that England would do great things for them; wherefore I found them all very friendly. I discovered that very few of them had any clear knowledge of their religious, or rather, au fond, irreligious system, a chief item of which is that all the Druses were created simultaneously, and have ever since remained the same in number. When a Druse dies they believe that his soul enters the body of an unborn Druse child, a transmigration which goes on from generation to generation. I consider this belief to be the cause of their utter indifference to all religion.

When I spoke to them on religious subjects they were perfectly apathetic; but on my mentioning the establishment of schools for their children they manifested visible interest, and some of them asked if I were ready to open the schools at once. But they usually began by inquir-init what was to be taught in such schools. When I told them that the object would be to communicate as much secular knowledge as possible, but that the Bible would also be taught every day, they seemed well pleased with the first part of the sentence, but at the mention of the Bible they became serious and taciturn for a while. Then, after a pause, one of them would ask in a soft, kind voice for the Druses of the upper classes are very polite " Do you intend to make oar children Christians? " To which I always answered that it was our desire that both they and their children might become truly Christian, believing that to be the only way of obtaining eternal salvation; adding that the English are a free people, who desire that all men should be free; consequently, we would teach the contents of the Bible to their children, but would leave them perfectly free either to embrace Christianity or to remain Druses.

Upon this two or three used to say, "Then you will not oblige our children to become Christians?" " Assuredly not. On the contrary, if any one tried to do it, we should be the first to oppose him." At this they always expressed their perfect satisfaction, and repeated their request that the work might be begun as soon as possible.

At that time these people were persuaded that, having been created Druses, not one of their sect could ever be persuaded to adopt any other religion; but when they heard that no constraint would be used, they had no objection to their children being taught from the Bible. More than this, they asked for the Bible and other books; and when they had received them, they used to retire to some corner to read. On my visiting their hhalweh (a retired place for their religious meetings) at Deir-el-Ivamer, I found a Bible on the table in the middle of the room.

I only met with two Druses who seemed to be attracted towards Christianity. Both were of noble family, and ajcaal, that is, intelligent. Besides five noble families to whom all Druses yield a willing and absolute obedience, the tribe is divided into two classes the AJcaals, or intelligent, and the Djahaals, or ignorant. The latter generally seemed to be mere animals, without any knowledge of their religion, or of anything but what relates to the body and the present life, and they are addicted to many vices. The Akaals are really educated, that is, they are not only instructed in the mysteries of their religion, but they are also taught to rule their own passions, feelings, and inclinations, and, above all, to keep secrets inviolable; hence the difficulty of discovering what their religion really is.

Having previously read the work of De Sacy, "La Religion des Druses," I could ascertain many points on which they agree with or differ from its founders, the disciples of Hakem ben Amr Allah, who lived about the year 1000 a. d. But I cannot here enter into this subject. Suffice it to say, that most of the Akaals are really intelligent, polite, and moderate. They neither smoke nor drink intoxicating liquors; and, so far as I could observe, they govern their families better than do most Arabs, and behave kindly to their wives and their dutiful children. But there is one terrible drawback to their morality, as taught in their works. Whilst they are enjoined to be moderate, truthful, and kind towards each other in every relation of life, they may commit any crime against non-Druses, provided they do it so secretly as to bring no disgrace upon their community.

I have said that I only met with two Druses who seemed to be attracted towards Christianity. I heard not long afterwards that one of them he, I believe, who had placed the Bible in the Khalweh of Deir-el-Kamer had died, it was supposed of poison. Of the other, a Sheik of the Hauran, I have an interesting anecdote to relate.

It seems that one of the books which I had distributed at Damascus had immediately found its way to the Hauran, and fallen into the hands of the Sheik in question, who read it attentively. It was "The Companion to the Bible," with the title in Arabic, ' Morshed et Talibeen," " Guide to Inquirers." The Sheik found it interesting; and as it continually referred to another book (the Bible), he concluded that the other book must be of the more importance, and therefore spared no pains to obtain a copy. Having been told that his book had been brought from Damascus, he hastened thither. But there he was told that the man who had brought both books had left for Balbec. So to Balbec he went; but arrived so far, he learned that I had gone to Beyrout. At Beyrout he was informed that I had gone to Deir-el-Kamer. Without inquiring whether he could get a Bible at Beyrout, he hurried to Deir-el-Kamer, where he found me, and related to me his adventures, ending by an entreaty that I would give him the book to which the " Companion to the Bible " referred.

I had only one copy of the Bible left, and this I thought I needed in my religious conversations with the people; but if I had had a heart of stone I could not have refused it to his supplications. After expressing his gratitude with a beaming countenance he became very serious, and asked me to advise him how to use the book most beneficially. We had an extremely interesting conversation of several hours' duration, after which he left me with his two books. I have never since had any tidings of him, but I have often prayed that God might bless His own Word to that Sheik's salvation.

Whilst I am now relating my experiences among the Druses more than thirty years ago, it may not be out of place to mention that, within the last two years, I have had two Druses baptized here, one of whom has been an efficient teacher in my Orphanage, and whom I have just appointed catechist at Eamleh. The other was baptized four weeks ago.

My work among the Druses was now done. I had held conversations, both in public and private, with all their men of influence, and could report that the door was open for the establishment of schools. But the next year the income of the Church Missionary Society had fallen so low, that, instead of enlarging their work, they were obliged to curtail it; and so my mission to that quarter remained without visible result.

Not long after my return to Malta I received a very kind letter from Mr. Coates, then Secretary of the Church Missionary Society, in which he intimated to me in the most delicate manner that I might do well to apply for episcopal ordination, by asking me if I did not think that such a step might enlarge the sphere of my activity.

It was a delicate question for one in my position; wherefore I thought it my duty to give him in my answer a detailed account of my views with regard to that subject. I deem it no less my duty to insert here an abstract of the contents of that letter. I know that my views do not agree with those of many of my brethren; but I hope they will bear with me, as I am ready to bear with them.

"I like Episcopacy; and if, when I was about to be ordained, I had been providentially guided, or if I had had a choice, I should most likely have been led to seek episcopal ordination; although I consider Episcopacy, as a distinct order, to have been introduced providentially to answer to the requirements of the age, but distinct from the divinely appointed ministry in general. So that, under other circumstances, a Church may, also providentially, be led to constitute herself a Christian, Scriptural, and Apostolic Church without Episcopacy, provided she place herself under the ministry appointed by God (see i Cor. xii. 28, and Eph. v. 11); and provided also that she abide in lively communion with the Head, the Lord Jesus Christ, the Apostles

"Wherefore the Protestant Churches of the Continent must be considered, like the Church of England, as true branches of the universal Church of Christ."

I ended my answer to Mr. Coates' letter by declaring that, as I considered the Church in which I had been ordained as a true, providentially constituted, Christian Church, and myself a minister duly authorised to exercise all the offices of the Christian ministry, I could not, without a sufficient reason, seek for or accept episcopal ordination without offending many dear brethren by seeminsj to declare their ordination invalid. I could only conceive one case which might lead me to accept episcopal ordination, viz., if I were nominated to an episcopal parish, or to any office or position previously declared to be inaccessible to all who were not in episcopal orders. I did not expect that such a case would ever happen, and yet it was realised a few years later.

The year 1842 was one of much sickness in my family; it was also notable for ns through the birth of our fifth child and third daughter, Dora, now the wife of Inspector H. Eappard, near Basle.

As already stated, the income of the Church Missionary Society had fallen very low in 1842, while some of their more important stations needed to be strengthened. Their books in Italian, Greek, and above all, in Arabic, having been multiplied to an enormous extent, there being then no means of distributing them among the people for whom they had been prepared, except through the agency of the missionaries at Cairo, the Society decided upon giving up their translating and printing establishment at Malta. Now, after an interval of more than thirty years, I am happy to be able to state that the work of the Society at Malta has not been in vain; for all those books have by degrees been disseminated all over the East, and have done much good, especially in Egypt.

In May 1843, after a long and tedious winding-up of the Society's affairs at Malta, which process included a vexatious lawsuit about the tenancy of the house, I returned with my family to Switzerland. Actiug on the advice of my good friend, Mr. Lillington, I went for the benefit of my health, which was much shattered, to Albisbrunn, in the Canton of Zurich, to try the cold-water system, then a novelty, and in high esteem. At Berne we stayed for the night at the Hotel du Eaucon, where the following incident had taken place a few days previously. Two young Englishmen had engaged rooms in this hotel for one night, and had retired to rest in proper time. Late in the night they rang their bell, and when a waiter answered the summons, they desired him to call his master. The innkeeper, however, did not make his appearance. After a while the bell was again rung, and the waiter desired, as before, to bring his master. This time the host did present himself, and asked what was wanted. " Just put this pair of boots on the chair," was the order given. It was good-naturedly obeyed, and after asking if anything else were required, the innkeeper withdrew.

Next morning, before departing, the young men called for their bill, which was handed them. All the items were moderate enough except one. " Eor putting a pair of boots on a chair, one hundred francs." Of course the young men refused to pay this; and when they found their departure prevented, they applied to the British Ambassador for protection. That functionary decided that as the service was extraordinary, it was but just that the payment should be extraordinary also; and the young travellers were obliged to pay the sum demanded.

I mention this anecdote, because I have more than once seen similar foolish and offensive behaviour on the part of young British tourists, and because such conduct is the cause of many inconveniences, and, I may add, of expense to respectable English travellers.

I spent three months at Albisbrunn, and derived some benefit from the treatment, but the root of my complaint, my old enemy, was not removed.

I then took a cottage at the foot of the Weissenstein, where I spent two long years with my family, in prayerful expectation that the Lord would give me work to do. I was soon invited to address missionary meetings in the neighbourhood, and before long was requested by the Committee at Basle to attend the meetings of their auxiliary Societies, so far as my health would permit, all over Switzerland. I have ever since been thankful to God for the great and lasting success with which He blessed my feeble endeavours.

I went home in September to be present at the birth of my sixth child, Maria, now married at Basle to Herr Kober, the successor of the late Herr Spittler, publisher of that town.

During the winter of 1844-45 I was obliged to spend much time at home, making only short tours in the Cantons of Berne and Neuchatel. I had intended to spend a part of the summer of 1845 in the Canton de Yaud; but in the beginning of that year, the Government and the mass of the people had suddenly declared themselves so inimical to religious liberty, and especially to the missionary cause, that no meeting for the furtherance of the latter object was tolerated. However, the good seed had been sown, not only by me, but by many faithful pastors, and is now bringing forth much fruit, particularly in missionary work.

The friendship and love which I everywhere experienced, though not unmixed with occasional insolence on the part of those who were hostile to my work, and the great success which had attended my labours, hindered me for a good while from feeling all the difficulties of my position. At last, however, my situation became a very painful one; and almost my only comfort lay in the assurance that I was where the Lord would have me to be. I had, in fact, no position. The Church Missionary Society allowed me ys and s Jot each of my four children, to which the Committee of the Basle Missionary Society added 2 per annum. This was amply sufficient for the maintenance of my family; but I had my misgivings as to my relations to both these Societies. After all the means attempted for several years for the re-establishment of my health, my state was such as to leave scarcely any hope to the Church Missionary Society that I could ever again be employed in a foreign mission; and yet I was not altogether an invalid. I could still do a good amount of work, provided I was free to abstain from time to time, for a short interval, from all exertion of a severe nature, and I was still young. I therefore found it almost intolerable to be obliged to live on a pension from a Society which had already been at considerable expense on my account, and in return for which I had accomplished so little.

On the other hand, I had received a hint that the Basle Missionary Committee had held a consultation concerning me one section wishing to appoint me permanently as their travelling secretary or preacher, while the other members, chiefly calculating merchants, objected, on the ground that I was in delicate health, that I might soon die, and that, in this case, my wife and family of young children would fall upon them as a heavy burthen.

The thought sometimes occurred to my mind that I ought to offer myself as pastor to some small congregation or parish; but, in the first place, I knew that my health would not allow me to discharge the duties of such a post with regularity; and, in the second place, I was so sure that I had hitherto been called and guided by Divine Providence, without any interposition of my own, that I was unwilling to emancipate myself from the same passive obedience to such guiding in the future.

While thus waiting upon the Lord, I received a letter from a dear friend in London, Dr. A. Crawford, with whom, when we were together in Malta, I had had many conversations about the desirability of establishing a Protestant College in that island. Dr. Crawford informed me that on his return to England he and his friend Captain Gordon had communicated on the subject with various persons of high standing and influence, the result of which was that a Committee had been formed, and the establishment of the College decided upon. The rules had been framed, and suitable premises had already been purchased, so that it could at once be opened. My correspondent added that he had been requested by the Committee of the College to ask me to accept the office of Vice-Principal, on most favourable terms. A Principal would not for some years be required. Dr. Crawford also intimated that I must be episcopally ordained, in accordance with the rules already passed and become valid.

Now, if the offer in itself appeared to me to be a Divine answer to my prayers, the last clause seemed to be a direct call of Divine Providence; for it was the very kind of case which I had mentioned several years before to the Secretary of the Church Missionary Society in which I would consent to accept episcopal ordination, but which I never expected to come to pass. I was thus able to accept the call without the least hesitation, but with humble thankfulness to the God who heareth prayer.

I was not altogether easy about the examination to which I expected to be subjected in England, having forgotten much of my Greek and Latin and other items of school-work, but I firmly trusted that the Lord would help me. Provided my health continued as it had been of late, I saw clearly that, with the help of my wife, I could easily fulfil the duties of my future position; and as for the branches of teaching in which I was conscious of being deficient, I thought I was still young enough to improve in proportion to the rising requirements.

I started for England in May 1845, and spent about three months, chiefly in London, visiting the members of the Committee and other friends of the Malta College. I was frequently invited, in company with Dr. Crawford, to breakfast parties, and on such occasions was always asked to take the lead in family prayer. I simply did as I had been accustomed to do at home: I read a portion of Scripture, gave a brief exposition, and ended with prayer. Sometimes I was allowed to choose the passage myself, and at others it was chosen for me. By degrees I discovered that it was a kind of examination to which they were subjecting me, but I continued just as before.

Those three months proved to be of lasting benefit to me, for I made many good and zealous Christian friends. Only two of them, both excellent men and Christians, have since dealt coldly with me in times of trial, just enough to remind me not to put confidence in man.

In August I was ordained Deacon by Bishop Blom-field, who, besides many other acts of kindness, exempted me from a preliminary examination. After my ordination I accepted an invitation to make a tour in Scotland, where I visited many spots of great interest and beauty.

such as Loch Lomond, the Pass of Glencoe, Fort St. George, Fort Augustus, Inverness, c. I was deeply interested in the spectacle of lovely Loch Lomond, wild Glencoe, Ben ISTevis, and other striking localities. But when asked which of the two countries, Scotland or my beloved Switzerland, I considered the more interesting, I always replied that, as there is no real likeness between them, no comparison could be justly instituted. Both are grand and beautiful, but each must be measured by its own standard.

I arrived with my family at Malta in October. I had been ordered, before leaving England, to make a tour, as soon as possible after my arrival at Malta, in Italy and Sicily, for the purpose of making known among the Protestant Italian and English families the existence of the College, and of inviting them to send their boys thither to be educated. I was also instructed to collect funds for the maintenance of the Oriental youths, who were to be educated gratuitously.

I started towards the end of October, and visited Piome, Naples, Leghorn, Florence, Pisa, and in Sicily, Palmero, Messina, and Catania. I spent nearly three months on this tour, and met, as a rule, with kindness and courtesy, and also with some measure of success.

I found many opportunities of preaching the Gospel in an informal as well as a formal manner in Italy and Sicily. So far as the people of all classes in the great towns were concerned, my prejudices against the immoral and irreligious character of Italians and Sicilians were confirmed. But with the country people it was different; for although very superstitious, and infected by the immorality which always accompanies superstition, especially where the confessional exists, there remains in them a foundation on which an enlightened preacher of the

Gospel may build with a good hope of success. Onlv let such a preacher beware of letting the people know beforehand that he is a Protestant, for that title is with them tantamount to that of an atheist, a willing servant of the devil.

I have often asked myself how it comes that among sincere Eoman Catholics a sense of sin, as the inward natural corruption of guilt, is more or less kept alive, while among the many members of the Greek Church whom I have known, I could seldom discover anything of the kind. I have come to the conclusion that the chief cause of this difference is the fact that the ceremonies of the Eoman Catholic Church, with their crucifixes, direct the attention of the people more often to Christ crucified; while the Greek Church, when she points to Christ, points to Him as risen and glorified. And it is not on Tabor, but on Calvary, that the nature and enormity of sin is revealed.

On returning to Malta towards the end of January I 846, I found that my dear wife, with the help of the late Mr. Innes, had purchased all the necessary furniture, and that everything was in readiness for the opening of the College, which ceremony took place on the 3d of February in the presence of a goodly company of friends and about a dozen boy-pupils.

The next day work began. But what was my surprise on finding how fearfully the boys had been neglected and their parents cheated! When I asked them whether they had begun the study of Latin, several replied that they had been at it for three or four years, and that they had read " Csesar " through. I opened "Csesar " at random and made them read and translate, which they did most fluently and with tolerable correctness, but not one of them had the least idea of grammar, and they did not know what declensions and conjugations were! All that they knew was a matter of mechanical memory. I was obliged to begin to teach them to decline "mensa." Neither had the boys any knowledge of geography or history.

However, affairs went on very smoothly, and the boys soon became attached both to myself and to Mme. Gobat, who had the management of the house. We were as one family worshipping together morning and evening, eating at the same table, and taking our walks in common.

Thus, after many trials, my family and I found ourselves comfortably established; and we were very thankful to God and man for having placed us in so desirable a position.

CHAPTEE VII.

NOMINATION AND CONSECRATION AS BISHOP AEEIYAL AT JERUSALEM. (1846.)

The quiet, peaceful days at Malta were not destined to last. One Sunday about the middle of March, when coming out of church, a letter with a large seal was put into my hand. Without examining it, I quietly put it into my pocket and walked home, without the least suspicion as to its contents. Arrived at home, I went into my room to open the epistle; but on reading the first line, "I have been commanded by my master, the King of Prussia," I allowed the letter to fall to the ground and exclaimed, "ISTo; never, never!"

It was an official communication from Chevalier (afterwards Baron) Bunsen, the Prussian Ambassador in London, informing me that the King, Frederick William the Fourth, had nominated me to the vacant See of Jerusalem, and requesting me to accept the appointment. The Queen of England had nominated the first Anglican Bishop (Alexander), and it was now the turn of the King of Prussia to appoint a successor to the late prelate, subject to the veto of the Archbishop of Canterbury.

It was a deep sense of insufficiency and unfitness for the important office which prompted the impulsive ex- clamation, "Never!" After reflection, I added, with Moses, " 0 my Lord, send, I pray Thee, by the hand of him whom Thou wilt send."

In the course of the week I wrote to Chevalier Bunsen, communicating to him my general reluctance, and my first impulse to decline the offer. I laid before him all that had passed through my mind since the receipt of his letter my scruples, my doubts; but added that, notwithstanding my utter unfitness, I was ready to accept and follow the call, provided I could reasonably conclude tliat it came from God. I should infer this partly if the Committee of the Malta College should not only give their consent, but positively advise me to accept the offer. I added that I should also desire the advice and consent of the Committee of the Church Missionary Society, with whom I was still in intimate relation.

Two days after this I received a long letter from tlie late Mr. Coates, Secretary to the Church Missionary Society, who had been my friend and chief adviser for more than twenty years, in which he anticipated all the objections which he supposed I might make, and tried in the most kind and friendly manner to invalidate them, advising, and almost commanding, me to accept the call.

At the end of that same week I received a letter from Lord Shaftesbury, President of the Committee of the Malta College, in which he not only advised, but desired me to accept the position, to which he believed that God had called me. Now, as I had always considered it my duty, and felt it to be a pleasure, to obey my superiors, so on this occasion I saw my way clearly. I concluded without hesitation that, as God had hitherto directed all my ways without any seeking on my part, so now it was He who, through His instruments, was. calling me to Jerusalem.

By the next mail I wrote to Chevalier Bunsen, informing him that, relying on the gracious help of my Lord and Saviour, I accepted the nomination of his Majesty the King of Prussia, and that I was ready to start for London, if desired, to be consecrated there.

A few days later I started from Malta, and immediately upon my arrival in London I called upon Bishop Blomfield. That prelate put into my hand a document which had been addressed, he stated, by influential persons to the Archbishop of Canterbury (Howley), and I was requested to answer its contents. It was a protest against my being consecrated a bishop of the Church of England, and contained eighteen folio pages of accusations of heresies, chiefly found, it was alleged, in my " Journal of a Three Years' Eesidence in Abyssinia."

The chief accusation concerned my views on Baptismal Eegeneration, as I had expressed myself in my conversations with the Abyssinians. All the rest was in-significant; the writers, who had not signed the paper, having drawn the most strange conclusions from words the most simple and innocent. I could not help smiling while reading the paper, and was delighted at the idea of answering it.

There was only one point which puzzled me. I knew that the Bishop was very decided as to Baptismal Regeneration, whilst I could not admit that doctrine in the meaning of the word regeneration as I find it in Scripture; and I thought that if my views were opposed to those of the Bishop, I must be rejected. Wherefore, before beginning my answer, I went to the Bishop and asked him what he understood by regeneration. He at once 1 Chevalier Bunsen's letter of proposal and the Rev. S. Gobat's reply-are to be found in full in " The Protestant Bishopric in Jerusalem; its Origin and Progress." London: B. Wertheim, Aldine Chambers, Paternoster Row, 1847.

said, "A change of position; that is, a passing from an uncovenanted to a covenanted state, by the person baptized being thereby introduced into the visible Christian Church."

To this I had no objection; I could even have gone a little farther.

The Bishop of London expressed himself perfectly satisfied with my formal answer. Two or three days later he came to me and stated that my opponents were, upon the whole, satisfied with my explanations; but that they complained that I seemed to attribute unfairness to them; he therefore asked me to change a few expressions in my answer. I replied, that as he had himself approved the original, I would willingly make such changes for his sake.

All difficulties seemed now over; but this was not so. I was to be ordained priest at a general ordination at St. Paul's; but a few days before that appointed for the ceremony, the Bishop sent me word that a party (unknown) had appointed a lawyer to protest at the cathedral against my being ordained. His Lordship therefore advised me not to present myself, stating that he would ordain me on another occasion. I learned afterwards that a lawyer had indeed been at St. Paul's watching the ordination.

A few days afterwards I was ordained at Pulham, with several other candidates, and a few days later I was consecrated Bishop at Lambeth by Archbishop Howley, the late Bishop Wilson of Calcutta preaching the consecration sermon on the text Isa. Ixii. i. In the afternoon of the same day I preached at the chapel of the Society for Promoting Christianity among the Jews at Bethnal Green, on the text which I had chosen as the motto of my life, "God forbid that I should glory, save in the cross of our Lord Jesus Christ."

After praying and receiving visits in London, I started for Berlin in obedience to the commands of the King of Prussia, with whom I spent several delightful and instructive days. I observed with great pleasure that not only was he not ashamed to confess Christ as his Lord and Saviour, but that at table he daily took advantage of my presence to introduce and maintain religious conversations, asking me questions about localities in Palestine connected with some works or sayings of Christ, and then introducing for consideration the most essential facts and truths of Christianity.

On one occasion I had the misfortune highly to displease his Majesty.

A question having arisen about the Holy Sepulchre, I happened to say that I did not believe that it was the sepulchre of Christ. At this the King became excited, afiirming the contrary. When I tried to reason with him, I perceived that, like other great men, he could not bear to be contradicted. I therefore said simply, "I once spent the entire Holy Week, even several nights of it, in the church of the so-called Holy Sepulchre, and after seeing the abominations practised there, it has always been a comfort to me to think that it is not the sepulchre of my dear Lord which is thus desecrated."

Upon this the stern expression of the monarch's face relaxed as he said, "I confess this is a strong argument in favour of your view."

On another occasion, though not in the presence of so many high witnesses, I again had the unhappiness of offending the King by mentioning the dissatisfaction of his subjects and their inclination to rebellion.

He interrupted me in an angry tone.

"What!" he cried; " do you say that my dear sub- jects are rebellious? No, no; they love their king as their king loves them."

"I beg the pardon of your Majesty," I replied.   " I may be mistaken, for I am imperfectly acquainted with the Prussian people. But on passing the other day through Magdeburg, I saw a great concourse of excited people; and, as I frequently do, I passed slowly through the midst of them to listen to their conversation, and I heard many hard and revolutionary expressions, such as have suggested my observation."

To this the King observed in a milder tone, "I hope there are very few malcontents."

This was in 1846, two years before the Eevolution, in which he suffered so severely.

I never can forget the kindness daily shown me by the King and Queen. On taking leave of them, they loaded me with their good wishes, and the assurance of their deep interest in the work intrusted to my hands in Palestine.

From Berlin I started for Malta by way of Switzerland, to take, as it proved, the last leave of my aged father. Notwithstanding my serious frame of mind, I was much amused by the naive pride evinced by the people of the Jura, Eomanists and Protestants alike, in that a Jura man had been made a bishop.

A kind friend at Geneva gave me a loo to purchase a Protestant burial-ground at Jerusalem.

I reached Malta at the beginning of September, where one of my first duties was to baptize my seventh child, James Timothy, born during my absence, now a medical practitioner in North Wales.

My dear wife had already made the necessary purchases and preparations for our establishment at Jerusalem, so that we were quite ready to start; but now patience was to be exercised to the utmost for the space of three months from the want of facilities for reaching Palestine. There were steamers and sailing vessels going to Alexandria; but between Alexandria and Syria there was absolutely no means of communication by sea, except the rare opportunities of small Arab boats, which could not have taken us with our furniture, not to speak of the dangers of such a mode of transit. Nor could I think of taking my wife and four young children through the desert.

At last, on the representation of Chevalier Bunsen, the Government gave me a steamer, the " Hecla," to take us to our destination. We embarked in the middle of December, and after six boisterous days reached Jaffa. Before gaining the shore we had to pass through short but severe trials, from which, however, a most kind Providence delivered us.

When the anchor was cast, the wind and the waves were so high that there was no possibility of landing; and the kind and sympathising captain told me that he had received orders, in case of bad weather, to remain twenty-four hours off Jaffa, but no longer; thence he was to proceed to Beyrout. We thus had the sad prospect of being taken to Beyrout with all our luggage and furniture. However, at mid-day we had a heavy shower, which calmed down the high waves, so that one boat ventured to put out from Jaffa to the steamer to take us. But by the time the little craft had come alongside, the rain had ceased, and the waves were rising again. I therefore hastened to lower my wife, four young children, and three servants into the boat, with a few small and necessary articles, leaving my children's tutor, the Rev. A. Schafter, on board to watch over the furniture, in case of the steamer being taken to Beyrout the next day. Each time that the boat was lifted up on the crest of a wave, my children were handed to my wife one after the other. When it came to the turn of the youngest, aged six months, he was about to be placed in the hands of his mother, when the boat suddenly dipped to a depth of ten or twelve feet. The sailor, supposing that my wife had caught the child, loosed him; and I shuddered as I saw him falling through the air. My wife, however, had the presence of mind to spread out the skirt of her dress to receive him, and he was saved.

Thus we safely landed, thanking God for His gracious protection, and were hospitably received at the house of an Armenian, which the missionaries at Jerusalem had kindly caused to be prepared for our reception. By eleven o'clock next day all our property was safely brought ashore.

It was Christmas Eve when we landed, so that we were glad and thankful to celebrate the Nativity of our Blessed Eedeemer the first day after our arrival in His own Emmanuel land. The following day being Saturday, we remained to spend Sunday quietly at Jaffa with the late Eev. J. Nicolayson, who had come the previous day from Jerusalem to welcome us.

We started for Jerusalem on the 30th of December, and as we approached the Holy City, many members of the small Protestant community, proselytes and others, came out upon the road to meet and welcome us. About two miles from Jerusalem we were met by the English and Prussian Consuls in uniform, accompanied by ladies and gentlemen on horseback. I was so deeply moved that I could scarcely speak, but I prayed inwardly. On reaching the city we went straight to the chapel, where I read the Litany, and then addressed the small congre- liiiliiillllllllllllllli:!; iwimi h i siiiiihiiiiiji- Ilii gation; after which all retired to their homes, having first expressed their good wishes to us.

On the 1st of January 1847 I fell ill of fever, which lasted three weeks, during which time I resolved to keep the anniversary of the arrival of the first Protestant Bishop (Alexander) in Jerusalem as a day of prayer and thanksgiving, not only for our community on Mount Zion, but for all believers everywhere who take an interest in the welfare of Jerusalem, the conversion and restoration of Israel to the covenant of God with His people, and the blessing which will follow for all nations.

A yearly circular letter has since been published, inviting all Christian brethren abroad to unite with us before the throne of grace in prayer and praise on every 21 st of January; and, blessed be God, that day and the opportunities it affords for self-examination and mutual exhortation has ever proved an occasion of blessing and encouragement to our whole community, and a chief means of keeping the members, originally of different denominations, united, so as to form but one Church.

I had earnestly prayed that I might be permitted at least to assist at the services of that first day of commemoration; and, behold, God did more than I had asked; for on the day previous the fever left me, so that I could preach freely, though with deep emotion, on the text, I John ii. 28, "And now, little children, abide in Him."

Till then I had hardly ever enjoyed good health for the space of twenty-three years, but from that time I recovered the vigour of my youth, which I have since enjoyed to this day; for, with the exception of a few fits of ague, I have had only two serious illnesses during the last twenty-seven years. God be praised for it!

Ever since I sat on the knees of my mother, who frequently spoke feelingly of the desolation of Israel, and especially since it pleased the Lord to reveal Himself to my soul, I have always taken a deep interest in the conversion of the Jews. Wherefore, before coming to Jerusalem, I resolved to labour in brotherly union with the missionaries of the Society for the Promotion of Christianity among the Jews for the spiritual and temporal benefit of the children of Israel, as it has been my privilege to do unto this day. During my residence at Jerusalem we have baptized nearly two hundred adult Israelites and many children. But I knew that it was not the object of those who had appointed and sent me to Jerusalem that I should restrict myself to the work of an ordinary local pastor or missionary to the Jews. Besides, I felt that, like St. Paul (though I am ashamed to mention my own poor name in comparison with his), I was a debtor not only to the Jews, but also to the Greeks and to the barbarians, to the wise and to the ignorant, Greeks, Eomanists, Armenians, Turks, c., whose wretched condition, spiritual and temporal, had been recalled to me during my visit to Palestine twenty years before.

I therefore at once began to meditate upon the means to be employed for the spiritual benefit of the ignorant and depraved natives of all denominations. The first idea which presented itself to my mind was to send colporteurs to disseminate the Word of God among the people; but alas! that would have been of but little use, for, with the exception of a few merchants and people connected with the corrupt Government, with the mosques, or with the monasteries, who on account of their evil practices, which they were unable to give up, did not care for a book that condemned them, with these exceptions, there were scarcely any men, and no women, who could read. Scripture-readers were desirable, but for a long time I could find none.

At last I made the acquaintance of a simple man who, several years previously, had received a Bible from an American missionary. He had studied the sacred book attentively, and had found in it so much that was contrary to the teaching of the Eomish Church, to which he belonged, that the priests, failing to bring him back to his allegiance, accused him of forgery. This was a crime punishable with death, but the local Governor or Pasha having no power to pass the capital sentence, he had been sent to Constantinople, and there kept in a dungeon for a whole year without a trial. He had there studied his Bible, no longer with a view to finding out the errors of Eome, but of discovering what he must do to be saved.

The Bishop's autobiography written at Jerusalem during the years 1869 to 1873, and slightly abridged in these pages, ends here somewhat abruptly.

The second part of the narrative has been written by another hand, but enriched with copious extracts from the Bishop's correspondence. Eng. Ed.

CHAPTEE I.

RETROSPECTIVE GLANCE AT THE ORIGIN OF THE EVANGEIJCAL BISH-OPRIC AT JERUSALEM.

Those readers who have perused with sympathetic interest the charming narrative of our venerable friend in the foregoing pages, will doubtless regret that he laid down his pen at the very commencement of his new and more extended career of usefulness. It has therefore devolved upon certain of the surviving members of his family to take up the thread of the story, and to portray as faithfully as possible, with the help of existing memoranda and personal recollections, the second half of his life, covering the period of his episcopate.

The narrative must now assume a different tone; the sphere of action has become widely expanded; and it seems to us that it will be no inappropriate prelude to our task if we take a rapid survey of the bishopric from its creation up to the period when Samuel Gobat was invited to undertake its responsibility.

The events of 1840 had a very decided influence upon the condition of Palestine. Mohammed Ali and his son, Ibrahim Pasha, had wrested Egypt, Crete, and Syria from the sovereignty of the Sultan, with the design of founding an independent

Mohammedan kingdom. Ibrahim, who had formerly rendered terrible service to the Turks in their struggles with the Greeks, subsequently gained a series of victories over the Ottoman power in Syria and Asia Minor. European diplomatists were consequently seized with the apprehension that Turkey, thus enfeebled, would no longer be able to withstand the ascendancy of Eussia, and that the Sultan would throw himself into the arms of the Czar, thereby turning the whole course of recent events to the advantage of the great Northern Power. In order to obviate this result, the other European Powers came to the assistance of Turkey. England and Austria stepped into the breach, declared war against Mohammed Ali, took Said, Beyrout, and the fortress of Ptolemay, the bulwark of Palestine, and obliged Ibrahim, against whom the people of Syria had also risen up, to retreat. The consequence of these martial successes was to place in the hands of the Western Powers the liberation of Jerusalem from the Mohammedan dominion, an object for which the Crusaders of old had made the utmost sacrifices. The liveliest hopes and wishes were now awakened among the Christians of England and Germany. Had not the time now arrived when a Christian kingdom ought to be established in the Holy Land? Or, if the supremacy of the Porte must absolutely be acknowledged, would it not become the duty of the European Powers to provide for the foundation of a semi-sovereign state under a Christian prince, analogous in position to that of the Danubian Principalities at that epoch? Or, if not this, could not at least a Christian administrator be placed in Palestine? The inclinations of the Philhellenistic party were in favour of the Christians of the East. A society at Berlin addressed a petition to Lord Palmer-ston praying for the restoration of the Jews to their own land. Among the Christians of Great Britain, the idea began to gain ground that the time of the prophesied conversion and restoration of Israel was at hand, and political events seemed to be opening a way for this consummation. But all these fair hopes and aspirations came to nought. The Holy Land was given back to the Grand Turk; and no Christian prince, no Christian administrator, was established at Jerusalem. Of the return of the Jews not a trace was to be discovered. The sole fruit of events so rich in promise was the founding of the Evangelical Bishopric at Jerusalem.

This was the work of King Frederick William IV. of Prussia. The plan originated with him; its realisation was effected in conjunction with the Government and Parliament of England. Evangelical Christians in Turkey had hitherto enjoyed no rights as such, no representation and no protection, while the Greeks were shielded by Piussia, and the Latin Christians by France. Now, however, similar advantages of protection were to be assured to Evangelical Christians by means of a Protestant Episcopate at Jerusalem, which, under the segis of the two great Protestant Powers, England and Prussia, would occupy a position competent to command respect.

It is true that as yet there were but few Protestant English or Germans in the East, but expectations were entertained of the formation of British and German colonies in Palestine. The Bishop was further to be empowered to take charge of all such missionaries of different denominations labouring in the East as should wish to place themselves under his care. There were already American missionaries actively engaged at Bey-rout, and Anglican ones busy in Palestine, Chaldea, Egypt, Abyssinia, and elsewhere. But above all else, Jerusalem was to be the centre from which the Gospel was to be disseminated among the Jews. In addition to this, the King of

Prussia cherished views with regard to the Christians in the East. It was the intention to promulgate among them Christian culture. The Bishops of England met the Greek Bishops half way, and it was hoped that in due time the way would he paved for a union between the Anglican and Eastern Churches, on the ground of mutual recognition. Finally, it was anticipated that a more favourable disposition would be engendered among the Mohammedans, who until then had held themselves entirely inaccessible to all Christendom, if the plan succeeded of building up within their borders an Evangelical community which should be wholly free from superstitious rites while adorned with Christian virtues.

Such were the intentions with which Frederick William IV. signed the document for endowment of the new See. He granted half of the necessary funds, to the amount of; 15,000 sterling. The Bishop was to be consecrated in England, and placed under the jurisdiction of the Archbishop of Canterbury. The right of nomination was to fall alternately to the British and the Prussian Crown. Evangelical pastors from Germany were under superintendence of the Bishops, to minister to the German Protestants and celebrate their services, alternately with the Anglican Christians, in the same church. This was the agreement entered into by the State and Bishops of England.

On the 6th of November 1841, the Act of Parliament for the establishment of an Episcopal See at Jerusalem received the sanction of Queen Victoria.""

Das Evangelische Bistum zii Jerusalem, Geschichtliche Darstellung mit Urkunden, Berlin, 1842; and Kheinwald-Repertorium der theolo-gischen Literatur, 1842, S. 368 ff., 1843, S. 85 If.

The first Bisliop nominated by the English Government was a baptized Israelite, Michael Solomon Alexander, born in 1799 at Schonlanke, in the Grand Duchy of Posen, and educated as a teacher of the Talmud. He afterwards became a Jewish private tutor in England, where he was instructed in Christianity by a clergyman named Golding, and was baptized at Plymouth in 1825. He was ordained priest in 18 2 7 by the Archbishop of Dublin, Dr. Magee. He then worked under the auspices of the Society for the Promotion of Christianity among the Jews, and as Professor of Hebrew and Rabbinical Literature at King's College, London.

The first candidate proposed for the new See was Dr. MCaul, of Trinity College, Dublin, and distinguished for Hebraical scholarship. He, however, declined it, on the ground that the Jerusalem bishopric ought to be filled by a son of Abraham; and it was he who recommended Alexander to the Government.

The consecration took place on the 7th of November 1841. The rite was performed by the Archbishop of Canterbury, and on the 21st of January 1842, Bishop Alexander arrived at Jerusalem. He was accompanied by Ewald, a zealous missionary to the Jews, who was by birth an Israelite, and who had already laboured at Tunis; by his chaplain, Mr. Williams, and his physician. Dr. Macgowan. They found in the Holy City Missionary Nicolayson of Schleswig, who had been sent out by the English Society for Promoting Christianity among the Jews.

Their first reception on the part of the Turkish authorities was not an unfriendly one. A paternal greeting from the Primate of all England, introducing the new Bishop, was presented to the Greek and Armenian Patriarchs. The Society for Missions to the Jews, presided over b Lord Asliley, found means, with the help of a noble-minded benefactress, Miss Cook, for the building of Christ Church on Mount Zion. This was the first evangelical church erected in the length and breadth of the Turkish dominions.

The beginnings of the united labours of these men were tedious, and without visible results. The building of the church was arrested by a prohibitory decree from Constantinople so early as 1842, the very first year of Dr. Alexander's episcopate; and it was only after years of effort on the part of the celebrated British Ambassador, Sir Stratford Canning, afterwards Lord Stratford de Red-cliffe, that a firman was obtained from the Sultan, in September 1845, authorising the resumption and completion of the building. But before the end of 1845 Bishop Alexander had already finished his course. He died while on a journey to England.

Such were the circumstances under which Gobat entered upon his episcopal duties, when he arrived at Jerusalem at the close of 1846. The congregation, which, during the vacancy of the See, had been taken charge of by Nicolayson, numbered only from forty to fifty communicants, and had hitherto assembled in an obscure private building.

A house belonging to a rich Israelite was taken and furnished for the occupation of the Bishop and his family. There existed a Hebrew seminary under the Rev. Douglas Veitch, who attached himself as chaplain to the new Bishop, and remained his faithfully devoted friend through life. In this college proselytes were instructed in theology and languages. Indigent Jews found work and instruction in useful handicrafts in a House of Industry established for their benefit. Of other schools there were none. No bishop had ever exercised sway over a sraaller community than that which fell to the lot of Samuel Gobat; yet none had ever been appointed to a wider field of action than that which stretched around him, for it comprehended Palestine, Syria, Assyria, Chaldea, Asia Minor, Egypt, and Abyssinia.

The sentiments of Dr. Gobat's friends when he was called to this important office may be gathered from the two letters here subjoined. One is from his intimate friend Pastor Karl Werner; the other from his father-in-law. The first sets forth, better than we could do it, the manner in which Gobat had been prepared through the Divine guidance for his vocation. Herr Zeller had at first felt misgivings as to his son-in-law's acceptance of the See. He seems to have felt much as Luther had done on hearing that his friend Staupitz was to be made a bishop. He was shocked; for it was his opinion that no bishop (as bishops then were) could be saved; the temptation to worldliness would be too strong. But we shall see how the apprehensions of the worthy inspector were calmed.

Karl Werner to S. Gobat.

"Grossheppach, March 30, 1846,

"Dear Brother, A letter from good Dr. Barth, received to-day, has brought me such important news concerning you, that I cannot refrain from writing to you without delay, which indeed I ought to have done long ago. He informs me that Bunsen, by command of the King of Prussia, has offered you the Bishopric at Jerusalem. Now, first and foremost, I am delighted that the identical thought seems to have struck his Majesty of Prussia as that which at once occurred to my mind when the episcopal office at Jerusalem fell vacant. I said at the time to a couple of trusty brethren that I knew who was the right man for the place, and that was no other than our dear Gobat, who would suit it exactly. It is certainly a ticklish position; I quite see that; and in your new sphere good times are as little to be expected as they were in your previous pilgrimage, when the Cross has often weighed heavily. But you are not a man who seeks his own ease; it is rather the fellowship of His sufferings' that you have chosen. The Lord has endowed you with prudence such as enables you to deal successfully alike with the high and the lowly, and to combine in the right way the wisdom of the serpent and the harmlessness of the dove. Moreover, it is not your own but God's glory that you seek; and therefore you need not fear the snares which beset your path. May He give you grace to bear His Cross where He has borne it before you, and may He rule your heart, that it may not strive against the burthen.

"And now I must tell you why I believe that you are the fittest man for the post. You have a strong love for the Jewish people; without nourishing enthusiastic anticipations, you yet hold fast the hope of Israel in its fullest sense. You are seeking no object of ecclesiastical ambition, for you hate that anti-Christian spirit which, among Princes of the Church and their partisans, manifests itself in a love of the power to rule over others. You will, therefore, strive to serve, not the exclusive interests of the Church, but the kingdom of Christ itself, which is built up of the lowly and wretched on the earth. You will ever preserve a brotherly heart, walk in evangelical freedom, love, and humility, and make room for others to walk at your side. Remember that many another on whom the choice might fall, in case yoa declined it, would act otherwise. This is my first and chief reason.

' Then you combine certain qualities which are rarely to be met with united in the same personality. You are allied in nearly equal measure by birth, education, and career to three great and distinct nationalities. By speech a Frenchman, you are a German in sympathies, and have become an Englishman by virtue of your connection with the British Mission. These circumstances confer upon you in your position important advantages which many other candidates might fail to possess. To these must be added your reputation in the East and in the West. Your name carries weight in both quarters of the world. This is again a special qualification.

"Finally, you are master of precisely those languages with which, in such a position, it would be most desirable for you to be acquainted. In short, dear brother, consider the matter in whatever way I will, I find you entirely calculated to fill up the gap. May the Lord vouchsafe to you freedom of heart and mind to give a ready assent!

"I must own that, in that case, I should find the solution to the mystery of your being led to Abyssinia; for then it would clearly appear that Providence had been guiding you through bypaths to the goal now in view, and preparing you by ways that you knew not. Moreover, your previous ordination in the English Church borrows a more important and significant force from this unlooked-for contingency.

"But enough said on a subject upon which you must be able to form a clearer judgment than I can do. Only, I could not forbear telling you my opinion; and I can assure you that all the reasons which I have here enume- rated are entirely the result of my own thouglits and convictions, unbiassed by the least hint from any other quarter. Barth certainly said in his letter that I ought to persuade you, but he mentioned no reason for my doing so. I am and must ever remain persuaded in my own mind that you are the man for Jerusalem, and I trust that the Lord has guided you also to this belief, and that He will make the matter clear to you. K. W."

Christian H. Zelur to his Daughter, Madame Gobat, at Malta.

"Beuggen, August 26, 1846.

My dear Maria, Those were delightful, but, alas! all too fleeting days of close and intimate converse which we enjoyed with your husband when on his way to London, and afterwards on his return from Berlin. We all observed with joy that he was kind and simple-hearted as ever, and that his promotion to the new episcopal dignity had not puffed him up, but that, on the contrary, he had preserved unimpaired his accustomed sincere humility. May God be praised and thanked for that. May He also bless you, dear Maria, with new gifts of His meek and humble Spirit, and with wisdom and grace,. that you may become a faithful handmaid of the Lord, and a loving help-meet for your husband in his new position. You will soon learn that his new dignity brings with it new burthens, not only for him, but also for yourself.

"We are sorry to read in the papers that there is great drought and consequent scarcity in Jerusalem, and that at Safet positive famine had set in. This is no easy beginning for you both. May God support you, and still more the multitudes of poor, with His gracious help! May He conduct you in the hour of need with

His mighty arm and angel-guards in safety over sea and land, till He bring you to that country which His holy feet so oft have trodden, and which once so blindly rejected Him. May the mighty prophecies concerning that city, that land, that nation, be brought to glorious fruition in His own good time, and may your husband's work be so blessed that it may prepare the way of the Lord. May the ninety-first psalm, in especial, be graciously fulfilled for you. The Lord be with you all. Amen.

"We send you our blessing, and abide in close communion with you through love and intercession. Think also upon us, dear Maria, and particularly upon your father in his advancing age.

"Christiax H. Zeller."

CHAPTER II.

DEVELOPMENT OF THE MISSION, AND OF SCHOLASTIC MATTERS UNDER BISHOP GOB AT.

(1846-1851.)

The fountain-liead of the history of the three-and-thirty years' activity of Bishop Gobat at Jerusalem is to be found in his annual circular letters. On each anniversary of his predecessor's arrival in Jerusalem, the Bishop addressed a " brotherly message " by way of New Year's greeting to distant Christian friends. An English version of these letters appeared in the Record, while a German edition of them was published in the Calwer Missionshlau, and in the Christian Volksbote. They were only omitted in those years when the Bishop was travelling in Europe, or when he was hindered from writing by illness.

These are supplemented by documents which have been found among Gobat's manuscript correspondence and elsewhere. A rich source of information concerning the Evangelical Mission in Jerusalem, Syria, Asia Minor, and Egypt is furnished by the valuable periodical entitled, Neiieste Nachrichten aus dem Morrjenlande, and published from 1857 till 1872 by the garrison-chaplain, Herr Friedrich Strauss, and since then by Herr Karl Hoffmann. Gobat himself abstained through delicacy of

"Latest Tidings from the East."

feeling and prudent foresight from the publication of histories of the conversions of persons still living, whereby the work of Divine grace may so easily be hindered and spiritual harm be wrought. In that periodical, however, more individual detail was ventured upon, and many an experience recorded in its pages may serve for the edification of the reader.

When Gobat discontinued his autobiography, he did this nob alone through want of time and strength. He had another motive for his silence. As Bishop he had to encounter much hostility, and to battle through many controversies. A lover of peace, he preferred to keep silence on all these points. In the present volume, however, these conflicts cannot be entirely ignored, because the truthfulness of the picture would thereby suffer; but we shall seek to treat them in the same spirit of conciliation as that which imbued the mind of the departed Bishop.

The reports of this first period, from 1846 to 1851, already present a striking picture of Gobat's manifold and increasing labours, of the material and spiritual poverty by which he was on all sides surrounded, and of the opposition which he had to suffer, alike from Jews, Christians, and Mohammedans. His path of duty, as representative of the Evangelical Churches of England and Germany, was occasionally beset with thorns; and we have high and competent testimony to the manner in which he demeaned himself in this difficult position, and to the general respect which he enforced not only for himself personally, but for the cause which he had to maintain.

The following extract is taken from the Tl ochcnhlatt des Johanniterordcns, Berlin, 1880, No. 47; and it was written by Dr. G. Rosen, savant and diplomatist, who, a Prussian Consul at Jerusalem since 1852, was a firm

STREET OF THE BAZAAR, JERUSALEJtf, WITH MOUNT OF OLIVES IN BACKGROUND. Pa re 235.

"If we take into furtlier consideration the fact tliat Gobat's mind had assimilated rich stores of theological learning, while his heart was filled with child-like faith,. that he was almost equally master of the three most important languages of modern culture, German, English, and French, that he possessed the advantage of an agreeable, sonorous voice, and that the effect of his dignified, earnest countenance was aided by a tall and imposing stature; it must be owned that he was furnished in an unwonted degree with the weapons necessary to combat the difficulties of his exalted situation.

"Gobat's presence in Jerusalem was to many people unwelcome; but. thoroughly peace-loving by nature, he lamented the discord awakened in all directions by his activity; though he was well aware that. reform and old routine cannot amicably co-exist. He regarded the actual conflict between the two as inevitable, but he was most careful to avoid visiting it on individuals. In the case of the hierarchies of the ancient confessions, for example, he ever cherished for them the most hearty good-will, notwithstanding the coldly repellant attitude maintained by them towards him."

So far Dr. Rosen.

Gobat left behind him an extensive collection of letters, from which we shall here give a selection. The most notable portion of it consists of his correspondence with King Frederick William. Gobat's own narrative has already made us acquainted with some of the particulars of interviews with his Majesty immediately after the former's nomination to the bishopric; the King himself observed at the time that he had seldom met with any man who had inspired him with such entire confidence as Samuel Gobat. This sentiment is exemplified in the letters above referred to.

Bishop Gohat to General Hose, Consul-General at Bey rout.

"Jerusalem, October 13, 1847.

"My dear Sir,. The subject of your letter has often occupied my thoughts for a long time past; and I fully agree with you that the combined efforts of French and Roman policy, of which education is the most powerful auxiliary, are calculated greatly to increase the influence of France in Syria. But the more I reflect on this subject, the more I feel our want of means to counteract that influence, either in a political or religious point of view.

"I do not think, however, that the greatest difficulty will be with the natives; although in this respect also the French emissaries, whether Jesuits or Sceurs de Charity, have a great advantage over us in the fact that they can begin their operations, wherever they go, with co-religionists, who not only have no prejudice of importance against them, but who have also been accustomed to look to them for protection. We, alike as Protestants and Englishmen, have no such nucleus to begin with; and it is well known that in every enterprise of this kind the beginning is the most difficult part. But still, it is not the field of operations which presents the greatest difficulties; with a little patience and perseverance existing prejudices would be removed, and in a short time people would discover that a lay education is better than one essentially clerical. I conceive that the great obstacle lies with us, and consists in our want of means, a difficulty which I already feel in my endeavour to establish an English school at Jerusalem.

"However important other questions on this subject of education in this country may be, whenever I think of it, the religious question is the first that presents itself.

as well with regard to the field of operation, as also with regard to the source whence we are to derive support.

If I were to express my conviction, I would say that consider education without religion as a j ositive evil, as the present state of my native country, Switzerland, abundantly proves. But then, with respect to this country, I do not mean by a religious education the teaching of creeds, catechisms, c., least of all the theoretical differences existing between different Churches, but the positive, historical, doctrinal, and moral truths of the Word of God, proceeding from a living conviction on the part of the teacher, and interwoven as much as possible with other branches of education. No so-called religious lessons, except the simple reading of the Bible, with short observations in a free conversational or catechetical manner. But I suppose that this view will not meet with any supporter. Pieligion ought to he the salt of education, seasoning other branches; never to be administered alone to children, except in small doses, to correct moral indigestion and to excite appetite.

"But as far as I am acquainted with the English public, from whom support is to be sought, I must consider such a system impracticable. One party will support schools in which a religious education is given, i. e., according to their views, where scarcely anything is taught but religion; I mean, a knowledge of abstract religious views as developed under a special form of ecclesiastical system. "Whilst others, less generous in action though more so in words, will have no religion at all in schools. Under such circumstances, where are we to get the means of establishing English schools? If we could show a prospectus of intended schools in this country essentially or exclusively religious, I have no doubt but some religious society would undertake to send cheap sclioolmasters, and to maintain them; but this would not do in this country. The schools would remain empty. On the other hand, if we stated that no religion, or at least as little as possible, should be taught, many people would applaud, while clever but expensive teachers would offer their services. In the latter case, we should be unable to find funds to meet the expenses, and the natives would scarcely be disposed to send their children to schools professedly irreligious.

If Government were inclined to undertake the matter, the middle course, which I conceive would alone be practicable as likely to prove useful, might be adopted. But will the Government do anything in this direction?

"In the year 1841 I was sent by the Church Missionary Society to ascertain whether the Druses were disposed to have their children educated on a large scale by the agents of that Society. I found them very well inclined in this respect, and willing that the Bible should be taught to their children. But before leaving Syria I received the intelligence that the receipts of that Society being far below its expenses, they could not think of putting that plan into effect; and since then nothing has been done.

"I conceive that the chief fault of the British Government in this country for years past has been to consider the inhabitants of Syria as a nation whilst there is no nationality, but only sects. This the French and Russians understand very well, and they both have their parties or sects or centres of influence in the Roman Catholic and Greek Churches. This cannot be changed.

"I believe that if the British Government would undertake to educate and protect the Druses, it would prove the means of getting a footing in this country similar to that of France and Russia. I should be sorry to see

Protestantism, whether episcopal or not, made a means of political intrigue, as is the case with. the above Churches. But, on the other hand, I am convinced that if England were to protect Protestantism, i. e., religious liberty, with a strong hand, such a course would be the means of acquiring within a few years the best-grounded, most just, and probably most powerful influence in this country. S. Angl. Hierosol."

Extract from Bisjiop Gohafs Circular Letter of 1847.

"Jerusalem, November g, 1847.

Samuel Gobat, Evangelical Bishop at Jerusalem, to all the brethren who love the Lord Jesus and look for His kingdom, but especially to those who yearn and pray for the salvation of Israel Grace and peace.

"When on the 21 st of January, the anniversary of the arrival of the first Evangelical Bishop in Jerusalem, I bent my knee before the throne of grace in grateful remembrance of abundant blessings bestowed in past years, it was my fervent prayer to the God of Israel, in unity of spirit with all the servants of the Lord who earnestly desire the building of Jerusalem, that He would vouchsafe His richest blessing to the growing Church upon Mount Zion. I also gladly formed the resolution to follow the example of my late predecessor, who, through the medium of an annual brotherly greeting, was accustomed to call to your remembrance the present needs and the future hopes of

Jerusalem. I would at the same time commend myself and the little flock committed to my care to jouv fraternal and Christian benevolence, to your love, and to your faithful intercessions.

' While availing myself of this opportunity to express my heartfelt thanks to all those who in past years.

have sliown me so much love and sympathy, I feel constrained to ask not only your general daily prayers, but also to invite you, in a special manner, to join with us in a spirit of supplication and intercession on the 21 st of January 1848, which day has been appointed by the congregation at Jerusalem to be kept as one of prayer and thanksgiving.

"Since our arrival here at the end of last year, we have enjoyed tranquillity and peace. Each one of us is actively working in his own proper sphere to proclaim the unspeakable riches of Christ to the unhappy sons of Abraham, and not to them alone. As far as we can discover, a lively spirit of inquiry after the truth is abroad among the Jews. I hear from time to time that many Jews are half convinced that Jesus is the Christ; many there are who secretly read the New Testament. There are but a few who have the courage to open their hearts to the missionaries, or even to visit or receive visits from them; while very few indeed have the heart to openly acknowledge their belief in a crucified Eedeemer. On the other hand, the difficulties which beset those Jews who believe in the Lord Jesus and desire to confess His Name are almost insurmountable. They must not only overcome their innate prejudices, but also see every bond of kinship and affection rent asunder. They must make up their minds at the very outset, that from the moment when they openly declare their belief in Christ, the love and attachment of their nearest relatives and friends will be changed into contempt and scorn and deadly hatred; and although they are almost all very poor here, they must yet renounce from that hour all the help which they, as Jews, w ould otherwise receive from their brethren after the flesh in different lands. Still there are a few whose conviction of the truth that Jesus of Nazareth is the Messiah enables them to surmount all these difficulties, and that without any prospect of the least temporal advantage.

"But it is a matter of course that, as long as we have a morsel of bread, we will share it with such, and, thank God! all the members of our little community are of one mind on this subject.

"In the course of the present year five adult Jews have been here incorporated through baptism with the Evangelical Church, among them a youth of seventeen, who had previously suffered persistent persecution and incarceration for the sake of the name of Christ, and who, we hope, has hajopily fallen asleep in the Lord. Since the year 1839, thirty-one adult Jews and twenty-six of tender age have been baptized. This is certainly a small number compared with the multitude of Israelites who are perishing in their unbelief and superstition. But when we consider that one single immortal soul is worth more than the whole world, how can it be asserted, even supposing that half of them are faithful members of the body of Christ, that success bears no proportion to the outlay and the efforts of the Missionary Society and the missionaries? Besides, it must not be forgotten that the past and the present time has been and is a season of clearing away difficulties and hindrances, a time of sowing. In the future we shall reap, if we faint not. I must own that these proselytes are still weak, and that they need our daily care, watchfulness, and intercession. On the other hand, I may venture to say, to the honour of God's grace, that some of them do walk worthy of their calling. Several are working as missionaries or assistant-missionaries in Egypt, Persia, and Palestine, and the blessing of God rests upon their labours. Of those who reside here, I must say that they work hard, and eat their bread in the sweat of their brow; and although very backward in their spiritual condition, they nevertheless strive to grow in the grace and knowledge of our Lord Jesus Christ.

"This leads me to the mention of one of our greatest difficulties, which of late has increased in magnitude. It has already been observed that a Jew, as soon as he confesses his belief in Christ, as a rule loses at once his means of livelihood. Now so long as isolated individuals come over to Christianity, we do what we can to protect them from hunger and nakedness. But as the Society for the Conversion of the Jews has been compelled through pecuniary embarrassment to give up the Hebrew College, and to materially reduce the industrial establishment or refuge for proselytes as, moreover, the missionaries only receive about 800 florins annually in aid of proselytes, it is clear that if our work meets with wider success we shall be placed in a most embarrassing position.

"At the present moment we have two candidates for baptism, who enjoy regular instruction and seem very promising. For these we must provide until their baptism a few months hence. But we have heard of several, of whole families indeed, who shortly intend to present themselves; and if they do so, we shall thereby find ourselves in very straitened circumstances, unless Christian brethren possessed of means come to our aid.

"I must therefore appeal to all the faithful, and remind them of their obligations; for in proportion as we promote the preaching of the Gospel among the Jews, so do we incur the duty before God of succouring according to our worldly means those Israelites who, in consequence of their acceptance of the Gospel, are exposed to utter want of all life's necessaries.

"I were almost tempted to beseech you, dear brethren, to refrain from causing the Gospel to be proclaimed to the Jews, unless you are at the same time prepared, in case of their conversion, and of their being therefore naked and destitute of daily food, to do more than to say, Depart in peace; be ye warmed and filled.

"But what is to be done? Should God hear out and your prayers, so that many of them might be converted, I know not how we should provide for them; and yet it is our duty to do so. It is clear to me that so long as our converts here are undergoing preparatory instruction, that is, previous to their baptism, they must be entirely supported by Christian beneficence; afterwards they must be taught to earn their bread themselves; but this again will cost both time and money. And I repeat that if those among the faithful who do possess means will not come to our assistance, the mission in Palestine and Jerusalem cannot thrive, the exertions of the missionaries will become crippled, and the congregation cannot increase.

' This is prosaic, but I cannot help it. Duty urges me to cry aloud to you all that the Lord shall arise and have mercy upon Zion; for the time to favour her, yea. the set time is come; and whether you come forward or not to aid in furthering the Lord's pleasure. He will yet gather together the people of His covenant, convert, feed, and clothe them, to the confounding of those who turn their backs upon them in the time of their need.

"No one can wish more earnestly than I to see the Jews delivered from every oppression which weighs upon them and rescued from all their misery. But to shower benefits upon the Jews, even were it with a view to lead them by such means to a belief in the Gospel, while the poor converted Israelites are neglected and abandoned to their fate, may perhaps be philanthropic, but it certainly cannot be called a Christian mode of procedure.

"In the course of the year now nearly expired, our services have been held with regularity and free from disturbance of any kind. On Sundays we have three services, two in English, which language is understood by the majority of our congregation, proselytes included, and one in the German tongue for the remaining converts and the six or eight Germans resident here. Every morning a Hebrew service is held. We celebrate the holy communion on all the great festivals, and on the first Sunday of every month. As several Arabs have attached themselves to us, and others seem to be so inclined, we are thinking of soon establishing a regular Arab service.

"In consequence. of the recent conversion of a Druse at Beyrout, we have received a fatuct (written declaration) from the Mufti of Beyrout, wherein it is expressly stated that it is permitted to the Jews and Druses, subjects of the Porte, to become Christians; and that all members of the various Christian congregations may migrate at will from one Church or party to another. This will certainly prove, like all the friendly firmans of the Porte, of little practical importance in the first instance. But we may, nevertheless, regard it as a further step towards the desired religious liberty in this country; and we may hope that good fruit may result, to the glory of God and salvation of men. This fatua is founded upon the Mohammedan axiom that there really exist but two religions, namely, that from God, which leads to God, and that from the devil, which leads to perdition. Now, seeing that all the unbelieving, i. e., non-Mohammedans, belong to the religion of Satan, it must be a matter of perfect indifference with which sect or party of this religion they ally themselves.

"The friendship and good-will which formerly arose between our community and the heads of the Armenian, Coptic, and Syrian Churches has uniformly continued, while the Greek Patriarch and his clergy hold themselves as much aloof from us as possible. The Patriarch does not even respond to ordinary courtesies. We have, however, come into no collision with them, any more than with the Latin Christians; whereas the Latin and Greek monks are in continual warfare with each other, so that on high festivals it is necessary to post one or two companies of Turkish soldiers in the Church of the Holy Sepulchre to prevent combats taking place between the two parties. No later than a week ago the monks at Bethlehem fought so fiercely that it was feared for several days after that the Greek Bishop would die of the wounds he had received.

"The people in general are kindly disposed towards us. They seem to perceive more and more clearly that a Church which rests upon the Word of God alone has juster claims than the superstitious communities of which they are passive members.

"A spirit of inquiry after the truth continually manifests itself among the members of the various Churches. Many who but a few years ago were in the habit of assembling for play, or to hear or relate marvellous stories, now meet together to read the Word of God or to discuss religious questions. A few months ago, therefore, I appointed an intelligent, well-read young man as Bible-reader; he has not formally seceded from his own Church, the Greek-Catholic, but he knows and loves the truth. He seeks to keep alive this spirit of inquiry, and to lead the people to the truth of the Gospel, without mixing himself up in Church matters, or in the least degree trying to proselytise. If, however, individuals become persecuted by the communion to whicli they formerly belonged on account of witnessing for the truth, then we receive them.

"This inquiring tendency has revealed itself not in this city alone, for many petitioners have begged me to send teachers and preachers to the country-folk. Only a few days ago the Sheik of a large Christian village came as a deputation from his congregation to request me, in the name of the whole community, to send to them a teacher, and to assure me that if I granted their prayer, they would immediately build a church and a school. As I have at present no means to enable me to meet their wishes, I must content myself with laying the fact before the Christian public, and leaving it for their further conscientious consideration.

"Another Bible-reader has been appointed to visit the Arabs beyond Jordan, and he finds a promising opening among them.

"I have also placed a converted Jew, Hershon, who has been trained in the Hebrew College, as evangelist among the Jews of Jerusalem, and they prefer talking with him on religious subjects to conferring with the missionaries. He will form an essential, and I hope a useful, bond of union between the missionaries and the Jews, and is at the same time active in promoting the growth of religious knowledge among the rest of the converts. We have two Bible repositories, one here and one at Jaffa, under the superintendence of two converts, who discharge their duty faithfully and well.

"The need of a school in connection with our Church has long been felt, but now the desideratum is to be supplied. A house furnished with all requisites stands in readiness to receive twelve poor children, who will be cared for in every way; and to this institution will be joined from the very beginning a day-school. An English mistress arrived a few days ago, while for the boys a pupil of the Hebrew College has been appointed. Tomorrow, if it please God, the school will be opened with about ten children. We have reason to believe that the number will soon increase. We wish this school to benefit Jewish children primarily, but not exclusively.

"May the God of Israel be gracious unto you, and grant His blessing to all who pray for the peace of Jerusalem. Your friend and brother, ' Samuel Gobat."

Bisliop Gobat to Herr von Bunsen in London.

Jerusalem, March 4, 1848.

"You spoke of passages in my letter to the Jewish mission which might be politically open to the charge of proselytising. Now, I confess that I am somewhat inexperienced in politics, never having, even in Abyssinia, met with difiiculties on that head; and the want of experience of this kind in the past appears to me as a sort of guarantee for the future.

"As for prosel tising, it is not so much my object as you seem to fear. My general principle is the following. It is the duty of every Christian, on the one hand, to confess the truth of the Gospel with prudence, but freely and openly, and if he meet with opposition, to give a reason for the hope that is in him; on the other hand, he is bound to warn his brethren, even though they may belong to other confessions, of the paths which lead to destruction. It is, however, the especial obligation of all the clergy, and particularly of a bishop, as the servants of our Lord Jesus Christ, to proclaim, to the extent of their opportunities, the Gospel with wisdom and freedom to every creature, no matter to what party any individual may belong; and I pray unto God to grant me tlie will and tlie ability to do this.

"In following out this principle, nevertheless, it ought never to be the preacher's aim to convert people to this or that Church, but to lead them to the source of all truth and life, even to the Lord Jesus, and to teach them to yield themselves to His guidance. This having been effected, let them remain in their respective Churches, and there confess their Saviour and His truth. If they are able to do this, then I do not wish a single one of them to come over to our Church.

"But if individuals are persecuted for their love to their Lord and their confession of the truth if they are anathematised and cast out by their own Church, and thereupon present themselves to us with the request that we would receive them, I do not see how we could refuse admittance to such without rejecting the Lord Himself, and in such a case no human consideration can avail.

You will no doubt approve this principle, irrespective of the serious difficulties which are inseparable from its practical application, and therefore I need not enter into details. Moreover,. as the Catholics here proselytise from the Protestants under our very eyes, I cannot see why we, at all events, where they are concerned, may not claim the same right, and you know that the Uniate Greeks are Catholics. That there can be no question of proselytising among the Moslems is a matter of course. Most respectfully, c., c. S. Angl. Hieros."

Extracts from Bishop G6ha s Circular Letter for 1848.

"Jerusalem, October 30, 1848. Whilst we were beholding from a distance the storm which was raging throughout Europe, the rod of the Almighty was stretched out over our own heads for a period of several months. Thousands and tens of thousands, on our right and on our left, in Egypt, Syria, and Palestine, have fallen beneath the scourge of the cholera. Thank God, Jerusalem has been spared, and we still live to praise the name of the Lord.

"Another ground of thankfulness, which will doubtless be shared by many Christians, is the reconciliation and mutual recognition of the three Patriarchs the Greek, the Latin, and the Armenian which took place at the beginning of this year. And although the motives of the Pasha who brought about this desirable state of matters are unknown to me, I nevertheless rejoice over the results of this reconciliation; for, with the exception of a few encounters between the Greek and Latin monks, the Christians have ever since avoided those ugly displays of hatred which in former years brought so much disgrace upon the name of Christian.

For ourselves, we enjoy the increasing respect, goodwill, and confidence of all parties. With regard to the heads of the various Churches, everything remains as it was a year ago. The Greek Patriarch and his clergy hold themselves as much aloof from us as possible. Between the Latin Patriarch and myself is a gulf which neither he nor I have created; but at least neither of us can complain of hostility, although the former began by warning the people against us. He held it to be his duty to do so, and was not very bitter. With the Armenian, and even with the Greek-Catholic Patriarch, as also with the Syrian Bishop, I stand upon a friendly footing.

"Our new Christ Church upon Mount Zion could not be consecrated, as we had hoped, upon the 19th of April, on account of unexpected causes of delay which inter-intervened, but I now know of no further hindrance, so that the consecration can soon take place.

' During the past year we have been quietly carrying on our work, each according to the gift he has received. We have had much intercourse with the Jews, many of whom, in the time of emergency and need, seem to look upon us as their best friends, which indeed we endeavour to be.

"The Jewish Hospital is a standing source of temporal blessing to thousands; and it has been so organised this year, that I venture to hope that it will become a means of spiritual blessing also to many sons and daughters of Abraham.

"Althouorh we have ao ain had numerous difficulties to contend against this year in providing for sundry Jews who are seeking after Christian truth, as well as in affording needful help to the poorer converts, we have yet been enabled, through the beneficence of many friends of Israel,. to relieve the most pressing cases of distress. And here I may gladly remark that through the generosity of the English Mission to the Jews an Industrial House will immediately be opened, from which I expect, with God's blessing, the best results.

"We have at the present time fourteen persons who have separated themselves from the Jews, and who are now being instructed preparatory to being baptized. Five of these have no means of subsistence; in accordance, therefore, with my resolution to baptize no able-bodied man who is not willing to earn at least a portion of his daily bread, I have apprenticed them to artisans to learn each a trade. Two others I declined to baptize, owing to their refusal to learn some handicraft. They both went eastwards, one to Constantinople in search of some one who would baptize him on other conditions; the other, Eabbi Jacob, has returned re- pentant, and is now learning the trade of a tailor. So I hope that from henceforth the Jews will understand that he who is, or who wishes to become, a Christian, must earn his bread by the sweat of his brow.

"I must here take occasion to observe that the German artisans who come here do not, on the whole, set a good example; for even when work is offered to them, the majority of them would rather live by begging than by honest labour. We have had swarms of such people here this year; and as many of them have fallen sick and are completely destitute, we find it at times no easy matter to provide them with necessary travelling-expenses, c. If we fail to do this, they add their quota to the disgrace of the nation to which they belong, and to the religion which they all, to some extent, profess. And while on this subject, I must express my especial thanks to friends in Berlin, who, by their substantial support, have enabled me to give something to each German artisan towards the further expenses of his journey. But why to each one without distinction? it may be asked. I do make a distinction in favour of the neediest, and sometimes of the most respectable. But as they are one and all in distress, and the deepest physical and spiritual misery speaks plainly from almost every eye, each one must be helped.

"From the foregoing remarks it must become clear to every one how desirable it is that a hospice should soon be established for the reception of such travellers, to aid them in their want and des radation. Then it is not fair that Protestant artisans should absorb the alms of Roman Catholics. If we had a German hospice, we could not only judge more correctly of the deserving-character of the applicants, and be enabled to treat them accordingly, but we could also influence them for good, which it is almost impossible to do under existing circumstances.

' I have during this year again employed three evangelists or colporteurs, one among the Christians, one among the Jews at Jerusalem, and one among the scattered Arab population. I am expecting a fourth to arrive from Beyrout in a few days. This work has not been without success, especially in dissipating the prejudice of the Jews and Christians in Jerusalem.

"When one of these evangelists, a simple-minded, faithful Arab, was at Nablus about a year ago, several men began to read the Scriptures together and to investigate. At Easter a few of them came hither in order to see and hear our service, and returned home again without having spoken much with us. Some weeks afterwards, however, I received a letter from Nablus, signed by eight or ten men, wherein they announced to me that they had resolved to leave the Greek Church (or, as they called it, the Church of the Patriarch), for if they remained any longer within its pale, they and their children must go to destruction through ignorance, c., and they had, therefore, decided to constitute themselves an Evangelical congregation, to take the Word of God as their sole rule of conduct, and to place themselves under my guidance.

"I answered that I was ready to do my utmost to aid them in their search after Evangelical truth, but that I could not countenance them in forsaking their Church. The only counsel that I could give them would be that they should continue to read God's Word with diligence and prayer, to make it their guiding rule of life, and so to remain in their Church until they were excluded from it, if matters should ever come to such an extremity.

"After some further interchange of letters, a mis- sionary went with our local evangelist to inquire more closely into the matter; and they found, as was to be expected, that the people had only a very imperfect knowledge of Scriptural truths, a deficiency which, however, the dear people themselves deeply felt. They learned also that several heads of families, who, with their respective wives and children, amounted to seventy out of the four hundred Christian souls at Nablus, had signed a mutual promise to hold together in their searching and following of the Holy Scriptures, and especially to do their utmost to obtain for their children an education based upon the principles of the pure Word of God. The document also intimated that there were other persons like-minded with themselves, whose signatures to the engagement they, from motives of prudence, had not solicited.

"To be brief, I shortly received a petition subscribed by twelve householders, and conceived in a humble, Scriptural spirit, in which they informed me that they would follow my advice, and abide in the communion of the Greek Church. But on that account they besought me yet more earnestly to procure for them the means of giving to their children a purely Biblical training, the want of which they so painfully felt with regard to themselves.

"As I had by that time weighed all the circumstances of the case, I determined quietly to buy a good house, large enough for a boys' and girls' school, and to accommodate a teacher and his family. I installed an intelligent, most promising young man, a native of Nazareth, but resident at Xablus, as master, under the supervision of two influential men of the Society. At the same time, while everything was as yet quiet, I obtained from the Pasha here, and from the Governor of Nablus, a written promise to protect my school and my agents, namely, the schoolmaster and his two overseers. The latter precaution was justified by the result; for as soon as the affair became bruited abroad, my chief correspondent and agent was brought before the tribunal. He was not only bitterly reproached for consorting with the foreigners, but was also accused by an influential Sheik of blasphemy against Islam. The matter was taking such an evil turn, that my poor friend was already expecting his sentence of death; when the Governor, who had just received my letter and that of our local Pasha, appeared on the scene and challenged the Sheik, who had probably been bribed, to name his witnesses on the spot. I will fetch them, said the Sheik. Yes, you are going to bribe scoundrels, replied the Governor; not so, but name them instantly, and we will prove them before they see you. Then the Sheik was forced to own publicly that he had lied, and the Governor made him kiss the Christian's beard, and ask his pardon before everybody.

"On the 5th of September the school was opened with one-and-twenty boys (there are now five-and-twenty). But on the very next Sunday an anathema-breathing excommunication was read in the church in the name of the Greek Patriarch against all those who should continue to send their children to the English school. This intimation was coupled with the threat that, even though they should afterwards repent, they could never again be received into the Church.

"I have reason to believe that the Patriarch knew very little of the contents of this bitter document of cursing, because he is only very imperfectly acquainted with Arabic; but why does he not learn the language of his flock?

"The effect of this anathema, which, in fact, was only aimed against God's Word, which alone is taught in the school, proved to be quite different from what was expected; for on the following day several persons met together with our friends, and asked leave to send their children to the same school.

"Immediately after these occurrences, cholera suddenly broke out at Nablus, and the correspondence was almost entirely cut off. I hear, however, that the school has gone on quietly, although several boys, the schoolmaster's father, and two other of our friends, have died. Sundry Christian inhabitants of the villages in the mountains of Samaria have decided to migrate to Nablus, in order to associate themselves with our friends, and chiefly in order to be able to send their children to a Christian school. We very often have to send Bibles to that neighbourhood.

"I mentioned last year that we were about to open a school at Jerusalem which was to be a kind of rescue-institution for poor children, w ho were to be committed to the care and instruction of an excellent English lady. This school was inaugurated on the loth November 1847. We now have the names of twenty-six children on our books, but have never been able to secure more than eighteen at a time. The reason of this is that Jewish parents, who would willingly have their children instructed, send them for one, two, or even four months, till they are persuaded by their friends and by the Rabbis to withdraw them again. But as this always happens against the will of the children, I hope that the impression which they take away with them will not be lost, and that some of the seed will bear good fruit.

"As yet we have only been able to take girls as boarders, and of them we have never had more than five at once, because the Jews do not like their children to eat the food of Christians. But that we may keep the boys in proper order and have them under supervision the whole day long, and also because they are almost all poor, we give them their dinner.

"After endeavouring for several years to obtain permission from the Turkish Government to purchase a Protestant burial-ground, we have at last succeeded in our design, chiefly through the efforts of the English Consul-General, Colonel Eose; and last spring I acquired for this purpose a large and beautiful piece of land on the southern declivity of Mount Zion, a few steps to the south-west of David's tomb. The graveyard will be, to the great annoyance of the Moslems, surrounded by a strong wall.

"It will cost in all about 3 50 sterling, of which the English Government has already promised me 100, and English private individuals 50. As, however, the burial-place is intended for Germans as well as for English, I should be glad if the former would purchase a right in it by their subscriptions, which, moreover, must be done soon, for in a few months it may be too late.

"A year ago I sought to advocate the cause of the poor converts, and, thank God, not in vain. I must now come forward on behalf of the eight to ten thousand poor Jews who are in danger of perishing during the coming winter in the city of David from hunger and nakedness. I must therefore entreat the Christian public to arouse the compassion of the wealthier Jews in favour of their suffering brethren in Palestine, and Christians and Jews alike to hasten to send help to those who are standing on the brink of the grave. Your faithful brotlier in Christ, 'S. GOBAT."

Bisliop Gohat to Inspector W. Hoffmann at Basle.

"Jerusalem, March 21, 1849.

"Dearly Beloved Brother, I have written to tlie Hessians what I said to dear Spittler years ago: If there were no difficulty with the Government or in the purchase of the land, I could nevertheless maintain no colony which was not strong enough to count at the least 500 well-armed fighting men. Since I wrote to you an occurrence has taken place about three weeks ago which must convince every one of the soundness of my opinion. In the very neighbourhood which Spittler as well as the Hessians has in view a ship was wrecked. There were about eighty or one hundred persons on board, of whom several perished in the water; but the greater number succeeded in saving themselves on planks and pieces of the ship, and they even rescued boxes and a very large sum of money. The inhabitants of the coast were, however, gathered together, and stole everything that had been saved, even all the clothes of the passengers, who lay about the shore naked and exhausted in the rain and the cold, till several of them died, whilst others, who refused to give up their last garment, were beaten to death.

One wore a finger-ring; without more ado, the finger was hewn off. They broke the arm of a sturdy monk who refused at the first word to give up his money. The Governor of Kaifa certainly took some of the ringleaders prisoners, but he released them next day on receipt of a gratuity; and before help could arrive from Beyrout on the summons of the Consuls, the robbers had plenty of time to place their booty in safety, and the ringleaders to hide themselves until the inquiry had blown over.

"And it is among such people that it is proposed to send poor, ignorant, unprotected German peasants! To be sure, they would not be robbed and maltreated every day; but, on the other hand, they would not enjoy a day's safety unless they were strong enough to defend themselves. Our good people certainly say that we must venture it in faith, and that the Lord is able to protect them; but Thou shalt not tempt the Lord thy God."

"S. A. HieROSOL."

Extracts from Bishop Gohafs Circular Letter for 1849.

"Cairo, Nov. i, 1849, ." Although we have been preserved from the sword, which has devastated various parts of Europe, and from the pestilence with which it has pleased God to visit the East, the past year has nevertheless been fruitful, in many cases, in painful experiences, but I trust also in salutary humiliations. In addition to a deficiency in spiritual life and in thoroughness of Christian culture among some of our converts, it has happened that two of them, too high-minded to listen to the faithful admonitions addressed to them, have not made their appearance in the house of God for several months past, and have rejected all Christian counsel.

"Several candidates for instruction have also conducted themselves in such a blame-worthy manner that we have been obliged to cease our operations in their behalf, and to withdraw our efforts in their favour. All this combined with the frequent derelictions (faults of weakness, I hope, rather than of wickedness) of those whom I considered as really converted and believing, has often filled my heart with sorrow and my eyes with tears.

"There is, however, a brighter side to the picture. It has been vouchsafed to us to detect indubitable evidences of the grace of God working in the heart and life of several of our proselytes; to say nothing of the fact that, not- withstanding the want of spirituality lamented above, the greater number of our baptized Israelites have striven to walk worthy of their profession. It will doubtless move the friends of Israel to thankfulness when they hear that in the course of last year nine adult Jews have been received into the Christian Church.

"In the external development of our mission, that is to say, in respect to the means of reaching Jews, proselytes, and others with the Word of Truth, sundry important steps have been taken. The first of these has been the consecration, after much opposition, of our Christ Church on Mount Zion, which took place on the 21st of January in the presence of a Palestinian Bishop, several priests, and a number of Jews and others. On the same day two Jews were baptized in the newly-consecrated church.

"Secondly, an Industrial House for converts was opened on the 2d of December under very favourable circumstances, and placed under the superintendence of a proselyte who has been trained in the Hebrew College. It is for the reception of Jews who are already persuaded that Jesus is the Messiah, but who desire further teaching from us. They receive lodging, clothing, board, and general care during the time of instruction until their baptism, and after that event until they have learned a trade. During their residence in the house they are apprenticed to handicraftsmen who belong to our Church tailors, shoemakers, watchmakers, silversmiths, c. and every evening they are instructed in reading and writing, English and German (the majority of them are German Jews), in arithmetic, and the like, but above all, in the Word of God. There are now eight of them, all with one exception young men, whose orderly conduct, diligence, and obedience afford us much encouragement.

Five of tliem were baptized last year, two of them are still unbaptized. This institution, which is now being maintained solely from the interest of a fund which a pious lady, Miss Allix, has devoted to it, places us in a position to provide much more easily than before for the wants of other converts, and of such as are thirsting for the truth.

"Thirdly, in the Jewish Hospital there is now a copy of the New Testament in Hebrew placed in each room for the free use of the patients, and daily prayer has been held through the past year, in which all might take part. The number of patients has not diminished in the least in consequence of this. Two of them are now receiving further instruction.

"The needy Jews received some help last summer from Sir Moses Montefiore, who visited Palestine, but thousands of them are still in great misery.

"The Diocesan School has prospered to an extent hardly to have been looked for under existing circumstances. It has, however, suffered considerably through the illness of an excellent mistress; but as an assistant-mistress is expected, I doubt not that the school will continue to be a blessing to many a lost lamb of the House of Israel and of other nations. The number of the children, almost all of Jewish origin, who have hitherto been received into the school amounts in all to about fifty; in the last few months twenty-nine has been about the average. Almost all of them are making encouraging progress in their acquaintance with the Word of God.

"The school at Nablus has also been in a very thriving condition through the past year, and has attracted the attention of the natives of all the neighbouring districts, so that they have repeatedly invited me to establish

Bible schools, as they call them, in their villages and towns. I believe there are few schools in Europe where the Bible is better known and understood; and through the boys a knowledge of the sacred volume reaches almost all the adult Christians in Nablus. Although the Samaritans, wlio had sent their children for a time to the school, have been obliged by the Mussulmans to take them away again, the school nevertheless counts more than forty pupils, including a few girls.

"I have recently opened a similar school also in Tiberias, which already at the end of last week numbered twenty-two boys.

"There was a school of older foundation at Salt, which I had made over, in the interests of peace, to a priest of that place; but as it did not answer, I have established another in the course of the summer, under a more efficient master. The Greek Patriarch has taken upon himself to defray the entire cost, and has further promised to retain the master chosen by me, and to admit no other books besides those which I had prescribed; only the natives were not to call it an English school!

"I deemed this the first step to approximation between the Patriarch and myself, and saw with pleasure that my first efibrts had incited him to establish in Jerusalem a model school under a very clever, and I believe very worthy, man. Unfortunately, I have since heard that the latter was to leave Jerusalem this month. In other respects the Greek Patriarch and I have remained as alien from each other as ever; but with the Armenian Patriarch and the Syrian Bishop I am on pacific, and even friendly terms.

' Of the Christians of the different Churches in Palestine and Syria I will not say much this time. I cannot omit mention of the fact, however, that from Aleppo to Jerusalem an almost universal excitement prevails. It is by no means exclusively of a religious nature, but still it has its source in the conviction of the people that they have hitherto lived in ignorance and error, that their Churches have degenerated, that their clergy, namely, of the higher orders, do not trouble themselves as to the spiritual condition of the flock, and that the latter must therefore look about for another Church or form of religion.

"The sense of a certain want oppresses them, but of its nature they can render no account. Two important decrees emanating from the Sublime Porte have recently been made known, in one of which the Sultan reproaches the higher orders of the clergy with the guilt of heinous transgressions, while in the other he proclaims to all his Christian subjects liberty to embrace any form of Protestantism, with promise of his protection.

"In consequence of this, I fear that before long great multitudes of people will set up a religion of their own, a sort of unbridled Protestantism, so soon as they get sufficient encouragement from without. Under these circumstances, all that I can do will be to spread the Word of God by every possible means; the j eople read it much more willingly than they used to do. I must also, to the extent of my power, establish schools in which the Bible shall be taught to the exclusion of all other religious books.

"I am writing this from Cairo, where I have been staying for some days past. In Alexandria I saw two of our Jewish proselytes, one of whom is already baptized; and I was rejoiced to hear from several persons that they walk agreeably to their profession, and that to the best of their capacity they witness for the truth in Christ in the presence of other Jews.

"There is in Cairo a small English congregation under the care of the missionaries of the Church Missionary Society. I was glad to make the acquaintance of the energetic lay missionary of the English mission to the Jews, Mr. Lauria. I visited several Jewish families in company with him, and found that he was everywhere respected and beloved. From what I have heard from him and from others, I believe that there is among the five thousand Jews at Cairo an open and most promising mission-field. Your humble servant, S. Gobat."

Bisjiop Gobat to King Frederick William IV.

"Jerusalem, July 30, 1850.

"Your Majesty will pardon me if I take the liberty of recalling myself most humbly to your gracious remembrance.

"It has often been the wish of my heart, after my correspondence with Herr von Eichhorn. was terminated by the sad events of 1848, to write to your Majesty, in order to express the heartfelt interest taken by myself and the little congregation here in the painful trials and tribulations to which you have been subjected by misguided men, and also in the consolation and the manifest mighty help which God has graciously vouchsafed to your Majesty.

"It was with shuddering horror that we finally heard of the frightful crime of a blinded instrument of him who was a murderer from the beginning, who made your Majesty the object of his bloodthirsty rage; but we were simultaneously impelled to thank our God for His gracious protection of your Majesty, and this we did with deep emotion publicly in the church immediately after receipt of the tidings. It is to tlie prince of darkness that so many people, even in our beloved German Fatherland, have sold themselves through unbelief and a carnal mind, and he it is who seeks to destroy all order, and with it all true light and fear of God. As God has called and chosen your Majesty to be an honoured instrument in His hand to uphold His people and His truth, we cannot wonder that the dart of the evil one is especially aimed against your person and office. Thank God, your Majesty still reigns by His grace; and so long as this is the case in actual verity as well as in accordance with the heraldic motto, your kingdom will subsist in honour. May God grant it! Amen.

"If, among the manifold great and important affairs and difficulties with which you have to contend, your Majesty could yet find time to think of the earthly Jerusalem, some information might not be unwelcome concerning the present condition and the slow development of the Protestant Bishopric.

"We have on Sundays as yet but two services, an English one in the morning, and in the afternoon a German one. On the first Sunday of every month we celebrate the Holy Communion at the English service; but the words of administration are always said in the language of the communicant, whether English, German, French, Italian, or Arabic. This, so far from having a disturbing effect, is most edifying. At every service, whether English or German, we pray for your Majesty, her Majesty the Queen, and for all the Royal Family, also for the ruler of this realm. I have always hitherto avoided mingling in the affairs of other Churches. A year ago I daily received petitions and deputations from all parts of the country, entreating me to take the people under my guidance and to give them teachers.

Of course I could not do so, but I exhorted tlie people to persevere in reading the Word of God and to remain in their Churches, seeking at the same time to purify them. I believe that many have followed my advice; but thereupon a new difficulty has arisen. They know that it is a sacred duty to receive the Holy Communion, but the priests render it impossible for them to do so, because they will only administer it to those who have confessed; and when they know that any one reads the Bible, they require him either to kiss a picture and kneel down before it, or to invoke the Holy Virgin or some other saint, or else to promise not to read the Bible any more. He who refuses to comply is excommunicated.

"There are some conscientious people who on that account have for the last year or two been unable to receive the Communion, and now they are imploring my help, begging for clergy who will administer to them the Lord's Supper.

"And now what am I to do? I have never wished to make converts from the old Churches, but only to lead to the Lord and to the knowledge of His truth as many as possible. From henceforth, however, I shall be obliged to receive into our communion such as are excluded for Bible-truth's sake from other Churches; and I trust that in doing so, even though men should blame me for it, the Lord will grant His blessing upon the proceeding.

The prayers introduced by Gobat, and mentioned in the foregoing letter, are as follows:

Prayer for the King and Royal Family of Prussia.

' 0 Lord God Almighty, who hast graciously put it into the heart of his Majesty, Frederick William, King of Prussia, Thy servant, to favour Thy Church and protect Thy people in this land; vouchsafe, we beseech Thee, to replenish him with the grace of Thy Holy Spirit, that he may alway incline to Thy will and walk in Thy way. Endue him plenteously with heavenly gifts; grant him in health and wealth long to live; protect him against all his enemies; and favour him with wise and righteous counsellors, that he may reign in righteousness, in Thy fear and love, ever confiding in Thy name; and that finally after this life he may obtain the crown of eternal glory. Bless her Majesty the Queen and all the Royal Family with health, peace, and godliness, and lead them by Thy Spirit to Thine everlasting kingdom, through Jesus Christ our Lord. Amen.

Prayer for the Sultan.

0 Lord God Almighty, who rulest over all the kingdoms of the nations, in whose hand is power and might; give Thy grace and Thy blessing to his Majesty the ruler of this empire, under whose sceptre we are graciously permitted to serve and worship Thee in peace and quietness; grant him long to live in happiness, and to govern the nations subject to his rule with benignity, wisdom, and righteousness. Lead him into the way of peace, that we and all Thy people in his vast empire may continue to lead a quiet and peaceful life in all godliness, through Jesus Christ our Lord. Amen.

Extracts from Bishop Gohafs Circular Letter for 1850.

"Jerusalem, Oct. 26, 1850,

"Beloved Brethrex,. I feel cod strained to ask your especial prayers on behalf of the following subjects:

"I. For the clerical and lay missionaries. Of the former class we have but two here at the present moment; of tlie latter, we have two sent direct by tlie London Society, and a Bible-reader under my orders, but maintained by the same beneficent English lady who has already done so much for the mission at Jerusalem.

"I can confidently assert that every one does his duty to the best of his knowledge and ability; but although we pray, preach, exhort, warn, and argue, we labour, alike among proselytes and others, frequently, nay, generally, without any visible success.

"2. The proselytes have occasioned us during the past year much distress, anxiety, and trouble. A few of the younger ones among them have indeed satisfied us upon the whole by their humble, steadfast, and teachable behaviour, and by their eagerness to acquire a more extended knowledge of Christianity. With regard to the majority, however, I have most reluctantly arrived at the conclusion that, although they possess an historical belief in Jesus the Messiah, they yet are strangers to the living, justifying faith in Christ which alone can enable them to overcome the world.

"But that which has saddened us most is that several of them have fallen into gross sins of various kinds; one in especial, from whom we had hoped for better things, but who has, I am thankful to say, expressed deep sorrow for his transgression, and, as I believe, sincere repentance.

"In this respect we have sustained an irreparable loss through the departure of the missionary, Ewald, whose love to his brethren after the flesh, and whose accurate knowledge of their mode of thought and peculiar characteristics, opened to him so direct an avenue to their understandings, hearts, and consciences, that he was able to exhort, warn, reprove, counsel, and console them with a degree of success to which not one of us who remain behind can ever hope to attain.

"When, therefore, beloved brethren, I invite you to pray for the proselytes, forget not, in the first place, to make supplication for those who are truly converted, in order that the Lord may keep them in His Name and preserve them from the evil; then for those who have the name of living, but who are spiritually dead; and finally, for such who, although they confess God with their lips, yet deny Him by their works.

"3. The Industrial House for converts promises to become an instrument of rich blessing and real advancement to its inmates, while it at the same time affords us an opportunity of forming a judgment as to the sincerity and general character of the candidates for baptism.

"4. The Jewish Hospital has been full throughout nearly the whole year, and has proved rich in blessing to many poor Jews during this season of unusual drought. I have heard more than once that this method of showing Christian charity and goodwill has brought about among the Jews a more favourable opinion of Christianity. The Christian faith is not obtruded upon them; kind treatment, and here and there a hint that such is the result of true Christianity, must have the most powerful effect.

"The New Testament is to be found in every ward; but it is left to the Jews' free option whether they will read it or not; only at times conversation upon religious subjects is introduced, if, namely, they show themselves inclined for it.

"5 The Jews are becoming more and more accessible, and conscious not only that we love them and seek their best interests, but also that we conscientiously avoid the employment of all unlawful and equivocal means. When, for example, a few months ago, the Rabbis forbade their people to work for the converts, to employ them as workmen, or to hold any intercourse with them whatsoever, we made it known that if this prohibition were carried out, we should be obliged to equalise matters, and give no more work to any Jew. Their answer was, Your conscience would not allow you to put in execution any such plan, which would be the ruin of many poor Jews.

' In the course of this year only two persons have been baptized, an old man and an old woman. Six other persons, chiefly young men, are receiving preliminary instruction. The poverty and temporal misery of the Jews continues unchanged, and this places a formidable obstacle in the way of the reception of the Gospel among them, because their impoverished condition renders them entirely dependent on the tender mercies of the cruel Rabbis. The latter have more actively opposed the Mission this last year than during several preceding ones; this may, however, be taken as a further proof that our labour is not wholly in vain.

"6. The Diocesan School continues to justify encouraging hopes for the rising generation.

'7. My school at Nablus has been and still is a blessing, as well for the parents as for the children. It has enjoyed a peaceful career, and the number of pupils is about the same as last year.

"I rejoice to be able to observe here that when, not long ago, some Greek monks stigmatised the English as heretics, the Greek Bishop of the diocese in which Nablus lies reproved them for it. In the presence of several bishops and many monks he declared that when, two years ago, I opened the school at Nablus, he had his own suspicious thoughts and prejudices; but that since then he had narrowly scrutinised all my steps, direct and indirect, and became convinced that my only aim was that of doing good. He further admitted that much good had been wrought in Nablus. Those present called him a semi-Protestant; upon which he replied, You say that as an epithet of opprobrium; I count it an honourable designation.

"The school which, as I mentioned in my last letter, I had established at Tiberias, was soon afterwards forcibly dispersed by the Uniate Greek Bishop of Acre and the Latin Bishop of Nazareth. They could give their flock no better satisfaction for this action than the consolatory assurance that as they were all poor, their children did not require any education.

' Besides the Bible-reader for the Jews of this locality, I have two at work among the Christians; the one travels about the country, while the other, who is at the same time my secretary, labours in Jerusalem.

"The great agitation among all classes of Christians in this country, to which I referred last year, and which indicated a seeking after better things than those to be found in their Churches, is at present less apparent, except in Nazareth, from whence I receive letter after letter containing the request that I would send them a schoolmaster and a clergyman. Many of these people have, since reading the Bible, forsaken the Greek and Latin Churches, and are now entirely without a leader.

' On the other hand, the Word of God is quietly making its way into the hearts of isolated individuals among the mountains of Samaria, at Cana of Galilee, and at Nazareth. They assemble themselves on Sundays in small companies in order to read their Bible and pray in common, on which occasions they make use of the English Liturgy translated into Arabic. May the Good Shepherd ever watch over them!.

"I have posted a well-instructed young man among the Druses, and have directed him to establish schools for that people. Colonel Kose has promised him his support. He has experienced a good reception from the Druses; they converse with him frankly on religious topics; but the time is as yet too short for us to be able to speak of results.

"At the beginning of this year I received letters from the King, from the Reis, and from several influential priests of Abyssinia, begging me to take their cloisters and their people here under my superintendence. I have since had many opportunities of preaching the Gospel to them, and they regard me indeed as their father and protector. I have placed over them a superintendent, a worthy man whom they themselves have chosen, as they are very numerous (about 100). I have given them several Amharic Bibles, and advised them to meet together morning and evening for the purpose of reading the Bible in their mother tongue. They have adopted this plan, and assemble themselves daily three times. The greater number of them have recently returned to Abyssinia, several of them impressed for good, and carrying with them the conviction that no one can improve the condition of their country except the English with the Bible.

"This affair has brought me into unpleasant contact with the Armenians, whose Patriarch, my friend, is now dead; it has, however, at the same time procured for me a glimpse at the abominations of the monasteries. Your servant and brother in the Lord, S. Gobat."

Xing Frederick William IV. to Bishop Gobat.

"Sans-Souci, July 23, 1851.

"Most Honoured Lord Bishop, I avail myself of the pilgrimage of the Pastor of Witbrietzen (not far from

Potsdam). to discharge in some measure a longstanding debt of thanks for your kind and interesting letters and communications from the Holy Land. I can recommend to you the bearer of these lines. He has changed an unruly, intractable set of people into a godly congregation amenable to Christian teaching. I therefore wish him well, and have favoured his journey to the East. His name is Liebetrut, a very old German-sounding patronymic.

"If you have time, most honoured Bishop, to write to me by Liebetrut, or by any other trustworthy messenger, I request you to do so. According to what Pastor Pliedner has told me concerning the state of things around you, it appears that the dreaded influences emanating from myself against the evangelical life which seemed to have been reviving in the bosom of the old, dead Churches in the Holy Land are beginning to assert themselves. I trust that you will not allow your courage to sink. Your idea of building up small national Churches from out of those communions, in place of compelling the awakened Greeks, Syrians, Copts, c., to become Anglican, Lutheran, or Swiss-Reformed, is a glorious, heaven-inspired, and truly Catholic one. You mtist not let it go. You will certainly summon into the lists both Pope and Emperor through this stirring up of fresh life in the ancient Churches;. but the King who rules over the one and the other will be on your side.

"One item of intelligence has especially interested me, because at the moment of its reaching me I was seeking a relief from unspeakable sorrow of heart by plunging, in my few intervals of leisure, into the ritual of the ancient Churches. The intelligence was namely this: I was informed that one of those men who are inclined to Evangelicalism had undertaken an evangelical revision of the

Greek Liturgy. The remark which I would venture to make to you,. in case that work should be carried through, is founded upon the well-known fragment of St. Irenffius on the Eucharist.

"In all the Liturgies of the ancient effete Churches, the Eucharist is the indisputable central-point in the Communion, representing, indeed, the repetition of the one, eternal, atoning sacrifice, just as in the Popish Mass. Irenseus teaches us, 1st, that in those days the Eucharist was offered according to the direction of the Apostles; 2dly, that the Eucharist is the spiritual, and therefore pure, fulfilling of the prophecy which announces for the time of fulfilment the universal j)resenting in all the earth of a pure offering; 3dly, that this presentation (of this offering) is the sjmhtual sacrifice of thanksgiving; 4thly, that the sacrifice was essentially distinct from communion and consecration; 5thly, that it preceded both these, but as an essential and necessary part of the Communion Ofiice (it seems to me, indeed, to be the most necessarv preparation for the Sacred Supper, according to the passage in the Psalter: Whoso offereth praise glorifieth me; and to him that ordereth his conversation aright will I show the salvation of God); 6thly, that the spiritual offering of the Eucharist was made at the moment when the elements of the Supper bread and wine were solemnly converted from being the possession of those who had contributed them, into the exclusive and undivided property of God.

"The Greek Church notoriously imitates the Jews in framing her ritual. She never abolishes a tittle of what she has once received, be it holy tradition, or rubbish out of the dark ages. I had long been struck with the extraordinarily prominent position accorded in her Liturgy to the Trisagion; for during the singing of this hymn nothing is going on in the sanctuary which could justify the importance with which it is introduced and uttered in reference to the voices of the four living creatures' of the Apocalypse. I have now arrived at the conviction that the Trisagion indicates the point at which, in the Primitive Church, the spiritual sacrifice of the Eucharist was made by the congregation, and that the Holy, Holy, Holy is the mode of expressing the unspeakable, that is, the deepest spiritual thanksgiving for such an immeasurable, everlasting blessing as the Redemption and the Sacrament.

"As all hope of seeing the offertory, and its complement the Eucharist, restored to their right significance and proper place in the Communion service, either in the Protestant West or in the Romish Church, has now vanished, I would ask you, Eight Reverend Bishop, whether your own persuasion would allow you, in connection with this evangelical revision of the Oriental Liturgies, to take Irenseus as your guide, and to attempt the re-establishment of the primitive rite? The question is borne in upon my mind. Who knows whether God will not permit the proper amplification and completion of the Protestant Liturgies to be brought about through the evangelical revision of the rites of the old Churches of the East?

"1 fear. you will deem me demented for having ventured to intrude upon a Doctor of Divinity with such theological lucubrations. But, believe me, you would but increase my high respect for you if, in your answer, you were to take me roundly to task, and set me right as to my absurdities, or even my heresies.

"I pray God from the depth of my soul that He will further the work of your hands, and pour out His richest blessing upon your head and upon all that you have at heart. Remember me in your prayers. I remain, with truest and most cordial respect, most honoured Bishop, your faithful friend, Frederick William, R."

Extracts from Bishop Gohat's Circular Letter for 18 5 i.

"Jerusalem, October- o, 1S51. ". In the course of this year a new branch of activity has been developed. Seeing that last year epidemic illness raged so fiercely for several months that there was scarcely one family free from dangerous illness, and as no suitable nurses were to be had, I wrote to Pastor Fliedner at Kaisers-werth, and begged him to send two deaconesses to tend our sick, to visit systematically our women converts, and if possible to take the place of our female teachers in cases of illness. In April came Herr Fliedner himself, bringing with him four deaconesses, two of whom are maintained by a Prussian women's association, and the two others by myself. They are to nurse our converts and also other patients. They live together, and receive into the house such patients as require special care and attention. Besides this, they visit regularly among our poor, more particularly the female converts and those who are anxiously seeking the truth. Good results are already visible. I expect much beneficial effect to follow upon their labours here; for their quiet, humble, kindly, and thoroughly Christian behaviour must make an impression upon the hearts and consciences of many Jews and Gentiles. Dr. Macgowan has kindly offered his gratuitous professional services to the hospital.

"The number of Bible-readers whom I have sent out this year is the same as last year. One of them. who is also my secretary, works chiefly among the better classes of Christians, and corresponds with various persons at a distance who are inquiring about the truth.

He is at tliis present time engaged, under my direction, in a most interesting interchange of letters witli the priest of the Samaritans, who is reading the New Testament very carefully, and bringing before us in a highly sensible, and, I believe, sincere manner, objections and difficulties which occur to his mind. For instance, in the speech of St. Stephen (Acts vii.) he found sundry statements which did not seem to agree literally with those in the Books of Moses; he was satisfied, however, with our explanations.

"This priest has recently applied to me for help in establishing a school for the benefit of his people, as the Mussulmans will not allow the Samaritans to send their children to my school. He has at the same time promised to have the whole of the Old Testament read in this school, though it is well known that the Samaritans look upon the Pentateuch as the only inspired Scriptures. I have made the condition that the New Testament is also to be read, and do not despair of his consent to this stipulation.

"This, my second Bible-reader, has been the means of awakening a spirit of inquiry among a considerable number of priests; they are, however, so sharply watched that it were not prudent to give a more detailed account of it here. I will only mention that a little while ago one of them, who could not quite conceal his attachment to the Gospel, was suddenly placed in confinement, and I have not yet been able to ascertain whither they have taken him.

"Although, in my last letters, I said that the prevailing excitement of the public mind had considerably abated, a door has nevertheless been opened in this country for preaching the Gospel to the native population; and I rejoice to be able to state that the Church Missionary

Society has resolved to send missionaries into this wide field of labour. One of them, Missionary Klein, has already been here two months, and is busy studying the Arabic language in order to qualify himself for the charge of the Protestant congregation at Nazareth. Another, who is well versed in modern Greek and Turkish (Dr. Sandrezki), is to arrive here in few days, and will in the first instance find his sphere among the thousands of ignorant pilgrims who annually flock to Jerusalem.

' In Jerusalem itself there are many, Latins, Greeks, and Armenians, who are more or less earnestly seeking the truth; but they are nearly all poor, and their dependence on the monasteries is a terrible hindrance. Not long ago, two families, who formerly belonged to the Latins, were suddenly turned out of their house forcibly ejected, in fact because they would not deliver up their Bibles to be burnt. When people are

thus forced, for the sake of the Gospel which we preach and p
dwelling-places, it would be too cruel if we did not seek to provide
whether they have up to that time given full proof of thorough heart
I usually pay house-rent for such, as long as they conduct themselve
my aid. If I have been mistaken in one or two cases, I yet can say wit
God that these poor Protestant Arabs, namely, the six or seven comm
well upon the whole. As long as their health is good, they claim hardly, any help from
me beyond their house-rent, and by their industry, frugality, and gratitude set a good
example to our Jewish converts.

"With regard to Nablus, I should have to write whole volumes if I wished to relate
all the intrigues, briberies, repeated promises, and threats of which the Bishops and
monks of the Greek convent have made use in order to hinder, and, if possible, destroy,
the good work there. On the other hand, I should need the same fertile pen to describe
the singleness of heart, good sense, and wisdom with which the Evangelical Christians,
by the grace of God, maintain their ground, and whereby they have frustrated all the
cunning and keen machinations of their adversaries.

"When the monks perceived that the people asked counsel in all things of our
emissary there, they tried every device to bring him on to their side; flattery, direct
and indirect promises, and threats, everything was set in motion to draw him into their
net. But in the midst of it all he acquitted himself as a man who submits to be guided
by Divine wisdom. I did not fear much from their threats, though all his friends most
earnestly entreated him to beware of poison; but I dreaded their promises.

"At last, seeing that nothing was to be done with him at Nablus, the monks invited
him to Jerusalem. He came, and for a whole month they tried every possible snare to
entrap him. They finally summoned him to the convent, where, in the presence of the
Bishops and monks, a document, drawn up by the chief secretary of the Pasha, whom
they had bribed, was placed in his hand. This he was required to sign if he did not
wish to incur their displeasure.

"He perused the document, and then, gazing earnestly at the superior of the convent,
Is this your religion? he asked; and do you suppose that for money I will become your
Judas? A silence ensued. He put the paper in his pocket, and came to me downcast
and sad. I am now in possession of the document. It is a kind of contract, in which the
convent promises to give my agent; 8o sterling per annum if he will hinder the children
of the Greeks from attending my school, and if he will undertake the superintendence
of their school. The cloister authorities offered him a present of ii ioO if he would
promise to raze my school-house to the ground within the next three months.

"However, when they saw plainly that neither threats nor promises were of any
avail, they became uneasy lest a great number of persons might leave them to declare
themselves Protestants. Accordingly, the Bishops wrote a friendly letter to Nablus,
begging the people to be at one, and not to say the one, I am of Apollos, and the other,
I am of Cephas.

"Since then everything has remained quiet; but my agent has had a long and
dangerous illness in consequence of these attacks. I may mention that although,
through his open-handedness, he is a poor man, and although he receives from me

y enough to cover his extra expenses for the school, the attempts at bribery
eemed not to produce the slightest effect upon him.

In consequence of the tyrannical treatment and persecution formerly suffered by
the people of Nazareth who read the Bible, about twenty families were brought to
the resolution of seceding from their Church and uniting themselves into a Protestant
congregation. They now, as such, enjoy the recognition and protection of the Government. The step was nevertheless a premature one, and I sliould not like to assert
that these Protestants are really converted people. Missionary Bowen has spent some
months at Nazareth this summer, and he has discovered that a large admixture of pure
and impure motives were at work in the matter. Still he is convinced that there are
among them people who are earnestly inquiring after saving truth; and at all events, it
affords a good opportunity for preaching the Gospel in Galilee. S. Gobat."

King Frederick Williara IV. to Bishop Gohat.

"Potsdam. November 29, 1851.

"Most Honoured Bishop, I commend to you the bearer of this letter, Pastor Valentiner, a Holstein man, whom the iniquity of the present Danish Government has
driven out of his Schleswig parish, which he ruled most successfully, and without ever
mingling in politics.

"I should like him to take charge of the few German members of your Church at
Jerusalem,. and I wish with all my heart that you may find him worthy of the office.
It is to be hoped that fresh ordination, according to the Anglican rite, will not be
exacted in the case of Valentiner. He has received ordination from the hands of the
Superintendent-General of Schleswig, Dr. Nielsen. Now it is well known that the
Superintendent-Generals of the two German Duchies in Episcopal Denmark are on a
footing of equality with the Bishops of the kingdom, and officiate as such at the royal
anointing and coronation. According to the principles which were received as fully
valid in the English Church down to the first decade of this century, it seems to me,
dear Gobat, that there could be no obstacle to his admission as member of your Church
and pastor under your jurisdiction. I have conversed at great length with Valentiner,
and if I associate the impression he has made upon me with the fair reputation he
enjoys, I think I may venture to hope that you will congratulate yourself upon this
acquisition.

"I hope that Valentiner will write to me soon after his arrival in Jerusalem. In that
case please to send me messages by him concerning the state of the ancient
Churclies in the Holy Land,. and more especially as to the progress of your
relations, personal and ecclesiastical, with your old royal friend of Abyssinia and his
Church.

"My prayers and ardent wishes are ever with you,. and with the beloved Church
of Jerusalem. The Queen sends you her cordial greetings, and most sincere thanks
to your wife for the pretty and curious articles which she transmitted through Pastor
Fliedner, and which have afforded my wife the liveliest pleasure.

"May that blessing and prosperity which the Lord alone can give rest upon your
rule, upon all your actions, and especially upon jour relations with Valentiner.

"I commend myself heartily to your prayers and blessing, honoured Bishop, as
your faithful and devoted

"Frederick William, E."

Bishop Gdbat to King Frederick William IV.

"Jekusalem, Dec. 29, 1S51. '. Your Majesty commands me to write. As, however, I sent to Herr von Bunsen at the beginning of this month a detailed report of the present state of things in this country in connection with the bishopric, and as I doubt not that gentleman will communicate to your Majesty whatever particulars of interest it may contain, I have nothing further to say upon this head, except that the Christians of Salt beyond the Jordan have again sent a Sheik to me to request that I would take them under my care. They wish no longer to remain connected with the Greek clergy, who not only do nothing for their instruction and improvement, but who have also destroyed the school which I had opened for their children. There are about 1100 Christians at Salt; and beyond that place are little groups entirely given over to wildness and ignorance. They have several times applied to me for assistance. I am sorry for the poor people. They are aware of their own ignorance and helplessness, but they do not know what they really need; they only have a dim idea that the thing of chief importance is wanting to them the Word of God, and the means to use it aright. I ought to have a Glitzlaff or a Krapf to send to them; such men as they are would, with God's help, work wonders. Mediocre missionaries could do no good at all.

"Your Majesty remarks that I shall certainly summon into the lists both Pope and Emperor through this stirring up of fresh life in the ancient Churches. Now, whether or not such august personages would consider it worth their while to condescend to look down upon the work which is being carried on among the poor people of this land, in great weakness in every way, but in firm reliance on the Almighty, I know not; but the spirit which actuates those institutions of which they are the heads is at all events very busy. I cannot say that, as yet, this activity is directed against me personally, but against the good work which I endeavour in faith to promote by means of God's Word. For when the Greek clergy here write to Nablus to warn the poor folk there against the wolf which, through the teaching of God's Word, is alienating their children from their Church and sacred traditions, they were obliged to admit, in answer to the questions of the simple creatures, that they know no evil of me. The Roman Catholic Patriarch, who returned from Europe a few days ago, is in too hot conflict with the monks respecting the question of meum and tuum to be able to think much about me at present; but after a while no doubt we shall not fail to come into serious collision.

"Be it so, then. I fear not those mighty, open adversaries, but rather rejoice in the strife; for in profound consciousness of my own weakness and impotence, I yet steadfastly believe that, as your Majesty says, the King who rules over the one and the other will be on my side.

"I hardly dare enter upon the principal points of your Majesty's letter, because I am too imperfectly acquainted with the subject. My work has hitherto lain too much in the direction of evangelising ignorant people, for me to have been led to the especial study of ritual and the Liturgy.

"My idea of appointing the Greek Liturgy, purged of its errors, for the use of Christian congregations in this land, simply originated in my personal experience. I was not only brought up in the Eeformed Church of Switzerland, but within its bosom

I learned to know my Lord, and to find life and truth. I knew no other Liturgy than her own, meagre enough indeed, and I was edified by it, as soon as I had found life eternal, in childlike faith. It is now nearly thirty years since I quitted Switzerland, and during that interval I have known and used several Liturgies, which my reason pronounced to be indisputably better than that of my youth; and yet, whenever I enter a church in which that Liturgy is in use, I find in it more edification and nourishment for my spiritual being than in any other. Therefore I consider it our duty to leave to the people of this country all that is good in what they have been accustomed to from their youth up, and, when possible, in the familiar form.

"Concerning the Eucharist, my view of it for years has coincided with that of Ireneeus, supported by Justin Martyr, namely, that the Eucharist was already in very early ages called a sacrifice offered to the Lord God; but at tlie same time I never could accept the doctrice that, after the atoning sacrifice of Christ once offered, there could be in the Christian Church any universal sacrifice whatever, save the spiritual sacrifice of thanksgiving. And as all lively members of the body of Christ have equal access to the throne of grace, i. e., are priests of God, it follows that the sacrifice must be of such a nature that they are all alike competent to offer it; that is, it must be purely spiritual.

"The gifts made at the offertory on behalf of the poor and of the ofiicers of the Church, and pre-eminently the elements of bread and wine for the impending Communion, are suitable outward signs of thanksgiving; they might also be regarded as a part of the sacrifice, but not essentially so, not being purely spiritual, and being, moreover, out of the power of many to offer.

"According to the view of Irenaaus, the Holy Communion seems to me to be a free gift of the grace of God, as is so clearly set forth in the Preface, and this in close connection with the spiritual sacrifice offered by His priestly people. This sacrifice of thanksgiving, if it is to be a pure one, includes the yielding up of ourselves to God, which is our reasonable service; and therein lies the cardinal condition of true and Christian communion. That saying here becomes true in a special sense and also collectively for a whole congregation, which at other times may be applied with reference to individuals; namely, if we give ourselves up unreservedly to God, He gives Himself to us. In other words, Whoso offereth praise glorifieth Ie; and to him who ordereth his conversation aright will I show the salvation of God.

"And now, if I have rightly understood your Majesty's analysis of the passage from Iren eus, I can gladly answer in the affirmative your Majesty's question as to whether my own persuasion would allow me. to take Irenseus as my guide, and to attempt tlie re-establishment of the primitive rite? My answer is founded on the hope that while the Eucharist, the thank-offering, as an essential part of the Communion Office, is explained to the people as the only sacrifice which the people of God can offer, so every idea of an atoning sacrifice or satisfaction may be eliminated from the sacrament. For the rest, I cannot, as I have already said, make any practical use at present of this view of matters. What is positively pernicious and erroneous in the Greek Liturgy I could, with the help of the person who has already on his own responsibility begun something of the kind, undertake to separate from it, and I could have the Greek Liturgy, thus curtailed, brought into use on the first opportunity. But with my slight acquaintance with liturgical lore, I would hardly venture to attempt anything new, or, what is nearly the same thing, to essay a radical reformation in this direction, without the help of one or more competent men.

"And now I beg your Majesty to pardon the length as well as the unsatisfactory character of this letter, and to graciously accept at this season my most heartfelt wishes for the temporal and eternal wellbeing of yoar Majesty, of her Majesty the Queen, and of your whole kingdom. From your Majesty's most obedient, humble servant,

CHAPTER III.

PROTEST FROM SOME OF THE ANGLICAN CLERGY AGAINST BISHOP GOBATS PROCEEDINGS THE BISHOPS VINDICATION.

(1852-1S53.)

We have already learned from Gobat himself that his nomination and consecration as Bishop in succession to Dr. Alexander had met with considerable ojdposition in England. The most serious attack, however, took the form of injurious aspersions upon Gobat's character and behaviour while in Abyssinia. The matter was brought before the Archbishop of Canterbury; and the result of a thorough investigation was to prove Gobat blameless, and to put his accuser to shame.

But although personal slanders were silenced almost as soon as uttered, prejudices of another kind continued to grow, and to increase the difficulty of the Bishop's position from the moment of his entrance upon his episcopal duties.

That position was not an easy one. The difference between the Episcopal Church of England and the Churches of Germany, which only recognise the pastoral office, and have delegated to the temporal ruler a portion of the functions properly j ertaining to the episcopate, is a fact which may be deplored, but which can neither be set aside nor treated as insignificant.

There existed at Jerusalem a kind of alliance between two independent Christian communities, one English, the other German. The same Bishop ruled over both. He was the head of the espiscopally ordained clergy, who were pledged to the XXXIX. Articles, and exclusively bound by the forms of the Book of Common Prayer. He was at the same time chief pastor over the Prussian clergy, who have subscribed to the Confession of Augsburg, who had been ordained in Germany, and who used in their German services the Book of Prayers and Hymns drawn up by Bunsen for the Prussian Embassy at Eome, and containing, for use at the celebration of the Lord's Supper, Lutheran and Reformed Prayers, to be selected at the discretion of the officiating pastor. It must be owned that the Bishop's position was a highly embarrassing and thorny one.

Gobat was pre-eminently qualified to surmount these difficulties. His large heart was full of brotherly love for the truly devout among the German and Swiss Evangelicals. He was also filled with reverence for the ancient, firmly-established ordinances of the Episcopal Church; a state of feeling which his office rendered obligatory, and his humility made easy. It was, nevertheless, impossible for him to satisfy all claims and to prevent every conflict.

Did he desire to ordain priest of the Church of England some candidate from Switzerland who had already received a quasi ordination at home, the step was disapproved at Berlin. Did he permit a non-episcopally ordained functionary to preach in

Christ Church, this was turned to his reproof in other quarters. He thus stood between two fires. For the Germans he was too Anglican, for the Andicans he was too German. He strove to meet these difficulties with patience and gentleness. He respected every conscientious conviction, and knew that there was something to be said in support of both sides. He was also aware that the fears of each party had some claim upon his attention. The Anglicans dreaded the stealthy inroads of German Neology, a fear which found its justification in Bunsen's increasingly obvious endeavours to introduce into England the Rationalism of the school of Schleiermacher; while the Germans were tenacious of the honour and riofhts of the German Reformation.

A second difiiculty in which the Bishop was involved arose out of the demands and expectations of the Jewish Missionary Society and the friends of Israel in England. At the very outset there was preferred against him in that quarter the singular complaint that he had no sympathies for the Jews a reproach which was afterwards repeated with striking acrimony. This is to be explained by the too sanguine, or, as Gobat expressed it, the poetical hopes entertained concerning the speedy and wholesale conversion of the ancient people. An idea was current among many that the return of the Jews to Palestine, their settling there, and the rebuilding of the Temple, would precede their acknowledgment of our Saviour as the Messiah. The return of the Jews to the land of their fathers was supposed to be near at hand, and the believers in this event sought to hasten it by framing plans for Jewish colonisation. An Agricultural Society was formed for the benefit of the Jews in Palestine. It was in contemplation to establish a hospital for Israelites, from which, in the first instance, the New Testament was to be excluded, so that the Jews might not be frightened away from it.

For such undertakings Gobat, as a Christian Bishop, would assume no responsibility, neither vrould he extend to them a helping hand.

He was forced to see the frightful degradation of the local Jews in Jerusalem. He stood firm in the resolve to require the true conversion of the heart as a condition of baptism. He maintained that converts, who until then had lived as beggars, ought, if their conversion were a reality, to learn some handicraft whereby they migrlit in future earn an honest living. He insisted upon the pure. Scriptural principle that the Israelite by birth when once baptized and received into the bosom of the Christian Church, can claim no special privileges above other Christians. He had had many sad experiences on the score of baj tized Jews; and he once said, I tremble whenever the missionaries send me a convert, for either he is insincere from the beginning, or, if he commences by being honest and in earnest, he will soon be spoilt by the flattery of the friends of Israel in England."

Gobat's heart was full of love for the Jews, but he possessed a remarkable degree of knowledge of human nature, and he eschewed false sentiment. His true feeling manifested itself in the vast scale on which he aided the Jews in the famine and cholera time, as well as in his paternal care for the hospital in which the sick of that nationality were tended gratis. These noble works are certainly the most important achievements of the Jewish Mission.

A third difficulty, and this was the greatest of all, sprang from the antagonism of the two great parties in the Church of England, the High and the Low. The former holds that the Church is grounded upon the Episcopate, and considers the Greek, Eoman,

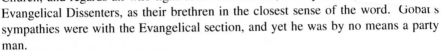

and Anglican communions as the three branches of the One Holy Ch
The Low Church party agrees with

Luther in viewing justification by faith alone as the article of the sta
Church, and regards all who fight under this banner, Presbyterians,
Evangelical Dissenters, as their brethren in the closest sense of the word. Gobat's
sympathies were with the Evangelical section, and yet he was by no means a party
man.

Hiofh Churchmen could not be reconciled to the Papacy, as it now exists, but they
were all the more strongly possessed with an ideal notion of a union between the
Anglican and the ancient orthodox Greek Churches. The work of Williams, formerly
chaplain to Bishop Alexander, "The Holy City," and of John Mason Neale, The Holy
Eastern Church," are the most memorable productions of this school. And who
would not share this noble aspiration, if the ancient hereditary privileges of the Greek
Church be taken into consideration? Her doctrines, founded upon the decrees of the
great Councils and the writings of the Fathers; her Liturgy, dating from Chrysostom
and Basil; the ancient rites which she has preserved, and the inexorable steadfastness
wherewith she confessed Christ in the most terrible days of Arab and Ottoman tyranny!
How glorious would it be, did but the existing reality and the present state of the Greek
Christians in Turkey correspond with the orthodox system! Unhappily this is not the
case.

When, like Gobat, we behold matters in close proximity, we see an entirely different
side of the question. The old, venerable walls, the institutions of Primitive Christianity, are still there, but the spirit and the feeling of the early Christians no longer dwell
therein. The fabric is overgrown with grotesque and spurious accretions; the superstitious worship of pictures, the invoca- tion of saints, and, lastly, the profound ignorance
of the laity and inferior clergy, produce a sadly discouraging-impression. Despotism,
especially Oriental despotism, ruins the character. The tyranny of a single individual
is less pernicious than that of an entire nation, which tramples upon the neck of an
enslaved people bereft of all their rights. The weak become the prey of the strong, and
there arises the temptation to gain legitimate ends by false and corrupt means. It is
from these evils that the Eastern Christians suffer. The majority of them do not know,
or have forgotten, the alphabet of Christian morals.

The Anglican admirers of the Greek Church reflected too little upon this side of the
question when they fixed their hopes upon a speedy union; but such persons as were
on the spot stumbled at every step against insuperable hindrances.

These fair hopes were touched upon in the Document of Foundation, dated December 7, 1841; and the commendatory letter written by Archbishop Howley, and
presented by Bishop Alexander to the Greek and Armenian Patriarchs, was conceived
in such harmonious terms, that one might have supposed that there was no conflict
to be feared, and as though the Anglican and Oriental Churches would immediately
clasp hands on the common ground of equal rights, and in token of perfect fraternal
fellowship. But assuming that this mutual acknowledgment was made in earnest, what
would be its practical issue? Firm stands the axiom, "Whosoever is admitted there
must also be admitted here; and whosoever is excommunicated there must likewise
be excluded here."

Here, then, appears at once the hard and insolvable difficulty which could not fail to render the position of the Evangelical Bishop a truly painful one. If persons were shut out from the Greek Church because they refused to kiss pictures and to surrender the Bible, were they to be debarred from admission into the Anglican Church, which rejects the worship of pictures, and founds its doctrines and its rites upon the Bible only?

We know the course pursued by Gobat in such cases, and it would be difficult to say how he could have acted otherwise.

But we can well understand the agitation into which the Anglican admirers of the Greek Church were plunged when it became known in England that Bishop Gobat was establishing Protestant congregations in various parts of Palestine, composed of those who had left the Orthodox Church. How did this proceeding agree with the declarations of the Document of Foundation? What was to become of the hoped-for union of the Churches? Every prospect of such a consummation seemed to be frustrated by these events.

Gobat's friends saw the storm gathering, and tried to avert it. Dr. Adair Crawford, Secretary to the Jews' Mission Society, and editor of the Record repaired in June 1849 to Jerusalem to warn the Bishop against a split between himself and the Greek Church; but once on the spot, he soon found that it was easier to give such advice than to follow it. Sir George Pose, formerly president of the Church Missionary Society, wrote in great anxiety in December 18 5 I to Dr. MCaul. The greatest prudence, he affirmed, was imperative. The Emperor of Russia might be provoked by Gobat's proselytising, and he would then forbid the Church Missionary Society to carry on its operations within his dominions.

In this dilemma Gobat chose the straightforward course. He appealed for counsel and help to his superior, Archbishop Sumner of Canterbury. He received in answer, on the 8tli of November 1850, a remarkable document. The Archbishop and Chevalier Bunsen had drawn up and signed at Lambeth an official " Explanation" of the 7th Article of the Deed of Foundation, which conferred freedom of action on the Bishop. It expressed the expectation that he would assume no hostile attitude towards the Greek Church, neither initiate any polemical war against her. But, on the other hand, the declaration was firm upon this point: 'If Greek Christians, dissatisfied with the state of their Church, desire scriptural fellowship, and are imbued with the belief that the Anglican Church in doctrine and constitution doth answer to this condition, it were unreasonable to forbid the Bishop to afford to such Christians his help and countenance. It were desirable, indeed, that congregations formed under these circumstances should be shepherded by like-minded priests of their original communion; if, therefore, the charge were undertaken by Anglican clergymen, this was to be looked upon merely as a measure of expediency, in order to preserve the seceders from complete spiritual destitution."

Unfortunately, this declaration was not made public; whether from mistaken prudence or not, it is hardly for us to decide. Gobat, at all events, was not responsible for its suppression. His position with regard to the High Church party remained as difficult as ever, so long as he was not permitted to make use of the declaration in his own defence.

At last, in September 1853, the celebrated protest against Gobat's proceedings, addressed to the Patriarchs and Synods of the Greek Church, and signed by more than a thousand members of the Anglican Communion, was put forth.

Against this serious attack, the most formidable that

Gobat had ever liad to endure, the four Angucan Archbishops, by a declaration dated November i, 1853, extended to him their protection. They were able to appreciate the difficulty of his position, and they justly observed that those who accused him of acting without authority, were themselves acting, in the case in question, on their own responsibility, and independently of authority.

In concluding this account of events which we would willingly have omitted from the biography of so eminent a lover of peace as Samuel Gobat, had we not deemed it but just to the Bishop's memory to briefly recapitulate the outline of the history, we may remark, that, in the matter of the protest, the Greek Patriarchs and Synods observed the same line of conduct as that pursued by them from the first in reference to the Evangelical See. They simply ignored it. The official proclamation of the four Metropolitans exonerated the Bishop, and no further unfavourable consequences ensued.

The whole affair awakened much sympathy for the Bishop, a sympathy which found vent in declarations of confidence and in generous gifts. When his school-house was completed, he might truthfully have said that it had been built for him by his adversaries.

The maintenance of the Bible-schools and Bible-readers, and the carrying on of the various institutions at Jerusalem, demanded a very large expenditure. There was no regular fund for these objects, and Gobat found himself compelled from time to time to visit Europe to arouse sympathy and interest by means of lectures. He accomplished the first of these journeys in 1852.

Concerning domestic events, we may add that two children were born to Gobat at Jerusalem Samuel Agenor, in 1848, who in after years studied at Oxford, became first his father's assistant at Jerusalem, and then a beneficed clergyman in England; and Blandina, in 1850, who eventually became the wife of the Kev. Theodor Wolters, missionary of the Church Missionary Society at Jerusalem. The youngest child was born in 1852 at Beuggen, and received, in compliment to an august sponsor, the names Frederick William; but he died in early infancy.

We deem it not unfitting if we end this chapter with a copy of the manifesto of the four Archbishops.

Declaration of the Four Metropolitans of the United Church of England and Ireland.

"Whereas certain clergymen have addressed a memorial to the Oriental Patriarchs and Synods, in which the Anglican Bishop at Jerusalem is accused of having exceeded the proper objects of his mission, and of introducing schism into the Eastern Churches.

"And whereas some of the names affixed to the said document are the names of persons who hold official stations in the United Church of England and Ireland; and it might be supposed, at least in foreign parts, that a censure of the Bishop, as having acted without due authority from his Church, would not be made by persons who were themselves acting without such authority: Therefore we, the Metropolitans of the United Church of England and Ireland, deem it expedient to make this public declaration, that the said memorial does not in any manner emanate from the said Church, or from persons authorised by that Church to pronounce decisions.

"We are induced to take this step, first, in order to guard against the danger which might arise to our own Church from the example of the irregular and unauthorised proceedings of the memorialists; and further, because we sympathise with our brother, the Anglican Bishop in Jerusalem, in his arduous position, and feel assured that his conduct, under the circumstances in which he is placed, will be guided by sound judgment and discretion.

(Signed) ' J. B. Caxtaur.

T. Ebor.

John G. Armagh.

KicHARD Dublin.

' Novemher i, 1853."

CHAPTER IV.

IMMEDIATE CONSEQUENCES OF THE CRIMEAN WAR GROWING HOSTILITY OF THE MOHAMMEDANS RESUMPTION OF THE ABYSSINIAN MISSION.

(1854-1857.)

Whilst tlie Revolution of 1848 and 1849 made all Europe tremble as witli the shock of a mighty earthquake, dwellers in the East enjoyed tranquillity; Palestine remained untouched by those portentous events. But when in 1854 the Czar Nicholas made his onslaught upon Turkey and lighted up the Crimean War, the state of matters changed.

What was the position in which the Evangelical Bishop at Jerusalem found himself at the outbreak of that terrible struof le? We learn from his well-known letter of the 20th of May 18 54, that, on the part of himself and his friends, one point of view alone drove all other considerations into the background. Under the feeble but benevolent sway of the Sultan, Abdul Medschid, who had every reason to show consideration for England, missionary efforts in Palestine were carried on entirely free from molestation; but it was feared that this freedom of action would be checked as soon as Russia usurped the dominion of the East. The Sultan was prayed for at Christ Church, Jerusalem, as it is the duty of all Christians to pray for and to seek the welfare of the ruler of the land in which they live, be that ruler Christian or heathen. Thus political events brought in their train a moral question very difficult of solution for Christians in the Turkish dominions.

In such cases, true wisdom enjoins upon the servants of Christ silence concerning political questions and the war of rights. Unfortunately, the Bishop's expressions in the letter above referred to were taken in the sense of a political and party manifesto.

But if the Turcophiles reckoned upon Gobat as a partisan, they found themselves very much mistaken. He knew the real state of Eastern affairs too well; he was too enlightened as to the respective essential characteristics of Christianity and Mo-hammedanism to believe in the ennobling of Islam, in the possibility of a good government in the Turkish empire, or in the civilisation of the East apart from conversion to Christ.

The result of the war, which had cost such frightful sacrifices, was laid down in the two memorable documents, the Hatti-Humayum, that is, the decree of the Sultan, signed with his own hand, dated January 26, 1856, and the Paris Treaty of March 30, in that same year. The Conference of French, English, and Austrian diplomatists, in which Lord Stratford played the leading part, had drawn up the outline of the Hatti-Humayum, and the Sultan was obliged by his position of dependence upon the European Powers to adopt it.

This document assured to Christians living under Turkish rule unrestricted freedom of conscience, equal rights of citizenship with the Mohammedans, and eligibility for all offices of state. Mixed, that is, Mohammedan-Christian, tribunals were to settle all disputes between Mohammedans and Christians, and the latter were made liable for military service.

By means of these and kindred " reforms," tlie Turkish empire was at one coup to be transformed into a modern civilised state, and a sort of cosmopolitan system of citizenship, embracing manifold nationalities and religions. Splendid fictions, in which no one who was acquainted with the circumstances could place any faith. The high value (!) of the Hatti-Humayum was proved by its fatal codicil, which declared that in no case were the said Powers to be allowed to interfere in the relations between the Sultan and his subjects, or in the interior administration of his dominions.

Bishop Gobat was one of those who were not to be deceived by the fallacies and emptinesses of diplomatic promises. His circular letter for 1857 and his general correspondence show that the position of matters was not improved, but rather made worse than before. The great war undertaken on behalf of Turkey had the most prejudicial effect upon the temper of the Mohammedans. Their pride was flattered by the favourite interpretation attributed to events by the Turks themselves; for the version of matters promulgated from Stamboul ran much as follows: " The Muscovite Giaour had the temerity to menace the Padisha. "Whereupon the Caliph ordered his vassals, the English Giaour and the French Giaour, to come and conquer them. They obeyed the command, and drove the Muscovite Giaour back."

Deeper-seeing Moslems beheld in the whole transaction the real humiliation of the Turkish power; they foresaw its approaching dissolution, and their wrath flamed high. " If the foreigners intend to take from us our land, they shall find nothing but a desert." The prophecy of far-sighted Europeans, who foretold that the proclamation of equal rights between Christians and Moslems would be the signal for sanguinary insurrection, had its sad fulfil- ment. In several places the Hatti-Humayum was not made known at all. At Nablns its publication on the 4tll of April 1856 excited a riot. Redress for the wrongs inflicted by the Moslems on the Christians was less to be hoped for than ever; for as (in the document) the separation of Church and State had been declared, the European Consuls, as civil officials, had nothing to do with religious disputes. According to the provisions of the Hatti-Humayum, the testimony of Christian against Moslem was to be received as valid; but as a rule the Kadi would hear nothing of it, and simply consulted his Koran. The Christian's liability for military service, ostensibly an honour and a ratification of the equality of rights, became, as the practice of buying off grew customary, a welcome pretext for endless pecuniary extortions on the part of the Turkish authorities. A Mohammedan who had received baptism could no longer, after the letter of the law, be brought to justice and condemned to death; but any Moslem who chose could with impunity shoot him dead in the open street. ' Certainly," observes Dr. Rosen, ' matters have improved since then. Progress, if slow, has been made by the nations of the Levant, more especially by the Christian peoples; but it has not been in consequence of pompous firmans or of the exertions of the Ministers of the Porte, but as a necessary result of intercommunion among the nations."

It was at this period that the Abyssinian Mission was revived. After the enforced retirement of Gobat through severe illness at the end of 1836 from that field, the work had for some time been continued in Tigre by Missionaries Isenberg and Blumhardt; but on the 9th of March 1838, these men, together with the newly arrived Missionary Krapf, were banished by Prince

Oubea, and missionary work soon came to a complete stand-still in that region.

Gobat had ever borne the welfare of the Abyssinians in his heart, and the Abyssinians in their turn preserved a faithful remembrance of him. The confidence which Gobat had earned from that people moved Eas Ali to the request, in I 850, that the Evangelical Bishop would assume the superintendence and protection of the Abyssinian monks and pilgrims, a task which Gobat fulfilled with many blessed results.

In consequence of a great political change in Abyssinia, the way seemed smooth for a renew ed effort of missionary activity. That kingdom, formerly ruled by one sovereign, had since 1780 been divided until the year 1855, when the whole country became re-united under one king. Our readers will probably remember mention being made in the autobiographical portion of this work of a savage Abyssinian grandee whom Gobat had successfully treated for fits of madness. This man's son, Casai, then a boy, was now grown up, and had distinguished himself under different princes as a bold and daring leader. He contrived to act a similar part to that played by Clovis among the Frankish princes. He became the son-in-law of Prince Eas Ali, whom he afterwards conquered and dethroned. He overcame his mighty adversary, Oubea, and caused himself to be crowned, February 5, 1855, "king of kings," under the name of Theodore II. The then Abuna, Salama, performed the ceremonies of unction and coronation.

Theodore was a remarkable man, possessed of kingly qualities. He had been from his youth favourably disposed towards the mission, and he was desirous of raising his people by means of European education.

The Missionaries Krapf and Flad, sent by Gobat, appeared before the King and the Abuna at Gondar, and presented the Bishop's letter of introduction, April 14, 1855. 1 gives his impression of King Theodore in the following words:

"The King was friendly in his demeanour towards me, and had various questions to ask about Europe and upon religious matters. He decided all judicial cases himself, and daily gave audience to dozens of petitions and complaints. Criminals were sentenced and executed on the spot. Numberless messengers received the royal orders for the Government officials. He could not write; he dictated sometimes two or three different letters at the same time, and for the slightest mistake the scribe was chastised with blows or with a great whip. Even officers, generals, ministers, received the same kind of punishment.

"The King was usually seated, in the simplest possible attire, on a carpet spread upon the ground; he wore neither head-covering nor shoes. He was of medium height, powerful frame, and moderately dark complexion. In the expression of his countenance there was something half savage, insincere, and crafty. His eyes were fiery, his nose strongly aquiline; when he was angry his face assumed a darker hue, and the three plaits of hair bristled upon his head. At such times I felt very uncomfortable in his vicinity."

Introduced into the presence of this Oriental despot, the two missionaries stood in apprehensive expectation.

"Is Gobat well?" asked the King. "His letter pleases me, and I wish him to send me three artisans, namely, a gunmaker, a palace-builder, and a book-printer. I do not intend to interfere in matters of faith; that is the business of the Abuna."

Flad, Zwolf Jahre in Abyssinien, oder Geschichte des Konigs Theodores II., 1869, S. 4 fif.

The latter functionary expressed himself in favour of receiving into Abyssinia persons who would disseminate the Scriptures in the language of the country. In the letter addressed by the King to Gobat, and intrusted for delivery to Krapf and Flad, his Majesty observed, "Thou knowest the circumstances of this country. "VVe were formerly divided into three parties, but I have now, with God's help, established unity in my dominions. Priests who would destroy our faith must not come, in order that love may not grow cold."

The King had banished the Jesuit Father Jacobis, who, according to Flad's testimony, was a pious and humble-minded man, besides sundry other Eomish missionaries who had gained some adherents in the northeast quarter of the kingdom, because they had occasioned a division.

These hope-inspiring invitations coincided with the wishes and plans of Herr Spittler at Basle, an indefatigable, enterprising man, ever active in the cause of true charity. The Bishop was highly satisfied with the Chris-chona Brethren, whom Herr Spittler had sent to Jerusalem; and he dispatched four of them Flad, Bender, Maier, and Kinzler after careful preparation and with excellent instructions, to Abyssinia, December 7, 1855.

Herr Spittler afterwards devised a bold project in connection with the revival of the Abyssinian Mission. He codceived the grand idea of establishing twelve mission stations in Egypt and Nubia, on the highway to Abyssinia, each station to be called by the name of one of the Apostles, and the whole to be collectively designated The Apostolic Way." By this means a regular line of communication with that distant land was to be maintained. This plan was, however, but imperfectly realised.

With wise precaution, Gobat abstained from ordaining any of tlie bretliren. They were to discharge no ecclesiastical functions, nor were they in any way to interfere with Church order, but simply to confine themselves to the duty of disseminating the Bible and of spreading Christian knowledge. The Abyssinians were to remain in their own Church, and it was hoped that that Church would, by degrees, become reformed from within. It was expected that, in time, King Theodore would favour such a measure.

The scheme was not devoid of dangerous elements. Many Christians looked upon the Bishop's compliance with the King's demand concerning the gunmaker as a hazardous step. It is true that the blacksmith, Schroth, who accompanied the second detachment of the brethren, died just as he had reached the Abyssinian frontier, but several of the brethren found themselves obliged by the King's order to labour at the task of repairing not only roads and waggons, but also guns, cannons, and bombs. The air of the court is an unhealthy element in Abyssinia as well as in Europe, and royal patronage is at all times dangerous to true Christianity.

The emissaries at first enjoyed so high a degree of the King's favour, that he exalted them to the rank of nobility, and endowed them with land. But he had at the same time tried to make them subservient to his temporal views. Gobat suffered great anxiety lest pride, vanity, avarice, and disunion should creep in among them, causing them to neglect their proper occupation of disseminating the Bible. These evangelical messengers found themselves, in point of fact, in a golden slavery. But ere long the King's mind changed, and his displeasure conduced to greater faithfulness in the fulfilling of their mission.

After the conclusion of the Crimean War, Gobat made a tour in Europe, visiting Basle, Berlin, and London. It was tlien tliat lie received tlie remarkable proposals of tlie King of Prussia, who invited him to consecrate as bishops certain German pastors. His Majesty thought by this means to transplant the episcopate into Prussia, and to pave the way for union with the Anglican Church.

Frederick William ly. had a just conception of the burthen and responsibility which rested upon him in his double position of King and supreme head of the Evangelical Church of Prussia. He was clearly persuaded of the anomaly of this arrangement, and of the advantages of the episcopal constitution. He cherished the intention of creating in his dominions dioceses of moderate extent, each one containing about 50,000 souls, and of placing at their head approved Christian ministers invested with jurisdiction. These men were to be chief pastors, curates in the original sense of the word, and fatherly friends to the inferior clergy and Christian community; they were to form, in short, an episcopate of the primitive type.

The intention was good, but the plan was not practicable. The simple, straightforward scheme proposed by Gobat would have been preferable. But the whole thing fell through owing to the opposition of public opinion and the disinclination of the men selected by the King to accept the episcopal office designed for them. The theologians of Germany failed to recognise the right principle which lay at the root of the King's wishes. Our men of learning have no appreciation of the deficiencies and injurious practical working of this unhappy Church system, in which the temporal power assumes the highest spiritual functions.

Bishop Gobat to Herr Spittler,

"Jerusalem, Sept 7, 1854.

"Dear Brother in the Lord,. The affair of the Abyssinian Mission seems to be now arranged, so that I need write very little on the subject. I do not think that I should meet with success were I now to attempt to form a committee for this mission; I shall not be able to do so until I have an opportunity of revisiting England. I must in the meanwhile undertake the matter on my sole responsibility, under the two conditions which you have. accepted, in the name of the Chrischona Committee.

"I am doing this in faith, for until my new school-house is finished, towards the end of the year, my coffers will be quite empty, unless Providence sends me special help, which He has never hitherto permitted to fail me. You must therefore send the six brethren to Jerusalem next month, and provide for their maintenance here for about twelve months. I hope that they will use this interval in such a manner that they will be able to begin work at once on their arrival in Abyssinia.

"Towards the end of September of next year, I intend to let them start from here with about; 400 for the expenses of the journey and for their first establishment in Abyssinia. I shall then try to arrange for them at Jidda or Massowa a moderate credit for future needs; for even if they labour with their hands, they will still require extraneous help for some years to come.

"With regard to the perils, ghostly and bodily, which will beset them, our dear brother Krapf has drawn them faithfully, though in somewhat darker colours than they appeared to me.,.

"The dangers which come from within are, in my opinion, by far the more important. I do not refer to tlie ordinary hazards to which each one in this world is exposed;. but I mean the one great danger, peculiarly mischievous in such an undertaking and transcending all others, namely, disunion among the brethren. For even here, where the two brethren, otherwise well conducted, are in comparative obscurity, as much harm is done by their discords as good is wrought by their presence. How then would it be in Abyssinia, where the whole population will subject the brethren to the strictest scrutiny? Should, therefore, any one of the candidates show signs of obstinacy, self-seeking, or pride, I would rather you did not send him. I shall, at all events, reserve to myself the right, if any of them manifest a spirit of contention while at Jerusalem, of refusing to allow such to proceed to Abyssinia.

' I also deem it necessary that on all occasions lulicn in ptohlic they shall treat one of their number as their chief,. who, in his turn, must undertake no enterprise or form any important decision without the concurrence of the others.

"They need not take many books with them; but those which they do take must be good, and worth reading several times over. They must not only be thoroughly and intelligently acquainted with the text of the Bible, but also know, as a rule, whence the passages which they quote are taken; for they cannot generally have their Concordance with them. A good knowledge of history and geography will be of great importance, and will form a means of attraction for young and old. But the chief thing, after the Bible, is a competent knowledge of the history of the Church, and especially of the history of dogma, during the first four or five centuries. Mechanical skill is very requisite.

"Your communications respecting the purchase of a steamboat, c., combined with what I hear from Germany, England, and America touching plans for the colonisation of this country schemes already in partial operation fairly bewilder me; and I am at a loss to know what I am to say to all these enterprises. But I must own that I feel uneasy and anxious when I think of them. No immigrant ought to dream of the vicinity of Jerusalem. In Jaffa there are already a few German and American families. The latter are handsomely subsidised from America, and by that means not only are they well off, but able to reduce the poor Germans to servitude; they make them work all Sunday, and keep Sabbath on the Saturday.,

"In short, the time for immigration into this country is not yet come.

"I am afraid you will think me over-cautious, and yet I must add one clause. You say that your steamboat is to transport pilgrims free of cost. To this I can only say, that if it is to transport them from here to Germany, we shall be for ever grateful to you; but the converse of this arrangement will, with very few exceptions, be most unwelcome.

"I nevertheless hope that success and a blessing may attend your enterprise; and I remain ever faithfully yours, S. Angl. Hierosol."

Extracts from Bishop Gohafs Circular Letter for 1854.

"Jerusalem, Novemlier 6, 1854, "The past year has been one of great trial and suffering in this country. We have experienced but little effect from the war,. with the exception of a few trifling disturbances at Jaffa and Beyrout.

"The land has, however, been visited by two severe scourges pestilence in the shape of smallpox, and if not actual famine, at least an extraordinary rise in the price of bread. During the past winter the smallpox has carried off about the tenth part of the population of Jerusalem.

' Last spring the Jews seemed to be deeply touched by the charity shown them on the part of the Christians, and their prejudices in that quarter appeared to be melting away. European Jews became alarmed for the possible consequences of this Christian charity, and they collected large sums of money, a part of which was to be applied for the immediate relief of the poor. The greater portion of the sum was destined for the founding of institutions similar to our own, in order that the bond which, in a certain sense, united many Jews to our mission, should thereby be snapped.

"The bearer of this money, who arrived in July from Paris, immediately proposed to establish a Jewish Hospital, to counteract the influence of that belonging to the English Mission to the Jews. Schools and a kind of Industrial Institute were also to be set up for the benefit of young Jews and Jewesses, in opposition to our own. The Jews were, moreover, urged in no measured terms to make themselves independent of the Foreigners. Of course, all this called forth great excitement and still greater party spirit."

Extracts from Bishop Gohafs Circular Letter for 1855.

Jerusalem, November 24, 1S55. " At present the country is quiet; but during the summer there have been great disturbances, attended with bloodshed and murder, in Galilee, the mountains of Samaria, and the district of Hebron. All this is tlie consequence of a bad, or rather of a weak, government; for it is universally believed that these riots are the result of a foreign influence. These circumstances, tosrether with the war and rumours of war, have told unfavourably upon the mission. Another obstacle to the spread of the Gospel is the difficulty of obtaining the necessaries of life for the people; for although the harvest was not a bad one, the price of every kind of food is high, in consequence of the exportation of the corn. Under these circumstances, the Jews, who almost all of them subsist upon alms, suffer most. Even in the summer and autumn thousands of them have suffered terrible privation. It is heart-rending to see the attenuated fathers and mothers, and to hear of the want which they and their children suffer. The little which we are able to do for them is like a drop in the ocean. No later than a few days ago a sickly Jew brought to me his favourite child, a sweet little girl of eight years, and wanted to give me the child to keep, as he had no food for her. The little girl attends my school, and I was able to help her; but from all sides 1 receive from parents similar offers of their children.

"It is better to trust in the Lord than to put confidence in man.

"It is better to trust in the Lord than to put confidence in princes.

But as the poor Jews in their blindness have rejected, and do still reject, the Lord, they cannot in sincerity put their trust in Him; hence their unwholesome propensity to put their trust in man, although such trust has often been put to shame. Our poor Jews here have recently experienced this truth in a very bitter manner.

Having in the foregoing spring read in the news- papers and elsewhere repeated announcements that Sir Moses Montefiore was about to visit Jerusalem, bringing with him 30,000 to be expended for their benefit, their expectations were raised to the highest pitch. Several times did the rumour spread that Sir Moses was on the way from Jaffa to Jerusalem, and the road to Jaffa was immediately thronged with Jews and Jewesses eager to greet him as their saviour.

' Had he given it out that he was the Messiah, they would have believed him, and obeyed his every behest. Their confidence became so assured that many of them began to throw off their characteristically downcast air, to carry their heads erect, and to look down with contempt upon other people. Nay, more; I know some poor families who spent all that they had, in the certain anticipation that they would receive it back again from Sir Moses in manifold proportion.

' How great, then, was the shock when they heard, on his arrival, that he was not come, as on former occasions, to distribute alms, but with the intention of founding institutions, buying land, and placing within their power the means of earning their own bread. To-day, to-day! they nearly all exclaimed in despair. We want instant succour for ourselves and for our children!

"In the meanwhile Sir Moses offered to many the value of a yoke of oxen if they would only till the land. A few accepted the gift, but by far the greater number rejected the proposal; and when the masses saw that Sir Moses would not read their begging petitions, or allow them to approach him to beg, they were for the most part seized with despair. After one of them had been beaten and cast into prison for having begged too clamorously, many Jews began to compare Sir Moses with the missionaries. When the missionaries cannot help us, said they, 'they at least give a patient ear to our complaints; but this man will not even listen to us.

' The position of Sir Moses must have been a very difficult one; for he could not have helped observing the profound misery stamped upon the features of so many of his brethren after the flesh; and yet the money which he had brought with him was not intended for the relief of their immediate necessities. Then he knew from previous experience that if he had divided among them the whole sum, it would only have assisted them for the moment.

Sir Moses Montefiore certainly means well; and his plans for founding almshouses, hospitals, boys' and girls' schools, and industrial homes, and for purchasing land, in the hope that the Jews will learn to live by agricultural labour, are in truth the best schemes that can be humanly imagined; but nevertheless I cannot expect from them any material improvement in the condition of the Jews in Palestine, because there is under the surface a tide of alienation from God, and of immorality, conscious or unconscious, which threatens to swallow up the intended blessing, or to change it into a curse. I am more and more convinced that it is the duty of all believers to do their utmost to help the poor outcast Israelites in their deep need, not because they are worthy (though, humanly speaking, many individuals among them are estimable), but because they require it, and because we all owe a large debt to their nation. But all that we can do is to alleviate their suffering; we cannot make them happy, for it is evidently God's will that they should be unhappy so long as they reject Him in the person of Jesus of Nazareth.

"This visit of Sir Moses Montefiore has had another prejudicial effect upon the poor Jews. Many of them have distant relatives and friends, who were formerly in the habit of sending them assistance, but this year these friends, having read in the papers what sums of money Sir Moses has brought to Palestine, have sent them, in place of the customary remittances, merely the verbal expression of their joy that so great a prince of wealth has visited Jerusalem.

"Such is the present condition of the Jews. Provisions are nearly three times as dear as formerly, and winter is at the door; when that season comes on, everything will, according to present appearances, be much dearer.

"S. AngL. HleROS."

Bishop Gobat to the Armishop of Canterbury.

"London, June 21, 1856.

My dear Lord Archbishop, Having received the important communication, which I mentioned the other evening, from Dr. Hoffmann, one of the chaplains of his Majesty the King of Prussia, written by order of his Majesty, I beg to lay the contents of that letter before your grace, and to ask your advice on this delicate subject. The letter runs thus:

"It is well known that the King desires to introduce an episcopal constitution into Prussia, to which he has a perfect right. He wishes to take advantage of your presence (at Berlin), as the sole Prussian Bishop now living, in order to have several men consecrated as bishops, with a view of having afterwards the fountain of further consecration in the land. And since three bishops are necessary to a canonically valid consecration, the King intends to ask the assistance of two bishops of the Moravian

Church. After this Mr. Hoffmann puts the following question, and asks me to answer it, viz.:

"Will a bishop thus consecrated by you and two Moravian bishops be fully acknowledged (as such) in England and America? After this Mr. Hojffmann continues thus: " But the doctrine of our Church (Prussian) is decidedly against the Eomish view of three orders. We know only of two orders (deacons and presbyters), and the bishop is merely a presbyter, but he is primus inter pares presbyter. Wherefore an ordination of a bishop by the imposition of hands is not to take place, but only a consecration by means of the sign of the cross and giving the right hand of fellowship.

' Now comes the second question.

Is it lawful for an English bishop so to consecrate as to avoid all appearance of ordination, and without any distinct or indistinct appearance of succcssio apostolica?

' We must remember that the plan of the King will make an immense sensation as soon as it is realised. The King thinks of realising it when you come. Wherefore you must be clear about what is to be done. It is because I see how difficult it will be that I write this beforehand, that you may have time and opportunity to ask the advice of the dear head of the Church of England.

"I wish also to know without delay your resolution and answer on this subject, that I may communicate them to the King before your arrival, in order to avoid the excitement of unpleasant feelings abroad.

"We must consider that the step which the King wishes to take is generally regarded here with abhorrence, as a step towards the Church of Rome, and that the Supreme Ecclesiastical Council, 'the Consistories and the ministers, are against it, and that the Crown Prince will be found in the ranks of the strongest opposition. May the Lord graciously direct you. I have ah eady expressed my doubt, and now the decision depends on your answer. ' Now please to consider this matter before the Lord, and to send me a clear and unequivocal answer, even though it should be a decided No, that I may communicate it to my gracious master.

(Signed) W. Hoffmann.

"Now, my dear Lord Archbishop, I should like exceedingly to oblige the good King of Prussia, but it seems to me impossible to accede to his present request; and besides, I think that at the present moment even such a consecration as he wishes would not be acceptable in Prussia. But yet I fear to answer the above letter in any way without your Grace's opinion and advice. I have, therefore, thus laid the whole case before you, humbly begging that you will give me the necessary advice and direction.

"It seems to me that, with the King's earnest desire to introduce Episcopacy into Prussia while he reigns, the best way for him would be to follow the example of the United States, and seek to have three or more men sent from Prussia to be consecrated in this country.

"But your Grace is much better qualified to give the best advice, which I earnestly solicit; and in expectation of which, I have the honour to remain, my dear Lord Archbishop, your Grace's obedient humble servant,

Extracts from Bisjiop Gohafs Circular Letter for 1857.

"Jerusalem, Nov. 24, 1857. " On the whole, the hatred of the Moslems against the Christians, whether Europeans or natives of this land, has during the past year increased; and since the outbreak at Nablus in April 18 5 6, it is no uncommon thing to hear them speak of an entire extermination of the Christians. About three months ago many Christians in Jerusalem closed their shutters for two whole days, and locked themselves into their houses, in expectation of a sudden attack by the Moslems, because two Koman Catholic Christians had slain a Moslem, and afterwards fled, with the help of the Latin Patriarch. A relative of the murdered man, an influential Effendi, held back the rabble, who were ready to fall upon the Christians. After the riot at Nablus, where an inoffensive old Christian was murdered and others were seriously wounded (the greater number had hidden themselves), my school-house was not only plundered, but partially destroyed; and among others, the house of the English agent was sacked. But all this is not to be wondered at; for although the rioters were frightened at first, yet now that they have seen that no one has punished them, and that to this day we English subjects have received no compensation for such of our property as they have stolen and destroyed, they have assumed an intolerably insolent and threatening attitude throughout the country.

"With respect to our Church at Jerusalem, it is my melancholy duty to announce that on the 6th of October 1856 it pleased the Lord to take unto Himself. the oldest missionary of this station, H. J. Nicolayson. It was a great loss in many ways. We all loved and esteemed this servant of God, not only on account of his manifold attainments and his experience in missionary work, but especially for his gentleness and piety. His successor in the incumbency of Christ Church is Mr. Henry Crawford."

It may prove an agreeable variety if we close this record of so many sad and serious occurrences with a charming idyll, a reminiscence of Bishop Gobat's family life at his country encampment, a sketch for which we are indebted to one of his daughters.

"My late father," says M. K. G., " was extremely gentle in his intercourse with us children, yet without ever derogating from his own proper position. On the contrary, although we knew that he very seldom actually punished us, yet his whole personality inspired us with such reverence, that we were perhaps less inclined to grieve or disobey him than we should have been had we stood in dread of bodily chastisement. He was extremely loving towards us, and manifested his tenderness in the joy which he felt in giving us pleasure. Of an equable disposition in general, he showed himself especially so in his association with us. We could rely upon him implicitly, repose in him our entire confidence, and in later years open our inmost hearts to him in all tha. t most nearly concerned us. With us children he could be as a child, although his whole manner and appearance, as far back as I can remember, had always an air of dignified solemnity. I still have a lively recollection of how, in the twilight hour, he used to play with us younger children in his study, enter into our games, and even take an active part in them himself; or how he would allow us to accompany him in his otherwise solitary walks, and would seek, with a degree of interest apparently equal to our own, the first green arum in the crevice of a rock, or direct our attention to the scarlet anemone blooming in the meadow.

"But above all, I remember those cosy winter evenings, when we children, some of us on papa's knees, others on the carpet at his feet before the blazing fire, were never weary of listening to his stories of the wonderful deliverances and answers to prayer experienced by him, varied by his comical adventures in Abyssinia, or by reminiscences of his childhood and youth.

"In summer our parents were in the habit for many years of spending a few months for health's sake entirely in tents, near the little village of Lifta, about an hour and a half's journey from Jerusalem. Those were delightful times for us children. We had no holidays, it is true, but our school-room was formed by the shade of a great carob-tree, under which a stone bench had been placed. Maps were hung upon the branches, and object lessons in natural history could be given whenever a great black lizard or a chameleon fell from the tree.

' Every morning my father rode to the town to attend to business affairs; he returned about four o'clock in the afternoon, and made one of our circle, looking on at our merry open-air games. Sunday afternoons were bright spots in those times. Our father then returned from the town about half-past one; and when the cool of the evening set in, we repaired with our parents either to a neighbouring olive-tree, called by us the Sunday-tree, or to our yet more favourite resort, the great fig-tree on the slope of the hill, directly opposite to the mountain, on the summit of which is situated Nebi Samuel, the ancient Ramah of the Prophet Samuel. Around this fig-tree lay great and small masses of rock, from among which each one of us selected a seat. We then had a children's service with our parents. We all in turn recited a hymn, or chose one to be sung. Then our father examined us upon some text or in Bible history, after which our mother read aloud something for our instruction. In the intervals of our sacred occupations, ! ilillli"i I'" iliilli f our eyes would roam over the lonely rock-strewn valley at our feet, or upwards to the dreamy heights of the sublime mountain of the Prophet Samuel; and ineradicable impressions, hardly clear as yet to our understandings, were stamped upon our hearts, and all was penetrated and sweetened by the blissful consciousness of being encompassed with tender parental love.

"Melancholy reminiscences are also connected with that stately fig-tree reminiscences which can never be forgotten by us children. One Sunday afternoon, late in the summer of 1857, we were seated upon this our favourite spot. All were there; not one was wanting, not one beloved member. Father, mother, the seven brothers and sisters, all were there. Yet a deep sadness had fallen upon us. In a few days Benoni, who had been at home for a visit of several months, was again to leave us in order to pursue his studies in England, and the approaching farewell weighed heavily upon us all. At last our father said, Children, this year the Lord has for the first time vouchsafed to us to meet together an unbroken circle; I feel that it will also be the last time. And so it proved. That which we had all unconsciously foreboded really came to pass. We children subsequently became so widely separated, that we never again were completely reunited, and now many of us have already hastened in advance to the Heavenly Jerusalem, the city of meeting after lifelong pai ting. Oh, in that abode may not one of us be wanting!

"In the year 1857 we took up our summer residence in tents for the last time. One reason for this might have been that in the autumn, just before our projected return to the city, we were molested by robbers. Two watchmen were posted; but whether they betrayed their trust, or how it happened, we know not. Thieves broke in one night, and entering tlie very tent in which a night-light was burning, stole money, clothes, c., without, however, personally attacking any one of the party. This was due to the manifest protecting love of God, which hindered any one from awaking and calling for help. A proof that murder was contemplated by the robbers lay in the circumstance that they had hea Ded sharp stones in front of each tent, wherewith any one might easily have been killed, and they themselves were armed with swords, which they brandished wildly at their pursuers. It was most remarkable that an otherwise extremely watchful little dog, who slept in our parents' tent, did not stir even while the robbers were plundering that very tent. If it had barked, of course our father and mother would have awoke, and what then might have happened cannot be conjectured. The manner in which, in similar cases, justice is dispensed by a Turkish Pasha, can be exemplified by this event. It was supposed that the robbers belonged to a certain Mohammedan village in the neighbourhood, whence sick persons had been wont to come to my mother with petitions for medicine. Without further investigation, the whole of the men of the village were imprisoned; whoever made a present of money to the Pasha was set free; the greater the sum the speedier the release; so that the only consequence of the whole affair was the filling of the Pasha's purse.

"Our father was always happiest in the family circle. When we were no longer little,. he always looked forward with us to the evenings, when we had a great deal of reading aloud. I can still picture him to myself in his comfortable arm-chair beside the fire, listening with wrapt attention when his weak eyes no longer allowed him to read in the evening, while we took each our turn to contribute to the general entertainment j and he never forgot, amongst it all, to maintain tlie cheerful blaze. If we ever went out in tlie evening without him, he would always say that we need not fear his becoming weary when thus left alone. In imagination he would make long journeys would visit his absent children, relatives, and friends would try to fancy himself in their place, and would always have much to say to his Heavenly Father on their behalf Thus employed, he could pace his room or the terrace of the house by the hour together, and then we knew that he was praying. Yea, truly, that was ever the favourite occupation of his lonely hours."

CHAPTER V.
DEVELOPMENT OF THE CONGREGATION THEIR PRESERVATION
AT THE TIME OF THE MASSACRE OF THE CHRISTIANS IN
SYRIA.
(1859-1860.)

The years 1859 and i860 were a period of prosperity for the Bishop and his flock at Jerusalem. Henry Crawford and Yalentiner worked together with their Diocesan in the most cordial unity, and a new mission station was founded in Bethlehem.

But while matters stood thus peacefully at Jerusalem, horrible events were taking place. The great massacre of Christians took place in the Lebanon and Damascus. Atrocities were committed which evoked throughout the length and breadth of Europe a feeling of horror and of the strongest sympathy for the victims. The newspapers of that period are filled with the records of these occurrences, the memory of which has not yet faded from the minds of surviving contemporaries. The most trustworthy reports are those contributed by Dr. Sandreczki to the Augsburger AUgemeinen Zeitung. We may here quote some passages from the communications of Pastor Kramer at Beyrout to the Ncuesten Nachrichten oms dem Morgen-land (i860, iii. Quartal.):

"To the various factors which combined to produce the outbreak of the late hostili-ties, we must add one which, according to our belief, was the sole cause that rendered the last war an unbroken chain of the most hideous and sanguinary cruelties a perse-cution of the Christians and a war of extermination in the literal sense of the word. Reference has already been made in former communications to the fermentation which was disturbing the various provinces of the Turkish empire; mention has been made of the bond which connected the butcheries of the Christians at Gaza, Tripoli, Aleppo, and elsewhere. This bond is the increasingly apparent hostility of Islam to Christian-ity. As, on the one hand, the victorious power of the Cross had become apparent for the past two years in conversions from Islam, especially at Constantinople, so, on the other hand, Islam tried to excite the fanaticism of its adherents against the Christians. That this hatred had a political motive at its root can by no means be denied; but it is in itself inadequate to move the great mass of the people. For this purpose religious fanaticism alone can suffice. That religious fanaticism was the mightiest lever of the Indian rebellion is now universally admitted; that the same cause was at work in the Syrian persecution of the Christians is also becoming more and more widely acknowledged. Maronites and Druses have often been in hostile relation to each other, and barbarities have been practised on both sides; but such a war of extermination, such a total annihilation of the professors of Christianity, has never before been witnessed.

'On the 29th of May i860, the Pasha repaired to the mountains; and at a spot near Hasmieh the devastations with fire and sword began before his very eyes. For a whole week we saw the smoke by day and the reflection by night of the burning villages, of which over a hundred were reduced to ashes. The towns which offered a more protracted resistance were surrounded, starved out, or surrendered through the treachery, false promises, and faithlessness of the Turkish authorities; all the male population, from the greybeard to the suckling, were slaughtered, and the towns plundered, then destroyed by fire. At length the Christians of Damascus were attacked, burnt in their own houses, or driven upon the knives of the Druses or the bayonets of the soldiery. The number of slain is computed at from seventeen to twenty thousand; of those who were despoiled of everything but life, at over seventy thousand.

". Shame, eternal shame upon a Government. whose only endeavour is to annihilate through faithlessness and treachery its Christian subjects! Yet greater shame upon the Christian diplomatists whose incapacity, self-interest, and jealousy have strengthened the so-called sick man for such deeds! We say it with full and deliberate conviction; the Syrian persecution of the Christians is the consequence of the Peace of Paris."

Jerusalem and the Evangelical community there experienced, even at the time of greatest danger, a marvellous immunity. They had a presentiment of a coming storm, but Gobat was resolved to remain at his post as a faithful shepherd with his flock. His wife was then at Nazareth. While the Mohammedans were attacking the Christian quarter at Damascus and murdering the inhabitants, a secret emissary was on his way to Jerusalem to stir up similar horrors there. But he fell ill at Tiberias and was laid prostrate. Thus it happened that the enemies at Jerusalem missed the right moment. In the meanwhile, English marines, who had landed at Jaffa, marched in. Soreya Pasha, the Governor of Jerusalem, was also amicably disposed, and promised to keep the peace. On the morning of the 20th of July, when the outbreak was hourly expected, Gobat was praying with his people, "If we must be chastised, 0 Lord, let us fall into the hand of God; let us not fall into the hand of man; " and so it came to pass. The peril was providentially averted, but on the evening of that same day Gobat was attacked with dangerous illness.

As at Beyrout benevolent institutions were established for the Syrian Christians and their children, so also at Jerusalem the now flourishing Syrian Orphan Asylum of Schneller was opened under Gobat's patronage.

The French expedition to Syria, the tribunal erected at Damascus by Fuad Pasha for the punishment of the recent outrages, and the installation of a Christian chief in Lebanon for the prevention of future disturbances, are sufficiently well-known historical facts.

The Syrian massacre had calamitous consequences in the subsequent persecution of the Arab Protestants at Nazareth by the Mohammedans and their Kadi, with the co-operation of the Latins, in i860 and 1861. At that juncture. Lord Dufferin, the new British Ambassador at Constantinople, successfully espoused the cause of the Protestants, as his predecessor. Lord Stratford, had done.

In 1861 Bishop Gobat made a prolonged tour in Europe, which lasted from the middle of April until late in December.

During the Bishop's absence the charge of the English community at Jerusalem was committed to Dr. Joseph Barclay, who had replaced Mr. Crawford on the 31 st of March 18 61, and been nominated by the Society for the Promotion of Christianity among the Jews incumbent of Christ Church and superintendent of the Mission to the Jews. He it was who, in after years, became Bishop Gobat's successor in the See. Born in Ireland in 1831, he was educated at Trinity College, Dublin, and proceeded in 1858 to Constantinople in the service of the Mission to the Jews. The diary of his missionary travels exhibits him in the most favourable light. He was pre-eminent among his fellow-missionaries for ripe theological learning, and some fruit of his studies was his translation of the treatise Middoth and an essay on the Talmud.

While at Jerusalem he tried to keep aloof from the bitterness of party spirit, and yet his relations with the Bishop were hardly cordial. Dr. Barclay possessed the self-esteem of the Englishman and the Churchman. He did not believe that a foreigner, who never had held an English cure, could be fully capable of discharging the duties of a Bishop. He considered that the English community was neglected, and that Gobat was too closely wedded to German interests. He was, however, studious to maintain becoming respect; and with Pastor Yalentiner he was on friendly terms. " Mien, nine years afterwards, he retired from his post and returned to England, he did so in consequence of his deep dissatisfaction with the measures adopted by the Committee of the Society for the Promotion of Christianity among the Jews.

Extracts from Bishop Gohafs Circidar Letter for i860.

"Jekusalem, Decembers, i860. " The past year has been one of great trial for our missions here, but especially for our labours among the Jews. We have not been able to accomplish much work. The late indefatigable Miss Cooper was called hence at the very time of my writing my last circular letter. Then our beloved Dr. Macgowan sickened, and was summoned to enter into the joy of his Lord on the 6th of February. He has left a wide and painful gap; for he was not only an instrument of blessing and consolation to thousands of poor Jews and others in his medical capacity, but also, as a humble-minded, fervent Christian, a pillar of our little Church. We feel his loss all the more as his excellent wife was obliged to return to England.

"A few days after his departure, Missionary Hefter left us for a necessary holiday, and only returned in the middle of November. Crawford, the chief missionary of the Society for the Promotion of Christianity among the Jews, was out of health all through the winter, but hoped for restoration at the return of warm spring weather. But as his anticipations proved vain, and his illness increased, he also was forced to leave this country.

"You will see from these details how, in a short time and in different ways, some of our most faithful fellow-workers have been taken from us. Dr. Atkinson, who was appointed to succeed Dr. Macgowan, left us a fortnight ago, having been called to another sphere of labour.

"I had intended to visit Europe in the course of last spring, partly on account of my health, and partly to stir up, with God's help, fresh interest in the work which has been intrusted to me; for I have very small means wherewith to maintain my schools, the orphanage, Bible-readers, c. I decided, however, to remain here, the mission being in such a weak state. But I was taught that God needed not my poor work; for he laid me low upon a bed of sickness, and brought me even unto death's door.

"Tet notwithstanding all these trials and hindrances, the Lord has not left our work unblessed. The services in the Church, and the various meetings for edification and instruction, have been continued without interruption, and even in times of sickness were pretty well attended.

"We have baptized eight adult Israelites, three of whom were brought up in our schools, and whom we find on the whole to be satisfactory.

' Missionaiy Bailey, whose special duty it is to instruct the sons of our converts, has also preached in English almost every Sunda, while his wife has a school for the smaller children, both boys and girls. The institution founded by Miss Cooper for the instruction and employment of poor Jewish women is being carried on by Miss James; and in the same house is a school for the daughters of Jews and proselytes, zealously taught by Miss Buckmaster. The Industrial Home, which during the past year has had to pass through heavy and depressing trials, continues to afford an opportunity of thoroughly investigating the characters of those who apply for baptism.

"Of the working of the Church Missionary Society here there is not much to be told. Their chief object, that of converting the Mohammedans, is at present unattainable, as all the Mohammedans are in a very excited state, and filled with fanatical hatred against the Christians.

"Missionary Klein is working as pastor of the Protestant Arab congregation here, and also occasionally visits the stations at Eamleh and Nablus, where little congregations have been formed. Dr. Sandreczki has of late been principally occupied in literary pursuits.

"Missionary Kruse, at Jaffa, preaches every Sunday in English and in Arabic, and affords medical relief to hundreds of poor sufferers. Catechist Gruhler is working with diligence and faithfulness at Ramleh, Lydda, and

Jaffa; the little Protestant congregation at Ramleli is thriving under his care. He also helps in the school, which now numbers over forty children. At Nazareth and the adjacent stations of Cana, Yafa, and Reneh there is an encouraging appearance of life among the Christians. The danger, on the brink of which they were hovering in the summer, seems to have had a good effect upon them, and Missionary Zeller is very busy; but it is too soon as yet to calculate upon the fruits of this present hopeful condition of things.

"The Institution of Prussian Deaconesses is working prosperously. Their hospital is open to all, but especially to Jewish and native Protestants. In their teaching department girls are instructed, clothed, and cared for, while the poorer pupils are at the same time trained for the position in life which they are eventually to fill. An Orphanage has been opened here by the Chrischona Brethren, in which a number of unfortunate boys, whose parents have fallen by the swords of the Mohammedans and Druses at Damascus and in the Lebanon, are received and educated. This institution is to be supported by subscriptions from Basle. Pastor Valentiner continues to work and pray in unity of spirit with us.

Of the special work which, I confidently believe, has been intrusted to me by God Himself, and which I am carrying on independently of all societies, I will not say much. I am firmly persuaded that a more or less profound knowledge of the Word of God is an indispensable preliminary to the conversion of sinners, and I have therefore endeavoured to post as many Bible-readers in this country as I can find men suitable for that employment. Mere colporteurs are of little use among a population ignorant of the art of reading.

"Several travellers who have visited this land have remarked witli astonisliment how much Biblical knowledge is now to be met with in many places where a few years ago the Word of God was entirely unknown.

"From Abyssinia and the seven Chrischona Brethren I rarely receive news, owing to the very unsettled state of that country. King Theodore has recently conquered Tigre and made peace with Oubea, the former Governor of Samene. He has also taken to wife Oubea's daughter, so that we hope that the country will soon be tranquillised; and that if the King remains true to his old love for the Word of God, mission work can be prosecuted in good earnest.

"As to the fruit of all these various efforts, I can humbly say that much Biblical knowledge has been spread abroad both far and near; that a considerable number of our people have begun to long for something better than the vanities of the world; and that some few have been really converted to the Lord. But the maintenance of the various institutions has been throughout this year, and especially during my severe illness, a source of great anxiety. About two months ago, my physician, in consultation with another medical practitioner whom he called in, advised me to proceed to Europe with as little delay as possible, that being the only hope for my restoration to health. But I could not go, for in that case I should have had to suspend all my work, upon which I trust God has vouchsafed His blessing. Besides this, the dismissal of my agents would, in these dear times, have plunged their families in want and misery. For even after greatly anticipating my private pecuniary means, I should, especially if my family accompanied me, have had nothing left over for them. But God has verily shamed our fears, for He has not only preserved me in life, but has also fortified my health in so great a degree as to encourage ttie hope that I shall soon be perfectly convalescent. For the future I am comforted by the precious promise, The Lord will provide.

"With the prayer that the Lord will have mercy upon all men, and that He will abundantly bless you, beloved brethren, I remain, your humble fellow-servant and brother, S. Angl. Hierosol."

CHAPTER VI.

UNINTERRUPTED WORK CALAMITIES IN PALESTINE THE ABYSSINIAN WAR. (1861-1871.)

The tranquillity of the East was but little disturbed by the great political events of this decade, and the mighty tumult of excitement aroused by the Austro-Prussian war in 1866, the fall of Napoleon III. in 1870, and the establishment of the German Empire in 1871, found only a faint echo in the remote regions of Jerusalem and its vicinity. The Germans of Palestine felt themselves exalted and secure since the name of Fricssiani had come to be feared by the Turks. A peace celebration was held in the Evangelical Church, and a German national demonstration took place outside the gates of Damascus.

Gobat's peaceful work daring these ten years was only interrupted by his journeys to Europe in 1862, 1864, 1867, and 1869. The first of these tours furnished him with the opportunity of re-establishing his health at the watering-place of Rippoldsau. While there he was invited to be present at the baptism of the Princess of Baden (now Crown-Princess of Sweden). On this occasion he was presented to King William of Prussia and to the Crown-Prince.

In 1867 the Bishop assisted at the Pan-Anglican

Synod at Lambeth. In 1869 Madame Gobat met with the serious accident described elsewhere,

The distress in Palestine increased during this period. To the calamities which have already been so touchingly described was added a fresh source of misfortune.

In his circular letter of 1866, Gobat was moved to the following complaint: " Whilst the British Government is sending help to the starving Hindoos, the Turkish administration is trampling upon her famishing subjects here. A new tax, Alms for the Sultan, has been levied. The peasants are now even poorer than the Jews."

Nevertheless, in the midst of these gloomy times, benevolent institutions were being multiplied. In 1866 the training-home " Talitha Cumi," for a hundred girls, was founded by Pastor Fliedner. In 1867 the House of Refuge for lepers was opened.

The long-wished-for colonisation of Palestine was now attempted. The first experiment had certainly an unfortunate issue. A number of Americans settled at Jaffa in 1866. They were misled by supposed spirit-voices, and by a deceiver in the flesh as well, and the colony broke up again in 1868. They were succeeded by the Friends of the Temple," who arrived in 1868 under the guidance of Christoph Hoffman and Hartegg. Their colonies at Jaffa, Haifa, and Jerusalem flourished. The spirit of enterprise and the honest labours of these settlers have been crowned with success.

About this time the number of European visitors to Jerusalem began to increase. The Prince of Wales arrived there in 1862. The Turks vouchsafed to him the distinguished honour of visiting Abraham's tomb in Hebron, a privilege never before accorded to a Christian. Prince Arthur followed his illustrious brother in 1865; his suite made a favourable impression by the Christian propriety of their behaviour. In 1869, at the opening of the Suez Canal, the Crown-Prince of Prussia visited the Holy Land, and the same privilege was conceded to him as to the Prince of Wales; he was permitted, in company with his interpreter. Dr. Sandreczki, to look into the grave of Abraham. The acquisition of the old Hospital of the Knights of St. John and the prospect of the opening of a separate German Church contributed to the motives of this visit, which Gobat missed, he being then in Germany.

In 1866 Pastor Yalentiner returned to Schleswig Holstein, after fourteen j ears of faithful co-operation with the Bishop. Sundry other changes also took place in Gobat's staff of fellow-workers.

It is now time to resume the interrupted history of the Abyssinian Mission. Martin Flad, the tried and faithful missionary, devoted himself, agreeably to Gobat's wishes, to the black Jews of Abyssinia, the Felashas of the region of Gondar, and found among them a blessed field of labour. He was aided in his efforts by the Chrischona Brethren, Steiger and Brandeis; and by degrees the number of baptized Jews amounted to sixty-five. These conversions were subject to the depressing condition of baptism administered by Abyssinian priests, and incorporation into the Abyssinian Church. From a moral point of view, the Felashas already stood higher than the majority of Abyssinian Christians; and it must have been a diflscult task for them to conform to a Church which maintains so many usages bordering upon idolatry.

Gobat had placed great hopes upon King Theodore; but the time came when he was fain to lament over the depths to which this man subsequently fell; and upon this moral degradation followed the tragic catastrophe of his career.

We may here insert a letter written at an early period ot tlie labours of the Chrischona Brethren in King Theodore's dominions, when, as yet, all was amity and confidence.

Bishop Gobat to King Theodore.

"Jerusalem, June 13, 1863.

"Your Majesty will be grieved to hear of all the wrong that is done to your subjects, the Abyssinian priests and pilgrims in Jerusalem. The Copts and the Armenians have already taken the chapel belonging to your Majesty, and now they want to take the whole convent by force. Formerly the English Consul protected the Abyssinians, but now there is a new Consul, who has no order from the Queen of England to protect them. If your Majesty would send and request the Queen of England to give orders to her Counsul at Jerusalem to protect your subjects, he would willingly do it.

"I am very glad and thankful to hear that your Majesty continues to protect and to be kind to the men whom I have sent to your country Bender, Wald-meyer, Kienzler, Mayer, Saalmtiller, and Flad; they all praise your Majesty's kindness to them, and am glad that your Majesty finds them useful in many things.

' When I was in Abyssinia, the Abyssinians were very kind to me, and I loved them much; but I grieved to see that they were very ignorant, both of the Word of God and of the arts and trades of civilisation, and therefore very poor; and what is worse, very corrupt, living in many sins,. and walking on the way to hell and eternal perdition. The priests were ignorant,

and tauglit all kinds of false doctrine to the people,. and yet I found many who wished to know the Truth and to be saved. Wherefore, I always prayed for Abyssinia, and wished to do good to your people, after that sickness had obliged me to leave your country; but I did not know how to do it, until I heard that it had pleased God to give the empire of Abyssinia to your Majesty, and that your Majesty loved and read the Word of God.

"Then, with the permission of your Majesty, I twice sent Bibles and New Testaments to Abyssinia through Mr. Flad, and eleven men to work for your Majesty, and to teach your people to work in iron, wood, and stone, as well as one clever man to found cannon and other firearms. But he, with his son, died on the frontier of your country, leaving a widow and four orphans.

"Now I rejoice to hear that your Majesty is pleased with these working-men, and that God has blessed my undertaking; for I learn that many Felashas have read the Word of God, and believed in the Lord Jesus Christ unto salvation; as also two or three Mohammedans, and that they have all been baptized in the Name of the Father, and of the Son, and of the Holy Ghost. I have heard with much pleasure that your Majesty allows Mayer and others to instruct the poor people in that Holy Word. May God reward you for it. He has intrusted the people to your care, that, by your example as well as by precept, you may lead them into the way of eternal life.

"I am getting old and my health is weak; wherefore I am constrained to beseech your Majesty to seek first of all the kingdom of God and His righteousness, that you may find the pardon of all your sins, for Christ's sake, who died for you. That He may give year Majesty grace to serve Him faithfully is the prayer of your Majesty's most devoted servant,

"S. Angl. Hierosol."

The degeneracy of the King was favoured by the possession of Oriental unlimited power; for the delusion that a monarch stands above, not under, the law is fatal in its effects. The mental equilibrium is lost, and the despot sets himself up at last, not above human law only, but above the Divine. Theodore's retrogression towards the savage state was accelerated by perpetual civil wars. Pretenders and rebels rose 'up against him in different quarters. In these conflicts he lost the two best men who at first had stood by him; they were the British Consul Plowden, and the Irishman John Bell. In order to avenge the death of these his frietids, the King gave orders for the slaughter of 700 (according to some reports 1700) prisoners; and this was the beginning of a series of barbarities. Martin Flad, in his 'History of King Theodore" (Basle, 1869), has described the course of these events, of which he was an eye-witness.

"Queen Tauabetsch," he informs us, ' who could tame the wrath of Theodore by her affection, and Mr. Bell, the protector of the Europeans and the faithful, shrewd counsellor, were both dead. Young people flocked to the court, and crowded out the old officials. Luxury and revelling were the order of the day. The first predisposing cause of the King's downfall was a tendency to excessive drinking. Formerly he had never touched any spirituous beverage until the business of the day had been completed; he now began to intoxicate himself almost every day with honey-wine and brandy. Formerly he had been the helper of the poor; he had rendered justice to every one, encouraged agriculture and trade, abolished the slave traffic, diligently read the Bible, and striven to regulate his life by it; he had promoted the spread of the Gospel in his dominions, protected the missionaries from the Abyssinian priesthood, and placed himself as a pattern at the head of his people by discarding polygamy and living with one wife, in whose company he received the Holy Communion.

"He now began to oppress everybody and to diminish the property of his subjects. He put a clog upon commerce by means of excessive imposts, allowed the slave trade to be carried on with impunity, the Bible was no longer read, prayer was neglected, sacred things were profaned; towards the missionaries he was first indifferent, then hostile; and instead of one, he had many wives. And now, because he had rejected God, God also rejected him, even as He had rejected King Saul, and permitted an evil spirit to come upon him, who transformed him into the greatest and most cruel tyrant known to history." (Only Ivan the Terrible of Russia can be compared to him.) " No rank, no profession, no age, and no sex was secure from the violent and blood-stained hand of the sovereign. All alike trembled before him, and every soul was filled with apprehension for the future; yet this was only the beginning of sorrows.

"He entered upon a successful war against the pretender Negusieh in Tigre, who sought safety in flight, disguised as a peasant. He and his brother were recognised by the country people and delivered up to Theodore, who had their feet and hands chopped off, and then ordered them to be exposed naked to the heat of a tropical sun by day, and to the alpine cold of Abyssinia by night. It seems that both victims survived for several days, until they were finally consumed by fire. Negusieli's officers had taken refuge in the free town of Axum. The King granted them an amnesty; but when they gave themselves up, the faithless despot had them all butchered in the most barbarous manner."

Until then the King had treated the German and English missionaries well, but his conduct now became altered by political and personal motives. A new English Consul, Cameron, had arrived, and with him a Frenchman, Bardel, a most mischievous fellow. Theodore was then at the summit of his power, and contemplated the cementing of relations with Queen Victoria, and also with the Emperor Louis Napoleon. He intrusted to Cameron a letter for the Queen, to Bardel a document for Napoleon III. Whilst he was awaiting answers to these missives a contretemps happened concerning the proselyte Heinrich Stern from Hesse. This man, a missionary to the Jews, of mediocre merit, had offended the King by the want of tact which had characterised his demeanour on two occasions when he had audience of Theodore. He was on that account beaten by royal command, wounded, and thrown into fetters. His papers were examined, and the suspicions of the King extended to the other missionaries; he believed himself to have been despised and contemned by them. On the 20th of November 1863 he held a great public judicial inquiry; the accused were threatened with death, but the King received conflicting advice, and the transaction was without result.

At the same time the English Government perpetrated a great blunder, the cause of which has never yet been explained. There came no answer from the Qaeen to Theodore. He imagined that she scorned him. Bardel riad, Hist. K. Theodore, pp. 26, 27. Cf. also Theophil Waldmaier, Erlebnisse in Abyssinien. Basle, 1869.

whispered insinuations into his ear that the English were the friends of the Turks. Cameron was seized, and Bardel did not escape imprisonment, for the King considered himself to have been insulted by Napoleon also. At first the number of prisoners was eleven; it increased by degrees. The arrest lasted, with fluctuating fortunes, for five years and a half. For a time the Germans were set free and made to work again for the King. Gafat was allotted to them as their place of abode, and they were not allowed to leave it without special permission. Then, at the caprice of the tyrant, some of the prisoners were again tortured. Part of the time they were at the royal head-quarters, but finally they were secured in the fortress of Magdala. The wisdom with which Gobat interested himself for the captives, and the earnestness with which he sought to work upon Theodore's conscience, are exemplified in the following letter:

Bishop Gdbat to King Theodore.

"Jerusalem, November 28, 1865.

"Sire, Having heard from time to time of your Majesty's kindness to the men whom I sent to you some years ago to teach your people useful arts and knowledge,. I take a favourable opportunity of thanking you for such kindness, and of sending you my blessing, with the assurance that I continually pray for your Majesty, that, as God has made you a mighty king on earth. He may give you grace to rule in His fear and love, in justice and mercy, in order that you also may obtain mercy, through our Lord and Saviour Jesus Christ, at the great day of judgment.

"The bearer of this letter is my friend, Theodore Beke, whom I commend to your gracious attention and protec- tion. He has seen tlie distress of the wife and young children of Mr. Stern, and of the relatives of the English prisoners in your country, especially that of Consul Cameron's mother, who has just died of grief before Mr. Beke left England. Moved by compassion, the latter has freely undertaken to go to Abyssinia to supplicate your Majesty to be merciful to Messrs. Stern, Cameron, Rosenthal, and their companions, and to forgive them their offences, as you pray that God may forgive you, and to set them at liberty that they may bless you.

"Mr. Theodore Beke has nothing to do with the Queen or with her Government; it is from Christian love and benevolence that he undertakes this long and perilous journey, relying on the goodness of God and on your Majesty's magnanimity for a free pardon. Wherefore I cordially unite with him in entreating your Majesty, for my sake, as a servant of God, nay, for the sake of our Lord Jesus Christ, to show mercy to those prisoners, and to let them go free, that the cry of their poor relatives and children may not ascend to heaven against your Majesty. The greatest glory of a king is to show mercy and to dry the mourner's tears.

"Again commending my friend, Theodore Beke, to your Majesty's favourable and gracious attention, I remain. Sire, your Majesty's most dutiful, most humble, and most obedient servant, S. Angl. Hierosol."

At last the sky seemed to clear when, on the 28th of January 1 266 an English embassage arrived at Theodore's court, consisting of Mr. Rassam, an Armenian, who had been British Consul in Syria, Lieutenant Prideaux, and Dr. Blanc; they brought with them presents and an autograph letter from Queen Victoria. By these means the British Government sought to redeem the past and to bring about the release of the prisoners. An order to that effect was in fact given by Theodore. All prepared joyfully for departure, when a mysterious turn of affairs occurred. On the way they were every one of them captured afresh. Another tribunal was held under the canopy of heaven, the captives were brought forward in chains, but released again the next day. They asked forgiveness, and the King did the same; he begged pardon prostrate before his late victims. This singular scene is hardly to be regarded as a farce; it seems rather that Theodore was really in a frame of mind resembling that of Saul, who threw the javelin at David one day, and who could say on the next, "My son, thou art more righteous than I."

The captivity continued notwithstanding, and even the ambassador, Rassam, contrary to the law of nations, was detained; he was to serve as a hostage for the good faith of the British Government. Martin Flad, who of all Europeans deservedly possessed the largest share of Theodore's confidence, was sent to England to ask for engineers, tools, and machines for the King. During his absence, which lasted more than a year, terrible things took place in Abyssinia, as may be learnt from the diary of Madame Flad, who remained behind in captivity. The power of the King was on the wane, and he practised the greatest cruelties upon those whom he suspected on political grounds. For example, the relatives of a fugitive official were burnt alive. The same fate overtook a number of deserters from the army. The hacking off of hands and feet became a common incident, whole provinces were devastated, the capital itself was plundered and set on fire, and even those provinces which had remained faithful to the King were ravaged, whilst he, like Belshazzar of old, held his revels.

Such was the nature of this tyrant, and we may judge from these particulars what was the position of the prisoners, who were like so many tennis-balls in his hands. Fladj who had had an audience of Queen Victoria at Osborne, came back with a very serious letter from her Majesty to Theodore. It contained a just reproof to the sable despot touching his conduct to Cameron and Rassam; there was but little confidence to be placed in him after his faithlessness; the desired engineers, c., were to be sent to him, but not until he had dispatched every European who wished to leave Abyssinia under safe escort to the frontier of his dominions. This message vexed the tyrant beyond measure. He clearly perceived that matters were becoming serious, but he trusted to the presumably impregnable fastnesses of his highlands. Whilst the disaffection in his kingdom increased, he gave way to still more abominable cruelties. Country people were burnt together with their houses; children, sick people, delicate women, and aged men were not spared; deserters from the army were captured to the number of over a thousand, and their throats were cut. More than two hundred soldiers who had intended to desert were condemned, with their wives, to be starved to death, their throats made fast with wooden forks. Several lived in this condition from ten to twelve days.

The engineers sent from England had already arrived at Massowa. They were there detained by Colonel Mere-wether, who demanded before all things the surrender of the captives. It was perhaps a blunder that he did not also send on the presents. Meanwhile, an English army, with cannon, elephants, and provisions, had landed from India under command of Sir Robert Napier. There were twelve thousand combatants, of whom one-third were British, two-thirds Indian troops.

The preparations for scaling those terrible mountains, with which we are already familiar from Gobat's descriptions, were carried on with the greatest foresight and energy, with the co-operation of Werner Munzinger, English consul at Massowa. Dr. Krapf was to accompany the army as interpreter.

And thus the storm of retribution gathered over Theodore's head. Slowly but surely the English moved from the north; onward they came against the mountain-fortress of Magdala. The prisoners, who expected each moment to be their last, were in a state of indescribable suspense. On Palm Sunday, 1868, the King spoke with Eassam at Magdala, and declared for decisive battle. On Holy Thursday evening, irritated by an insolent word, he ordered three hundred and eight Abyssinian prisoners to be slain, and the bodies, together with several living jdeople, to be thrown over a vast precipice.

On Good Friday, April the loth, 1868, the battle took place. The ill-fated, poorly-armed Abyssinians fell in troops before the sharp fire and rocket-practice of the

English. Sir Eobert demanded that the King should surrender himself to the Queen of England, and bring all the Europeans into the English camp. In return, he and his family were to be honourably treated. At this decisive moment a wonderful dispensation of Providence was manifested. Theodore, who might have all the prisoners slaughtered at the cost of a single word, experienced at the last moment a noble revulsion of feeling. While his Abyssinian counsellors were advising him to put the captives to death, he set them at liberty with the words, "Let them go; these people have done nothing amiss." They descended from the rock of Magdala unhurt into the British camp, fifty-nine persons in all, counting the children.

To surrender and submit to be a prisoner of war, Theodore refused. His troops were utterly dispersed, and they laid down their arms before Sir Eobert. The King wanted to continue the struggle with the little host of followers who had remained faithful to the last. On Easter Monday, after a bombardment which lasted two hours, the English stormed the walls and took the fortress. When Theodore saw that all was lost, he killed himself by a pistol-shot through the head. A few minutes previously he had said to his arms-bearer, "I believed hitherto that God was with me, and I thought that I was fulfilling His will in all that I did. I now see that it was not God, bat the Devil, who was with me, and urging me to be so cruel."

Magdala was plundered by the wild Indian troops; even the graves were robbed, and finally the fortress was set on fire. Then the English commenced the retreat. The Abyssinians breathed freely, and marched, with their priests at their head, to meet the English, whom they greeted as their deliverers, and they sang in their old Ethiopian dialect the triumph-song of Moses the man of God over the destruction of Pharaoh and his host.

The English evacuated Abyssinia, and did nothing further for that unhappy country. On this occasion they had no intention of making conquests; they had only the twofold object, to rescue the captives and to maintain the prestige of British power in the East.

A son of King Theodore, eight years of age, was brought to England to be educated, but he died some time after his arrival.

The Protestant Mission in Abyssinia came to a standstill in consequence of the events just narrated. Sir Robert showed no further interest in it. The missionaries returned to Gobat at Jerusalem, leaving behind them anarchy and confusion. So early as October 1868, the Bishop ventured to send two of the brethren into Ethiopia.

A second Casai, who had rebelled against Theodore in Tigre, favoured the English during their campaign, and was rewarded by Sir Eobert with a considerable present of arms. With these he succeeded in subduing Abyssinia, and in January 1872 he had himself crowned at Axum, under the title of the Emperor John II. The manner in which he won over the Abuna to his interests is characteristic. He placed a pistol at the breast of that functionary with the words, "Dear father, give me thy blessing!"

Roman Catholic and Protestant missionaries are labouring for access to John, and also to Menelek, to whom in all probability the succession will fall. Intercourse between Europe and Abyssinia is on the increase; and there is a danger that among that ancient Christian people the pernicious influences of a civilisation devoid of Christianity may find an entrance. May God grant that Christian culture, such as Samuel Gobat sought to disseminate, may find an abiding-place among the Abyssinians!

Queen Elisabeth of Prussia to Madame Gobat.

"Sans Souci, Se t, 24, 1863. "I have received your letter of the 14th of July, and read with sincere pleasure and sympathy the information it contained concerning the condition and progress of mission-work at Jerusalem of work which is identified with the noble task of re-kindling and reviving the light of the Gospel and the knowledge of salvation on the very scene of the manifestation and redeeming work of our Lord, where they had been overshadowed and eclipsed in successive centuries by the abomination of desolation. My Yliole soul is filled with the grand and exalted thought of this enterprise; it swells in harmony with him who, in joyful trust and ardent love to his Saviour, has now finished his course, and of whom you make mention in your letter with such touching and affectionate appreciation. May God continue to bless this noble and sacred work, and may He with His Spirit and His strength ever abide in you and in all your fellow-workers mightily and with quickening power. Eest assured of my lasting and lively sympathy for you all, of my prayers, and of my hearty good-will, which latter I hereby emphasise with especial reference to yourself and to the Lord Bishop, your excellent husband. Elisabeth."

Bisliop Gdbat to Pastor Sarasin-For cart at Basle.

"Jerusalem, June 1865.

"I spent the evening of the 11 th of May among the Protestant men of Eamleh (there were about fourteen of them), in edifying conversation.

"On the 12 th, I took an early ride to Jaffa, where I met the steam-packet, and took passage in it for Haifa, where, the wind being contrary, I did not arrive until nine o'clock in the evening. There met my son-in-law, J. Zeller.

"On the 13th we started betimes for Xazareth; but had scarcely ridden half an hour before we encountered a messenger from that place, who brought us the tidings that on the previous day the Eoman Catholics had mustered in great force and had attacked the Protestants; they would have killed the native catechist if he had not had just time to fly. The Turkish Governor took part with the Eoman Catholics, because not long before

Zeller had refused to bribe hira with a present; and yet the Cadi declared that the Protestants were in the right. Since the persecution at Constantinople a year ago, there is no more justice for Protestants under the Turkish Government; and whilst the French and Eussian Consuls are always ready, the one to protect the Eoman Catholics, the other to defend the Greeks, even when they are in the wrong, the Protestant, and particularly the English Consuls, dare not say a word in favour of their co-religionists.

"During my thirteen days' sojourn in Galilee everything was quiet. Indeed the Governor of Nazareth came to Zeller to apologise; but four days after my departure the Koman Catholics, with a Syrian monk at their head, renewed the attack. I do not yet know what has happened since."

"Jerusalem, July 13, 1865.

"On the 27th of May, after having visited the ruins of Sebaste (Samaria), among which I counted more than a hundred pillars, though few of them were of marble, we traversed the fruitful valley up to Nablus. The valley was swarming with locusts, which had already devastated a great number of olive-trees, besides other vegetation. The whole population of the adjacent villages was employed in driving them away;

it was one universal shrieking and howling to frighten the locusts and drive them to perpetrate their ravages elsewhere. For nearly an hour as we passed along, the roads and trees were quite covered with these creatures, and the air of the entire valley was so full of them that we could hardly descry the neighbouring mountains, and the sun could give but half its light. That was a sad sight, worse than hail.

"On Sunday the 28th we had divine service at eight o'clock in tlie morning. The large room, which serves as a chapel, was thronged with men, and an adjoining apartment with women, who were all attentive and devout, although many of them were not Protestants. Zeller preached a thoroughly evangelical, practical sermon on the words, Because I live, ye shall live also. After service I examined the school children, who assembled in another room, which does duty as a schoolroom; and it was a pleasure to me to see how heartily and correctly they answered all my questions, not only upon Bible history, but also upon doctrine. The schoolroom was afterwards filled with inquiring Protestants, Greeks, and Samaritans, with whom I conversed until one o'clock, chiefly about the Word of God and the cardinal truths of Christianity. I found even among the Greeks a very fair knowledge of Holy Scripture.

'I learned that not only Protestants, but also several Greeks have for some years past had family prayer in their houses, at which the Bible is daily read and extemporaneous prayer offered, when they do not use a translation of the English Liturgy. Moreover, the priests of Nablus seem much more tolerant of late towards those who repudiate the errors of their Church, out of simple fear least the people should become Protestant. At three o'clock in the afternoon we had service again, and the worshippers were as attentive and almost as numerous as in the morning. A convert, who had formerly been a Greek priest, preached a Scriptural, telling sermon on the necessity of renouncing all that is vain and sinful, and clinging to Christ. Zeller, to whom this man had hitherto been a stranger, was quite prepossessed with him; he accompanied him next day to his village in the neigh-hood of Sebaste, and spent the night under his roof. This further acquaintance only tended to increase Zeller's respect and regard for this humble-minded and zealous man.

"This priest had had an extraordinary career. About sixteen years previously I had made his acquaintance, and discovered that he possessed absolutely no knowledge of the Word of God. I spoke v ith him seriously, gave him a Bible, and exhorted him to read it diligently and prayerfully. When I saw him again, after the lapse of some years, I found him well versed in the whole Bible, and especially in the New Testament, whereby he had already detected many of the errors of his Church. He was then minded to leave the Greek Church, although no one had encouraged him to do so. Yet even then there was more light in his intelligence than life in his heart. He would have liked to discuss matters with his superiors, but they were unwilling to allow this, and knocked him down instead. One Bishop placed his foot upon his neck, and forced him to promise that he w ould remain a priest of the Greek Church. At the same time, as the man was poor and had a family, this Bishop lent him a sum of money, with the observation that if he remained true to the Greek Church the capital would never be claimed, but if the recipient failed to fulfil this condition, the return of the sum would instantly be demanded, with heavy interest. A ith this the priest was dismissed from the interview.

"After this he began to have a sense of his misery and sinfulness. He seemed to himself like an apostate, and yet he was bound with golden chains, and could not free himself, for he had paid other debts with the Bishop's money. And so he languished for some years. He frequently visited the Protestants of Nablus, as being like-minded with himself; and whenever one of my catechists visited his village he invited him to preach in his church.

He himself began, by little and little, to read the Scriptures in his church, and often to testify against the errors of the same, till at last he was found out, and placed under the ban by the Patriarch. (He had in the meantime cleared himself from his debt.)

"He then went to the governor of Nablus and declared himself a Protestant. His congregation sided with him; but when they heard that the Patriarch had declared all those who should follow the seceder to be under the ban, the majority of them drew back for a time.

"I have lately appointed him evangelist in the mountains of Samaria, and he is now going from village to village preaching the Gospel amid shame and persecution. But he bears everything with deep humility and love.

"On the two Sundays that I spent at JSTazareth we had two Arabic services, with about sixty worshippers in the morning, and fifty in the afternoon. After the services the greater number of them came to me, and we had long conversations, in the course of which I perceived with joy that most of them were well acquainted with the Scriptures.

"I also visited the smaller congregations in the neighbouring villages, upon each of which occasions we partook of an Arab repast in a numerous company. Eice and sour milk formed the staple of the banquet. I was at Yafa, Pteneh, and Kefer-Kana. At Eeneh, an hour's journey from Nazareth, the Protestants have a nice school-house, which also is used for a chapel. It was built, with the help of a few private contributions, by Zeller and Huber.

"On the 18th I rode with Zeller to Shef-Amar, a large village four hours' ride west of Nazareth, where I have for some years had a capital catechist and a congregation of five-and-thirty men, who have remained stead- fast, various discouragements notwithstanding. Unfortunately they have no school-house, and they assemble on Sundays, and also in the week, in a dark and gloomy chamber, incapable of holding many persons. I was much pleased with these people, although their conversation continually turned uj)on the necessity of building a school-house, for which they have no funds. They wanted me to undertake it, to which I would consent with all my heart had I but the means to do so.

"S. Angl. Hierosol."

Extracts from Bisjwj) Gohafs Circular Letter for 1865.

"Jerusalem, November 13, 1865.

"When Thy judgments are in the earth, the inhabitants of the world will learn righteousness' (Isa. xxvi. 9).

"With the fervent desire that the truth of the Divine Word may be abundantly realised in this land, and surrounded as I am by the dead and dying, by poor widows and orphans who have lost their sole earthly stay, I address these lines to you, in order to commend Jerusalem to your remembrance and to your Christian sympathy, and to invite your prayers for us during these days of trouble. In the course of this year the Lord has visited this country, and Jerusalem in particular, with heavy judgments.

"As early as last spring the late rain fell, and we consequently suffered in Jerusalem from oppressive drought. Then came the locusts, which in the months of May, June, and July covered the land from Gaza to Lebanon. Happily they found the wheat and barley too far advanced and too hard for their teeth; but they devoured, except in a few districts, everything green, all the vegetables and summer fruits, as well as the leaves and tender twigs of the trees. But in the midst of justice the Lord remembered mercy. For althouo-h the locusts had more than once consumed the first tender blades of the Dhurra, which forms the staple food of the country people, the crop recovered itself; and when in July the locusts suddenly decamped eastwards, it yielded a fair harvest; so that with this, and with the vegetable crop which was sowed after the locusts left, we have been preserved from famine. But all provisions are very dear; and as, during the last four months, the Government, through fear of the cholera, has prohibited the sale of vegetables in the city, and trade has consequently been suspended, the poor people have been unable to earn anything; and but for the help which has been sent to me, chiefly from England and Holland, hundreds of the poor would probably have died of want. Thank God! these charitable gifts enabled me to provide more than two thousand Jews, within the last three months, with regular supplies of rice and water; and I was also in a position to render occasional but material aid to Jews, Christians of various denominations, and Mohammedans.

"But all this misery was as nothing beside the cholera and its terrible consequences. After the locusts had suddenly disappeared in July, the cholera first showed itself at Jaffa, where it has raged frightfully, also at Gaza, ISTablus, and in several villages. In August and September we had daily from one to four deaths from cholera, but fewer cases than usual of other diseases at that unhealthy season. When at the end of September very cool weather set in, we thought that Jerusalem would remain exempt; but the customary great heat of autumn came in with October, and the cholera assumed a more virulent character; so that, from the ist to the 2ist of that month, we had daily about fifteen fatal cases. During this time thousands of Jews fled to Hebron and Jaffa, but several of them died there.

"On the 22d of October forty-two, and on the 25th a hundred and nine, persons died. From that day forward it was forbidden to publish the number of deaths; but from the data which I have been able to collect, I conclude that the number of deaths reached a daily average of sixty, out of a population of fourteen thousand (not counting the fugitives). From the 6th of this month up till to-day, the disease has rapidly decreased; and we now hope that in a few days it will have entirely disappeared.

"I have referred to the consequences of the cholera, but it is impossible to describe them, for they are heartrending. Among the Jews the distress is especially great; for each burial costs them about eighty francs, which obliges many families to sell all the little household articles they may possess, and this involves endless poverty. If the father of a family dies, the widow must, in accordance with Jewish customs, throw away all the water that she possesses, and she remains inactive, often with six or eight young children, or else she soon dies of want and misery, because she has not sufficient energy and courage to seek for help. Others do seek for help; but where is it to be found, now that the greater number of those who could have rendered assistance have fled? The Consuls of England, Prussia, Russia, and France do what they can, but their resources will soon be exhausted. The Jews have certainly received considerable sums of money from distant co-religionists; but the numerous Rabbis always take the lion's share, so that the portion which falls to the poor is very small. I have appointed three dear, faithful brothers to gather information respecting the circumstances of the poor, and to distribute to the neediest, out of the funds committed to me, supplies of water, wheat, rice, and to the sick and convalescent coffee, tea, and sugar.

"It is estimated that at least one-tenth of the inhabitants of Jerusalem have died of cholera since July, chiefly Mohammedans and Jews, but also many Greeks and Latins.

"I tremble at the prospect of the coming winter in the face of the great dearness of food and the utter failure of employment.

"Missionary Carabet has travelled much in the course of the year, and has visited the various congregations that have been formed in Syria and Mesopotamia. He possesses a special gift of bringing the Gospel home to the Mohammedans, wherever he may be. While he was in Beyrout last winter, a goodly number of Mohammedans used to assemble every evening to hear him preach the Gospel and refute the Koran. Fifteen men had already decided to openly embrace Christianity, and Carabet was beginning to instruct them previous to their baptism, when two Mohammedans, who had been converted some time before, were brought to Beyrout and delivered up to the authorities. One of them was sent forthwith to Constantinople, and nothing has been heard of him since; the other (a young soldier) was taken to the barracks, and the same night, in the presence of the fifteen, murdered in the most barbarous manner. In consequence of this melancholy circumstance the baptism was postponed. It is remarkable that the Mohammedans in all quarters, in Palestine, Syria, Mesopotamia, and Bagdad, are no longer satisfied with the miserable Koran, and that they are beginning to inquire after the truths of Christianity. Had they not the persecution of the Turkish Government to fear, many of them, I am persuaded, would come over to our sacred faith. Oh, that God would raise up to us at Constantinople a second Lord Stratford de Eedcliffe! S. Anql. Hiekosol."

Bisjiop Gobat to Queen Elisaheth of Prussia.

"Jerusalem, July 21, 1866.

"Most gracious Queen, Your Majesty will, I trust, allow me to offer my sincere thanks for the most welcome and valued present which your Majesty condescended to send to me by Professor Strauss, namely, the Manual of Communion Prayers, once the property of the illustrious, and to me the ever-beloved King.

"Truly I needed no outward token to preserve a vivid and grateful remembrance of that incomparable monarch, or to keep alive the sentiments of affection in my heart, upon which his image is distinctly and deeply graven. But none the less is this little book of inestimable worth to me, as also the letters, so full of weighty matter, which were addressed to me by that august personage, and which from time to time I peruse with my dear wife and children, always with fresh edification and profit.

"Alas! most beloved and honoured Queen, of what a cup of sorrow has it been your Majesty's portion to drink! How often, since those memorable days of 1856, have I been with you in spirit, both beside the couch of sickness and in the chamber of death,. and cast myself down in supplication before the throne of grace!

"Since then I have been four times in Europe (twice on account of my health), but have never had the courage to revisit Berlin. Often during the long illness of his late Majesty have I taken the pen in my hand in order to address some words of sympathy, and, if possible, of consolation to your Majesty; but an inward voice would always whisper, No; pray rather that both may be endued with patience, resignation, comfort, strengthening grace, and healing by Him who can bestow far beyond what we ask or think; and I feel persuaded that the Lord has heard my feeble prayers, and that your Majesty has realised that the dark path. was yet the path of salvation and of peace, and that through the ages of eternity your Majesty will thank and praise Him as well for the sufferings of late years as for the joys of earlier days. Everything must work together for good to them that love God.

"And now, in the blessed hope of one day meeting your Majesty and the departed King in the mansions of everlasting peace, I remain, in most faithful obedience, your Majesty's most humble servant,

"S. Angl. Hierosol."

Bishop Gohat to his Daughter Maria.

"Benhall Lodge, near Saxmundham, Suffolk, November 8, 1869.

"My dear Maria,. You will already have inferred from the tone of this letter that I am about to impart to you some sorrowful intelligence, and this indeed is my painful duty.

"Last Saturday we were ready to leave here for London, where I was to preach twice yesterday,. when your dear mamma, who had gone up to our room to bring down some little trifling articles, slipped in coming downstairs and fell over several steps. No one was at hand. Mrs. Holland happening presently to pass through the hall, found her lying with her head upon the lowest step, and bleeding profusely. I was called to the spot, and beheld your poor mamma lying in a pool of blood. We sent for the doctor, but more than half an hour elapsed before he came, and when he arrived he had not brought the necessary things with him. He had to send for them; and all that he could do in the meantime was to arrest in some measure the copious flow of blood.

"When his assistant came with the requisite instruments, the wound was probed, and it was ascertained that an artery above the temple had been, not exactly severed, but crushed. A compress and a bandage were made, which took up a considerable time, but all went on well until eight o'clock in the evening, when a fresh effusion of blood burst forth. Iortunately the physician and his assistant were in the house, and they applied a new bandage, which, up to the present moment thirty-eight hours afterwards has proved efficient, so that we now have the best hopes of a happy result, although. the danger is not quite over as yet.

". Dear Mrs. Holland and her servants are indefatigable in doing everything for your mamma in the most affectionate manner. Pray for us, and join us in giving thanks to God. Ever your affectionate father,

"S. Angl. Hierosol."

Extracts from Bishop Gohat's Circular Letter for 1870.

"Jerusalem, October 28, 1870. "This year has been one of great distress throughout the whole country. In consequence of the drought in December, January, and February, the vegetable crops entirely failed, and bread and water were so dear that the poor had to sell their little property, even to their clothes, to buy bread and water, till at last one universal cry of distress arose. In the time of greatest need and anxiety, I instructed my chaplain in London, the Eev. Thomas Smith, to insert in the Record an appeal for assistance. The speedy and generous response to this appeal enabled me to assist many hundreds of sufferers, and, I believe, to rescue many Jews, Christians, and Mohammedans from death by famine.

"I continue to employ four missionaries. The Eev. Stephen Car abet lives at Diarbekir, where the members of his congregation built a chapel last year, and they have undertaken the support of the school.

". A member of our congregation, so writes Mr. Carabet, went to Gawendach, to remain there for a time. He gathers the people together on Sundays, and preaches the Gospel to them. A Mohammedan of that neighbourhood, who wanted to raise a disturbance in the meeting, entered, and stationed himself near the door. When, however, he heard the words of the Gospel of St. Matt. v. 34-48, he became attentive, and requested that they might be read again, for him to hear them once more. This done, he said, I came here to interrupt you, but when I heard those words I could not help trembling, for they taught me that God's law commands us to love our enemies. Such doctrine I had never heard before. My religion teaches me to kill my enemies, and to seize their wives and their possessions for myself. Oh, forgive me my evil intentions, and allow me, in future, to join your meetings.

"The brethren heard this with astonishment and joy, and willingly acceded to his request. The Armenians, hereupon, begged the colporteur to preach to them in their church. We went thither, and they collected forty piastres to purchase a Turkish Bible. Their services are held in the Armenian tongue, which the common people do not understand.

"When an Armenian Bishop visited the place, they put the Bible into his hands on Sunday, and requested him to read aloud from it. But he could not read Turkish; and threw the sacred volume upon the floor with the words, May God curse this book, and all those who have been concerned in bringing it here! At this, the Mohammedan mentioned above stood up to reprove him, and an instant tumult in the church was the result. Some said that the Bishop's beard ought to be shaven (a mark of the greatest indignity), because he had thrown God's Word upon the ground and cursed it; others said he ought to be hunted out of the place. The Bishop was ashamed, and asked the Mohammedan to make it possible to apologise before the whole congregation. The colporteur then read St. Matt. vii. 13 23, and after he had expounded it, peace was restored. On that day many souls were won, and they now worship God according to the forms of our prayer-book. They earnestly desire a reformation of their Church.

"So far Carabet's report. The Mohammedan has since made a public profession of Christianity.

"My fourth missionary is my dear brother Megher-ditsch, formerly an Archbishop of the Armenian Church. Por the last five years he has had the charge of the Protestant Episcopal congregation at Aintab, where, I believe, he was born, and where for twelve years he held the office of Bishop. Besides discharging the duties of his pastoral office. Archbishop Megherditsch maintains an extensive correspondence with a great number of priests who are dissatisfied with the state of their own Church, and who, with their congregations, would like to follow his example and join the English Church.

I can now reckon this Archbishop, who for Christ's sake has become poor, among the number of my ordained missionaries. S. Angl. Hierosol."

Extract from Bishop Golat's Circular Letter for 1871.

"On my visitation tour, which I recently made through Samaria and Galilee, I consecrated the beautiful Gothic church at Nazareth. The church was filled with devout worshippers, as many native Protestants came from the adjacent villages,. I ordained three candidates for orders, of whom two were natives of that region; the third was a German, who has long worked as a catechist at Nablus. After the ordination we celebrated the Holy Communion. S. Angl. Hierosol."

We will close this chapter with a description of Bishop Gobat's character, sketched by Herr Lie. Superintendent Karl Hoffmann, who entered into closer relations with him in his later years, and who counts his reminiscences of Jerusalem among the most agreeable of his life. The portraiture refers to the years 1866 1869, and we avail ourselves, with thanks, of the permission to insert it here.

Recollections of Bishop Gohat in the years 1866 1869, hy Lie. Theol. K. Hoffmann, Superintendent at Franen-clorfj Pomerania.

"The Bishop, at the time of my appointment as pastor of the German Evangelical congregation at Jerusalem, was already approaching his seventieth year; but he produced the impression of a thoroughly strong and healthy man, only that he was not so alert in his movements as he had been in the earlier years of his eventful life; for much walking in the heat and on the stony roads about Jerusalem had become irksome to him. Yet he was no infrequent visitor at the Zion School, which was situated beyond the city boundaries, and which was especially dear to his heart. He also appeared on all other occasions, whether anniversary festivals of the different institutions, mission lectures, or weekly prayer-meetings of the united Evangelical congregations. Never was his countenance wanting if by any means he could arrange to be present, and he accomplished even the longer distances to the suburbs of the city almost invariably on foot.

"His missionary activity in the Holy Land had to a certain extent reached its close, in that his work lay more especially in maintaining the various mission schools and other means for the evangelisation of the Arab population already founded by him, and the burthen of which lay almost entirely upon his own shoulders, as well as the continual necessity of collecting pecuniary contributions for their support.

"Among all the different congregations of the Evangelical Mission, any members who had petitions to prefer, but especially those who needed help, went to the Bishop in preference to any one else. Sometimes Arabs would come from Jerusalem and Bethlehem, sometimes converts, or teachers and evangelists from the various schools and mission stations scattered over the country, all seeking counsel and aid; or even Abyssinians, for whom, as it was said of him, he had always retained a certain prepossession. With the greatest calmness and patience he would give audience to even the importunate and intrusive. In many cases, however, his faithful wife was able to relieve him of this burthen and annoy- ance (for such it often truly was); for she was unwearied in sharing with him the care of the mission, particularly all matters connected with economics, and with the alleviation of poverty and distress.

"His official apartment in the house opposite to David's Tower was close to the door of entrance, and so immediately accessible to all comers. It never was to be seen otherwise than in exemplary order; just as in all money matters accruing from the Mission he was a man of the most methodical punctuality.

"In his intercourse with his fellow-men, even with Arabs and proselytes, of whom it is so difficult to form a right judgment, and with whom many well-meaning missionaries have lost their patience, his compassionate love and long-suffering shone most conspicuously. Although he was a shrewd observer and a sjood discrimi-nater of character, he never allowed his equanimity to desert him, though he was not exempt from some bitter experiences and disappointments. (The physician. Dr. Chaplain, affirms that he never saw him in a passion.) This equable, quiet, and dignified de-meanour seemed natural to him, and was, in my opinion, innate. If anything vexed or wounded him, he preferred being silent, and awaiting the proper time when he could talk the matter out. On several journeys through the Promised Land, in which I had occasion to accompany him, his character appeared to me especially remarkable and instructive. The calm taciturnity with which he used to sit upon his horse and ride at the same deliberate pace until he had reached his destination, in itself gave one the impression that he had long been accustomed to far and tedious journeys.

"I remember a visit to Eeneh, near N"azareth, where the little Arab-Protestant congregation determined to give some outward expression to their joy at the advent of the Bishop. We entered the school, and could see from thence how the Arabs were hastening from the different corners and alleys with dishes and vessels, each family bringing some contribution to the meal which they were anxious to prepare for the Bishop. How well he knew the art of kindly and gratefully accepting, yet without making too much of it. He was also capable, on occasions, of givinsj a sfood lesson to those about him, without expending many words. He had one day returned from a journey, and the porters and servants were disputing as to whose duty it was to carry the luggage up the steps. Without a word, the Bishop seized a trunk in each hand and hastened to ascend, whereupon they all rushed after him, vying with each other which should take his load from him.

"His position in Jerusalem was not always an easy one. Not that the people there are more sensitive and captious than elsewhere; but there are so many different nationalities living not only side by side, but in close relation to each other. The intimate connection that existed among the Protestant congregations at Jerusalem, or at least among many members of the same, rendering the whole evangelical community more like one large family, and rarely to be met with elsewhere, had its reverse side; for, owing to the weakness and imperfection of human nature, it easily led to piques and discord. Great prudence and Christian tact, in things both great and small, were necessary for discerning the right course to be pursued, and Gobat possessed these qualities in an abundant measure. It may be said with truth that all sincere and well-meaning Protestants of every nationality maintained for him an equal degree of affection and respect.

"I always found it in the truest sense of the word edifying when, in the weekly meetings for prayer, he, as a veritable priest, offered up to God the petitions of the people; or when, at Christ Church, he read those portions of the Liturgy, especially of the Communion Service, which he was accustomed to read in virtue of his episcopal office. The worshippers could not but hear and feel that the solemn words were spoken by him from the very depths of his heart. He occasionally preached, sometimes in English, sometimes in German; and his manner of addressing his congregation was the faithful mirror of his character; simple and terse in expression, but rich in Scriptural thoughts and pointed applications. His wide Biblical knowledge here showed itself; and that which spoke most impressively to one's heart, in the pulpit as in the prayer-desk, was the deep and sincere response which he awakened in his hearers.

"The effect of his sermons was but little impaired by the circumstance that he read them, instead of preaching extemporaneously. He also made use, in his latter years, of his earlier discourses, after he had remodelled them. I mention this because, in his open-hearted humility, he told it to me himself. He said that he felt as he grew old, what he had never experienced in his younger days, the difficulty of having to speak in the various tongues, German, English, Arabic, c., acquired by him in mature age, and of hardly ever being able to use his mother-tongue. This obliged him frequently to have recourse to previously written sermons.

"The fact of the French lancruagje havinsj remained the mother-tongue of his old age was often impressed upon my mind when, in his family circle, I heard him recite his native Protestant hymns, of which a great number were stored in his memory, and which he could repeat with quite remarkable warmth and vivacity. At the same time, the fluency and facility with which he expressed himself in different languages was very singular. It is true that in the East, where no particular dialect has the predominance, the ability to clothe one's ideas in several of the current tongues is nothing rare; but this very facility, at first so striking among educated Orientals and Europeans naturalised in the East, is one of the great disadvantages to intellectual life there, and a hindrance rather than a help to sound intellectual development, because all conversation evaporates in mere surface-talk, and in the endeavour to learn the languages themselves every stimulus to real culture dies away.

"Gobat's gift, however, was not of this nature. So far as I am in a position to judge, it was his talent to appropriate from various tongues all that was simple and natural in expresssion, not mere sounding forms of words and phrases. He once happened to give me the key to the secret of his linguistic acquirements. In the last year of my stay at Jerusalem, he invited my wife and myself to spend an evening in each week with his family, in order that we might pursue the study of Italian under his direction. After having learned the elements, we read the psalms in the Italian Bible, and he once profited by this opportunity to explain that the Bible was the best book from which to learn any language. He had studied the language which he had been obliged in later life to acquire chiefly from the Bible, and thereby perceived what a treasury and diversity of thoughts and expressions for all the more important matters and contingencies of life are contained in the Word of God.

"This reminiscence brings me to his home and his family life. As a regular Sunday-evening guest, I had abundant and memorable opportunities of learning to know him in the intimate associations of the family circle. At that period there were only two of his children, daughters, at home, so that the substantial-looking house in the square near David's Tower was sufficiently large, though not superfluously so, for his needs. In many books of travel this mansion is erroneously designated as the Episcopal Palace, for it was by no means a palace, and, moreover, it did not belong to the Bishopric. While the English and the German pastors had each a dwelling attached to their cure, the Eishop (after 1862) had to rent a house, the property of a rich Armenian. Frederick William ly. had certainly promised to have a proper house built for the Bishop at Jerusalem, but by reason of the King's sickness and death the intention eventually fell into oblivion, and Gobat was not the man to recall it to remembrance, although he would naturally have liked to have had a settled place of abode. Here, then, in the narrow circle of the domestic hearth, he appeared in all his kindliness and sociability, sometimes relating particulars of his past life, or emulating his daughters in reciting poetry, with which his memory was stored, or perhaps listening to sacred music.

"He could also be very silent at times, especially when matters were discussed in which he took but little interest. For example, he had no pleasure in the hackneyed questions concerning the topography of Jerusalem, invariably debated by strangers. When twilight came on, he was in the habit of mounting to the roomy terrace which occupied the whole of the flat square roof of the house, and was surrounded by a balustrade. On this convenient promenade he would pace up and down for about an hour every evening, generally alone. On Sundays I was often his companion, and it is this twilight hour upon the high terrace, commanding a magnificent view of the whole of

Jerusalem and of the encircling mountains as far over as Moab, that has impressed itself most deeply upon my mind. The solemn silence was only broken by the report of the cannon which announced from David's Tower, about thirty paces distant, the setting of the sun and the Moslem's hour of prayer. At such times one might heatr and learn much from him. He had also watched and studied Nature from this exalted post of observation. He knew at what season and at what hour the great flocks of crows would take their flight from the low lands about the Dead Sea to seek the eggs of the locust; or he could tell whether a sirocco was on the way, and many similar things which I have forgotten. Experienced also in sea voyages, he could tell the bearings of a ship, and once astonished a fellow-traveller Pastor Sarasin-Forcart when sailing the Mediterranean, by remarking in open sea, and out of sight of land, that the ship was not holding a right course. In fact, he had hardly made the observation when the vessel tacked, proving the correctness of his assertion. He was, moreover, an acute observer in other directions. When in church he occupied his episcopal chair, it never escaped him if any members of the congregation. failed in their attendance, which was happily an exceptional case, and he took the earliest opportunity of remarking upon it.

"I am indebted to him for many a wise and fatherly counsel. I will mention one rule which he laid down to aid me in my studies and conclusions concerning Oriental life; it is characteristic of him, and, like much that he used to say, it contains more meaning than at first appears. Many who come to the East, he said, think they will wait until they have become accustomed to their new surroundings before they note down their impressions; others form an immediate judgment upon what they see. The right plan, however, is to note from the very beginning everything that strikes one as remarkable; for in proportion as one becomes familiar with Oriental life, one is apt to lose insensibly one's acute perception of its peculiarities as distinguished from conditions of existence in the West. On the other hand, one must not be too ready to jump to a conclusion respecting all that is new. The balance of judgment, and a correct estimate of the whole, can only be learned by experience.

"Swift to hear, but slow to speak, is a characteristic trait of Christian perfection which especially suggests itself to my mind when I think of the departed Bishop, as I knew him in his latter years. It was not only a natural and happy union of a clear and honest mind and a ripe and deliberate reflection; it was also one fruit of his God-fearing life and of his rich experience in the service of his Lord."

CHAPTEE VII.

THE bishop's jubilee THE LAST SEVEN YEAES OF HIS WORK, AND HIS ENTRANCE INTO REST. (1871-1879.)

The Bishop had suffered during the past decade from several severe attacks of illness, which seemed to predict the speedy termination of his earthly career. Contrary to expectation, after he had attained his seventieth year he was blessed with a tranquil and protracted eventide, which lasted, with gradual and gentle decrease of strength, until the close of his eightieth year.

In the few last years of the Bishop's life there was no serious outbreak of the Mohammedan spirit of persecution, but ever-increasing care and anxiety were not wanting. The labours of Gobat and his helpers in the Bible-schools and Protestant congregations continually took a wider range, and in the same proportion, of course, the responsibilities and pecuniary expenses increased. The See was certainly well endowed, the Bishop and his family were provided for, and he was placed in a position to exercise beneficence on a generous scale; but still there was wanting that which every Christian country has possessed from time immemorial, namely, an established fund for churches, schools, and the relief of the poor.

He himself used to say, in a modest and sorrowful tone, "I am really no bishop; I am only a missionary."

The expenses, which grew from year to year, particularly in the years of famine, had to be defrayed by the voluntary offerings of the societies and of private individuals. But these contributions, instead of increasinjz, decreased. The original enthusiasm for Evangelical undertakings in the East declined in proportion as the hopes with which the enthusiasts started seemed to fail of realisation. Hence the painful necessity under which the Bishop laboured, of constantly urging the claims of his diocese upon his Christian brethren in his circular letters and general correspondence, and in sermons and addresses while on his travels. Yet, trusting surely in the living God, and guided by proper feeling, Gobat avoided as much as possible making direct appeals to individuals. But his friends in England, Messrs. Veitch and Smith, who acted for him as his chaplains, and his friends in Wtirtemberg, were forced to adopt such measures. In the course of his later journeys through England and Germany in 1872, 1875, and 1878, the Bishop could not divest himself of the sad impression that among his Evangelical sympathisers love had cooled, faith had waned, and that a certain worldliness had crept into their views.

In 1876 and 1877 a new Kusso-Turkish war disturbed the East. The abuses of the Turkish government and administration had gone from bad to worse. The commands and challenges emanating from Constantinople, and insisting upon just and righteous dealing, proved to be a deceitful scheme, just clever enough to silence diplomatists and to appease public opinion in Europe. Pressed by the European Cabinets, Midhat Pasha, the Turkish reformer, in 1870 played off the farce of an Osmanli Paiiiament. The insurrections in Herzegovina, Bosnia, and Bulgaria, and the Servian war against the Turks, complicated the position. At this juncture Alexander II. believed that the time was come for him to walk in the steps of his father, Nicholas, and to summon his people to the grand struggle against the Turks, with the ulterior aim of once for all establishing the rights of Christians in the East. A repetition of the Crimean War was by this time impossible. The public mind of England had been too clearly enlightened to be again led astray as in 1854.

Under these circumstances, the Eussians, though at a terrible sacrifice, succeeded in marching to the very threshold of Constantinople. Before the gates of the capital they halted, held in check by the English fleet and by the warnings of the European Cabinets. The fruits of victory conceded to them by the Porte in the Peace of San Stefano were deprived of much of their value by the Berlin Congress of 1878. A patchwork of provisional arrangements was put together, and the bounds of the Turkish Empire were certainly contracted; yet in essentials the prestige of that power was maintained, the settlement of the Eastern question was once more postponed, and the position of the Christians in no way assured. Our friends at Jerusalem were witnesses of the frightful misery caused during the war by the forcible raising of levies, and the increase in the rates of taxation.

Yet, all this notwithstanding, the posture of affairs in Palestine has improved in the last decade, and many evils have been ameliorated. The credit of these marks of progress is not, however, due to the European Powers, but to the mightily increasing intercourse with other nations. Since the opening of the Suez Canal in especial, the East has been thrown open to the people of the West; and as in ancient times, after the conquest of Alexander, Grecian culture pervaded the East, so now, by means of multiplied facilities for cosmopolitan association, the influence of European thought and customs is brought to bear. The highway from Jaffa to the Holy City has been completed, certainly by Pharaoh-like measures of cruel compulsion on the part of tlie Turkish Government, and it has now become an almost perfectly safe enterprise for a traveller, armed with Baedecker's (or, still better, with Socin's) handbook, to wander at will through Palestine. The future rulers of Great Britain, Germany, and Austria, the Grand Duke of Mecklenburg-Schwerin, and other Christian princes, have visited the principal localities of the Holy Land, and extorted respectful demonstrations of welcome from the Turks. In Jerusalem stately edifices are rising, surmounted by the Ptussian or the Prussian flag. The mosques are open to foreigners. A number of Jewish benevolent institutions, never heard of until recently, are springing into existence. In the Greek Church solid theological learning finds here and there an entrance; the Eoman Catholic Missions in Syria are developing an extraordinary activity. Palestine has become more familiar to us through a great number of excellent accounts of travel; whole hosts of tourist parties traverse the country, and the many-sided archaeological investigations have not been devoid of success. At Jerusalem itself, conferences of German Evangelical preachers take place. There is a German school, an institute for higher education founded by the "Friends of the Temple," a social union of the Germans, and a museum of antiquities arranged by them.

Bishop Gobat is one of those who, by untiring labour and patient waiting, have paved the way for a new order of things. The condition of his schools and missions is evidenced by his circular letters. We venture to borrow the words with which his friend Dr. Eoseu closes his obituary tribute: " Wherever Gobat went he succeeded in making the light of pure evangelical doctrine shine through the darkness of ignorance and superstition. Under his refining influence the Jewish Mission at Jerusalem became transformed. Many an Arab Christian becomes convinced of the truths of Scriptural doctrine, yet without breaking the bonds of his hereditary faith. The Cfood seed once scattered abroad, neither storm nor frost can destroy it. It was Gobat's privilege to watch its gradual growth through a long chain of years, until He whom he had served in such immovable trust called the octogenarian to Himself. When, half a century previously, he had begun his missionary career in all his youthful vigour, and was for long detained in Egypt without being able to tread the soil of Abyssinia, the land of his vocation, he wrote in his diary at the end of the first year, Annum j erdidi. But we can testify at the close of his earthly course, Vitam non i erdidit!"

One point we should like to refer to and press upon the notice of the reader. It was not alone Gobat's nobly endowed and saintly character whereby he was enabled to carry on such a grand and many-sided work in the East. His dignified official position as Bishop contributed to its success. It gave permanence to his work and weight to his words. It imparted a tone of unity to the enterprises of the different societies; it inspired the Turks and Jews with respect; it placed him in the position of spiritual pastor and guide to the missionaries and teachers; it empowered him to be their father and protector. Thus the institution of the Evangelical

Bishopric proved itself a benefit; it ministered to the promotion of God's kingdom. Who would not concur in the hope that this institution will be perpetuated? The position gained by England in Egypt in 1882 furnishes a special reason why she should not pursue the interests connected with money and power only, but should fulfil a higher, more truly philanthropic and Christian destiny. It seems to us that to give up this post at Jerusalem would be equivalent to unfaithfulness to this call.

Be this as it may, whether the Eastern Evangelical Bishopric survives or not, one thing we hope, that the seed sown through the agency of Gobat may bear for many imperishable fruit. His labour was not in vain in the Lord, and the remembrance of him is blessed.

Pastor Weser has furnished us with an interesting and graphic account of the jubilee festival which was held on the 30th of December 1871 at Jerusalem, in honour of the Bishop's having completed his twenty-fifth year of office.

"Besides the Christmas feast," he writes, " we have just celebrated another day of rejoicing that of the twenty-fifth anniversary of Dr. Gobat's first entrance into Jerusalem as Evangelical Bishop. Notwithstanding many bitter experiences, it has been the Bishop's successful task to maintain a true Evangelical alliance among Protestants of all denominations, and of German, English, Arab, and Hebrew birth. Next week, the week of intercession, all Protestants will assemble in the Arab chapel, and expression will be given in the most dissimilar lancTua es to one common faith. This circumstance suggested the idea that on the day of jubilee an address should be presented to the Bishop by the whole united Protestant community in the four languages spoken by its respective members. This address was to bear a Latin superscription, and it was to be accompanied by the gift of a model in silver of Christ Church, the first Evano'elical church erected in the land.

"We waited on the Bishop at his residence in sundry detachments, being too numerous to attend in a body.

"Every family belonging to our community had sent a representative, for each one felt heartily grateful to the Bishop for his teaching and example during the long period of his episcopate, whether in the sacred precincts of the sanctuary or in the intimate communion of personal association and friendship.

"In accordance with Oriental custom, two Kawasses, with long staves in their hands and trailing swords at their side, headed our procession from the Consulate through a respectful and unobtrusive crowd of Arabs to Dr. Gobat's dwelling. Arrived there, the proceedings began with a speech from Consul-General Petermann, in the course of which he handed to the Bishop an autograph letter from the Emperor William, together with a presentation vase of gilded porcelain, manufactured at Berlin, and enriched on one side with an excellent likeness of the imperial donor, and on the other a picture of the Emperor's palace at Berlin.

"With emotion the Bishop expressed his thanks for the honour which the Emperor and his late brother, Frederick William IV., had always paid to the efforts for evangelisation in the East, and, above all, for the sympathetic interest which, on this day, his Imperial Majesty had manifested for the Bishop personally.

"I then read the address drawn up by the Supreme Church Council at Berlin, and coupled with it the thanks and good wishes of our local community.

"It was all deeply touching, especially when the Bishop, in a truly evangelical spirit, laid at the feet of his Lord his thanks for all that he had been permitted to achieve. He only sought to clothe his whole life, so rich in earnest labours, in the grace of God, where alone shelter and forgiveness are to be found; and he ended by praying that the Divine mercy and the love and intercessions of his flock would continue to bear him up in the time of his old age.

"I further presented to him a written address from the Jerusalem Union, and then each individual offered to the aged, though still vigorous and robust man, his personal congratulations.

"A supplementary festivity took place on New Year's day, on a more limited scale, at the Imperial Consulate.

"At a preliminary meeting which preceded the great public demonstration, the Bishop had recently exhorted his people to abide in unity of spirit, in order that each separate person should be a living member of the body of our Lord Jesus Christ, imbued with one spirit and joined together in the bond of peace. This was the fervent desire of him who could look down upon his flock as a father upon his children. May he one day be suffered to appear before the throne of the Eedeemer and to say of us all, Behold, here am I, and the children Thou hast criven me!"

The Em peror William to Bishop Gohat.

"Berlin, Dec. 17, 1871.

"My deak Bishop Gobat, It is with sincere pleasure that I express to you my cordial sympathy with the interesting celebration of the day which will complete the twenty-fifth year of your exalted and onerous duties as Bishop of the Protestant Churoh at Jerusalem. You have justified in the most honourable manner the confidence evinced by my late brother in his nomination of you to the See; and I add my thanks to those of the German Protestant community at Jerusalem for the faithful care and affectionate sympathy which you have bestowed upon them. I beg you to regard the vase with my likeness upon it, which will be presented to you by my Consul-General in my name, as a token of my personal high respect and esteem. William, I np. Bex."

Extract from Bishop Gohafs Circular Letter for 1873.

"Jerusalem, Nov. 7, 1873.

"This year has been a season of deep sorrow and severe sickness for my family, and we are still bowed down by the painful blow that has smitten us in the sudden death of my beloved eldest son, immediately after the announcement of his preferment from the incumbency of Isycoed (in Wales) to that of Seaforth. We, his parents, cannot choose but weep, yet, so far as he is concerned, our tears have no bitterness; for, judging from the contents of his letters and from the trustworthy reports of friends, we have the certain hope that he has fallen asleep in the Lord. But we are oppressed with the thought of his forlorn widow and his three young children, whom I would especially commend to the prayers of the children of God.

"During my seven months' sojourn in Europe in the past year,. his Majesty the Emperor of Germany granted me an audience at Ems, in which he strongly encouraged me by the interest he takes in the Palestinian Mission. I moreover had an opportunity of communicating some particulars as to my work, in the presence of the two English Archbishops."

Extracts from Bishop Gohat's Circidar Letter for 1876.

"Jerusalem, Nov. 17, 1876.

"On the previous occasions of my addressing you, it has always been a great pleasure to me to be able to inform you of the progress of Church and Mission work in this land; but it is now my unhappy duty to acknowledge that we have in many points retrograded, under the burden of difficulties, opposition, and repression. In consequence of reawakening fanaticism among the Mohammedans, fewer children are sent to our schools. At Nablus, the Pasha has expressly forbidden our missionary there to receive Mohammedan girls into our school, and has further threatened the parents with a fine of 250 francs in case they should dare to send their daughters to it. The Mohammedans at Lydda, instead of, as formerly, sending from thirty-five to forty of their children to my school at that place, now insult my schoolmaster in every possible manner.

"On the other hand, the Eussians have opened schools at Nazareth and ISTablus; and as they give money to whatever poor children they can pick up, they have succeeded in enticing many pupils from my school to theirs. However, as many parents are beginning to compare to our advanta i e the different modes of teachimx in the respective schools, we hope that this unsatisfactory state of affairs will not last very long.

"Several of our congregations also, especially those of Nazareth and its dependent branches, have been disturbed by the missionaries of a secular society. The main object of this association seems to be that of stirring up the poor people against their teachers, the missionaries, and against our Church order, and to introduce amonsf them false and dano erous doctrines. The Arab congregation at Jerusalem has not escaped this pernicious influence, which aims at the relaxing of all Church discipline and order, to the promotion of carnal liberty and independence.

"Eespecting our mixed but united community of English people, Germans, and Israelitish proselytes, I believe I may thankfully say that in many ways it could compete with the best communities of Europe.

"I certainly wish that a higher spiritual tone and greater missionary zeal were to be found among its members; but, on the whole, they strive to lead an orderly Christian life, they dwell in peace with each other, are always ready to render mutual help, and to avail themselves of all opportunities for edification.

"The London Society for Promoting Christianity among the Jews has accomplished less than usual in the last two or three years. As their sole missionary, Herr Eriedlander, has spent last summer in Europe, this station has been without any missionary at all.

"Before leaving the subject of Palestine in this letter, I must not omit to mention the mission station at Salt in Gilead, beyond Jordan. Three years ago I resigned it to the Church Missionary Society. It has a school and cono'reo'ation under the care of a converted Greek priest; my son-in-law. Missionary Walters, is, however, shortly to be transferred to that charge. There is in that district a great field, apparently ripe unto the harvest.

"Archbishop Megherditsch and his flock at Aintab have been greatly persecuted for many years, and treated like outlaws, chiefly because a former Armenian prelate stands at their head.

"The leader of the Independent congregation informed the Pasha that the Episcopal Church was not Protestant, and that therefore it had no right to the protection extended to Protestant bodies. N"ot long ago, when the Archbishop was at Constantinople, the members of his congregation had occasion to write to him; but when the letter was taken to the post, the post-office servant, himself an Armenian, read the letter and tore it up. When the writers of the document complained to the Pasha, he told them that they had no right to be protected, and he drove them away like so many dogs. They have to pay higher taxes than other Christians, and twice after they had hired a building in which to celebrate their services, repaired it and paid the rent, they were forbidden, on all kinds of ridiculous pretexts, to make use of it.

"Finally, I received six years ago from an English clergyman the munificent present of looo for church-building purposes. With the help of the English Consul at Aleppo, a suitable site was purchased, and building was at once commenced. But wdien the ground was marked out, and the foundation walls were raised to the level of the earth, all further progress was forbidden under the pretence that the building was planned too near to a Turkish mosque, and that we must first obtain a firman from the Sublime

Porte. The firman was refused upon the same grounds, and when, after a lengthy correspondence, it was proved that the distance from the mosque gave us a legal right to proceed with the building, other objections were advanced. I have had to fight out this battle for the last four years, but I gave the Ensrlish ambassador no rest until, about three months i o, he succeeded in obtainincr the firman which gives US leave to complete the work. Dear Bishop Megher-ditsch has now recommenced building. I have been rejoiced to hear that the Independents, who were previously opposed to him, are now working with him."

Bishop Gobat to his Grandson, Theodore Gohat.

"Jekusalem, August 8, 1877,

"My dear Theodore, To-day we celebrate the anniversary of your dear father's removal from his tabernacle of clay to his heavenly home; and my first thought when I awoke this morning was about you, your dear mother and your sisters, praying that the Father of the orphan and the Judge (that is, the refuge) of the widow may be very near, in the midst of you this day and always, to comfort and bless you all four, and to give you His Holy Spirit, the Comforter, that He, the Spirit of Truth, may lead you into all truth, and so make you the children of God, that you may throughout your whole life be enabled to cry Abba, Father, and to commit yourselves to His protection and guidance under all circumstances. Oh that you may choose Him especially as the guide of your youth, to preserve you from falling into temptations whilst you are preparing for your future vocation! Before all things, use all diligence to make your calling and election sure; for if you do these things, you shall never fall. For so an entrance shall be vouchsafed unto you into the everlasting kingdom of our Lord and Saviour Jesus Christ, there, in the fulness of joy, to meet and be for ever with your dear father, whose absence you surely feel deeply to-day.

"These expressions of an old grandfather's love will reach you a very few days before your fourteenth birthday, on which I heartily congratulate you, thanking God for all the good He has hitherto given you a loving mother and sisters, a healthy body, and, I trust, a sound mind and a loving heart and also for graciously providing you with the means of receiving a good moral, intellectual, and religious education. And I pray that He may give you the will to duly improve all these tokens of His love and His care for you. May you, on entering into a new year of your existence, give your heart to the Lord, who has redeemed and hitherto blessed you, that He may fill it with His love and the joy of your salvation, that is. His salvation granted unto you.

"I hear that you are now living with your mother and sisters and your uncle Timothy. I wish you happy and cheerful holidays with them; and I hope that you will always endeavour to be a comfort to your mother by setting a good example to your dear sisters now, and by not only alleviating her present cares for you, but also by continually remembering that you are her only son, and that, consequently, after due preparation, you are to' be her help, her stay, and her comfort. This thought will stimulate you to activity in your studies, so that you may acquire all the qualifications calculated to make a Qucm of you. I mean a man of God, thoroughly furnished unto all good words and works, that you may be a blessing in your generation.

"But now I fear you are tired of my preaching, which, however, is not intended to prevent your seeking and enjoying all the innocent pleasures and recreations suited to your age. On the contrary, I would remind you of the simple words, well adapted to young and old,

Work while you work, and play while you play, This is the way to be happy and gay.

"But I wish you to keep this letter, and always to read it on the 8 th of August and on your birthday.

"My dear Theodore, my heart beats warmly at the remembrance of you. Of my eighteen grandchildren, of whom two are gone to their eternal home,. you are the only 07ie who will bear my name; wherefore I am exceedingly anxious that you should do well and prosper, walking in the way of your father, in the fear and love of God, and in benevolence towards men. For the present, your chief duty is to acquire knowledge by earnest and persevering study. Blessed be God, who has intrusted you with talents sufficient, if duly improved, to raise you at any rate above mediocrity, if not to the top of the ladder. But you must never forget to accompany your endeavours with earnest, believing prayer for God's blessing. We hope next year to leave Jerusalem,. to go to Switzerland and England, when I intend, D. V., to pay you a visit at Canterbury, when I should be very glad to find you at the head of the school, so that you might have a well-grounded hope of being sent direct from Canterbury to Oxford or Cambridge.

"And now good-bye, my dear boy. May God bless, keep, and prosper you, to the joy of all your friends and relations, and especially to the comfort and joy of your grandfather,

S. Angl. Hieeosol."

From Bishop Golafs last Circular Letter.

"Jerusalem, November 1877. " Samuel, by Divine Providence Bishop of the Church of England at Jerusalem, to all the brethren who call on the name of our Lord Jesus Christ in all places, but especially to them who desire the rebuilding of Zion and the raising up of her walls, and who pray for the salvation of Israel Grace, mercy, and peace from God our Father, and from our Lord Jesus Christ.

"Dear brethren, God be praised that while a great part of the Turkish Empire is the scene of war, murder, devastation, and desolation, we have as yet been preserved in peace, only disturbed here and there by rumours of approaching danger, which have afterwards turned out to be groundless. These very rumours, however, combined with our knowledge of the newly awakened murderous hate of the Mohammedans against the Christians, are calculated to exercise us in watchfulness and prayer, so that, come what may, we shall be enabled to commit ourselves and our work with entire trust to the mercy of our gracious God and Saviour. In the mean season we endeavour to improve our time and opportunities to sow the Word of Life in the hearts of the blinded men among whom we dwell, and to offer the same to our Protestant congregations and schools.

"I here repeat what I wrote three years ago, namely, when I compare the present state of the world and of the Church, and particularly the horrible decimating war now being waged in Turkey when I compare this condition of matters with the word of prophecy, I feel more and more convinced that the time appointed of God for His showing mercy unto Zion, for taking back His ancient people of Israel into His covenant of mercy, and for hastening His kingdom, is near, even at the very door;

which blessed time must be preceded by the time of Jacob's trouble, as foretold by Jeremy the prophet.

"I therefore feel very deeply and earnestly how much my brethren and I need the grace of the Holy Spirit to enable us to bear witness to these things and to Jesus, the King of the Jews, according to the will and word of God, before Jews and Gentiles, with power and unction.

"By reason of the differing tongues, we have now three congregations in Jerusalem, to wit, the German, presided over by Dr. Eeinicke, their pastor, sent from Berlin; the English, chiefly composed of Jewish proselytes, under the superintendence of the London Society for Promoting Christianity among the Jews; and the Arabic, under the care of missionaries of the Christian Missionary Society. But, thank God, all these different pastors and congregations dwell together in brotherly love, although small, trifling, personal misunderstandings sometimes arise.

"In consequence of my advanced age, and because I found increasing difficulty in collecting the necessary means for the carrying on of my work in Palestine, I was very anxious to arrange such plans as would ensure its furtherance on similar principles after my departure, which cannot now be far distant. I have therefore assigned to the Christian Missionary Society nine schools, and my missionary and catechist at Nablus.

"I cannot refrain from adding a few words concerning the present miserable condition of the inhabitants of this land. Last winter we had very little rain, particularly in Judea and beyond Jordan; the harvest consequently was very scanty, and wheat rose to a high price; while the heavy imposts, old and new, consume the last resources of the poor ruined people, so that many are hastening on the road to starvation. The Mohammedans are the worst off, as nearly every able-bodied man of them has been pressed into the war in the most outrageous manner. At first, those who could pay 1250 francs 0) were exempted from the conscription; after a short while, when a new contingent became necessary, they could only escape by bribing the medical authorities to certify to their being invalids; and in the end they were forced to serve if they had no influential patron. The poor people were impressed without ceremony, if they had not already fled to the Bedouins.

"Of those who had to march to the seat of war, many, deserted on the way, but most of them were recaptured. Even out of the barracks here many contrived, by the help of little bribes, to desert; but this plunged their poor wives into the greatest misery. It seems that the oflqcials have ill-treated and beaten them, partly by way of punishment for the desertion of their husbands, and partly to force them to point out the deserters' hiding-places. Then the creditors who had advanced money for bribes (perhaps those very officials) demanded their money back again; and now thousands of poor women and children, whose husbands and fathers are gone to the war, languish in the last degree of misery. Some of us are trying to help them, but what can we do for so many? Every month new conscriptions take place. At first there was nothing to be heard anywhere but one universal weeping and lamentation from men and women alike; but now the new recruits are to be seen, often bound together in couples, going forth in dumb despair. I mention this by way of commentary upon the news in the papers that the recruits march to the seat of war with joy and exultation!

". With the help of Christian friends in Europe, I have already devoted more than 7500 francs (; 30o) to the relief of poor Jews and proselytes. But now my purse is empty, just at the beginning of the winter, which will be a terrible time for the poor. I can do nothing except most heartily commend the poor creatures to God, and to your Christian compassion.

"The mission at Aintab in Cilicia, so promising but a few years ago, lias been, during the last five years, a great load upon my heart. The difficulties with which Bishop Megherditsch had to contend in his church-building have already been mentioned. When at last the requisite firman was obtained, and the walls had reached a height of twelve feet above the level of the ground, the w ork had again to be stopped through want of funds. Yet the real and chief object of the mission, namely, the spiritual, prospers in and around Aintab; so that the good, humble-minded Bishop is persuaded that when the church is built at last, it will be too small to contain all those who are prepared to join the congregation.

"And now, my dear brethren, who have aided me by your prayers and alms in extending the kingdom of God in this land, and in the relief of the needy, I thank you with all my heart for your kindness and confidence. May the God of Abraham, of Isaac, and of Jacob, our beloved Saviour and Ptcdeemer, requite you a thousandfold. Pray, dear brethren, in these days of distress and disquiet, for the peace of Jerusalem, and especially for the servants of the Lord in Emmanuel's land, among whom forget not to number your servant and brother,

"S. Angl. Hierosol."

We are now approaching the closing earthly scene of this long and fruitful life, when the aged Bishop was to be called to his well-earned rest; and we cannot do better than borrow the touching words of his son Samuel in the followinsj brief record:

"The Bishop, now in his eightieth year, feeling that the time of his departure was fast approaching, determined, in May 1878, to visit Europe for the last time, in order, as he said, to see all his children and grand- children, and his old friends once more; and then to return to Jerusalem, there to die. Up to September all went well, but in that month, while he and Madame Gobat were staying on a visit at the Castle of Casteln in Switzerland, a slight attack of apoplexy, to which he was then subjected, prepared him and his wife and children and friends for the end, which, it was felt, would not now be long delayed. He managed, notwithstanding all weakness of body, to bear the many fatigues of the journey, and he arrived in Jerusalem once more on December lo, 1878.

"He never rallied from the effects of his first attack, but grew more and more feeble in body, though remaining strong and joyful in spirit, and peacefully he awaited his Lord's summons.

"On Easter Day 1879 he for the last time appeared in Christ Church, and after Holy Communion once more pronounced the benediction. Soon afterwards his illness assumed a new phase, and his strength gradually sank, till early on Sunday morning, May 11,1879, the Master called His faithful servant home, and he was indeed in the Spirit on the Lord's-day. His end was very peaceful and happy, and his last words, full of power and faith, not only showed his own strong and childlike confidence in his God, but also filled the hearts of those who were with him with gratitude and joy.

Thus, e. g., when his son reminded him that he, as a child of God, had no need to be afraid of any evil in the dark valley of the shadow of death, the Bishop smiled and whispered, It is not dark.

"All Jerusalem and Palestine mourned his loss, and felt that a father in Israel, a good soldier and servant of Christ, one who throughout his long Episcopate of thirty-three years had been a true friend and shepherd to all who had been committed to his charge, had gone to his home.

"Three months after his death, on August I, 1879, his wife, who had earnestly and faithfully laboured with him for forty-five years, followed him, and they were laid side by side under an olive-tree on Mount Zion, there to rest in the Lord, and to await their joyful resurrection."

The announcement of the Bishop's death, sent by the family, in accordance with foreign custom, to relatives and friends, concluded with a few words expressive of Christian thankfulness for the rich life just withdrawn, and of pious hope for the departed. It bore the following signatures:

Maria Gobat, 7iee Zeller.

Johannes and Hannah Zeller-Gobat, and family.

Heinrich and Dora Eappard-Gobat, and family.

Paul and Maria Kober-Gobat, and their infant son.

James Timotheus Gobat.

Samuel Gobat.

Theodor and Blandina Wolters-Gobat, and their little daughter. Dorothea Gobat-Arnott, widow, and family.

We will conclude this long record of a noble life with a few appropriate reminiscences of the Bishop's faithful and worthy helpmeet, a sketch for which we are indebted to one of the daughters, D. E. G.

"Our mother was so entirely one with our dear father, that his portrait would be incomplete without hers. She clung with all the fidelity of her heart to the husband to whom the Lord had given her to be

OLD MISSION-HOUSE, BASLE; BISHOP GOBAT S TOMB; ST. JULIANS MISSION-HALL. MALTA. P 5re 390.

a helpmeet. His work was her work; she did nothing without his advice and permission, and she was a true daughter of Sarah, who obeyed her husband, calling him lord. Yet when she found it necessary to do so, she could act decidedly, in sincerity and rectitude. Our father in return gave her his fullest and most affectionate confidence, and bestowed upon her a fathers tenderest care; and we children had the happy privilege of beholding in our parents the realisation of a truly blessed union, where the supremacy of the husband was combined with the most lovinsf consideration, and the submission of the wife with joyful, perfect confidence. The Lord had brought them together, and prepared them for each other; to Him they gave the glory.

"Maria Christine Eegine, second daughter of Christian Heinrich Zeller, then director of the educational institution for girls at Zofingen, was born on the 9th of November 1813. When seven years of age she accompanied her parents to Beuggen, the future scene of their valuable labours during a period of forty years; and there she spent the quiet, happy time of her girlhood and youth.

"Under the careful guidance of her mother, Maria grew up in the midst of a large circle of brothers and sisters."

"In matters of food and dress the children of the inspector were treated exactly the same as those who were being trained in the institution, though the father was even more strict with his own children than he was with those of strangers committed to his care, and

A sketch of that mother's life has appeared under the title Mutter Zeller, Basle, 1882; of the father's under that of Grossvater Zeller s Lehen, Bade, 1876.

frequently punished them with severity when he judged it requisite to do so.

'When Maria was fifteen, she was sent with her elder sister and her cousin, Helene Bertschinger, to spend three years at Locle under the care of a serious-minded and deeply religious instructress. In 18 3 i she returned to Beuggen, to be the steadfast, sensible, and ever-cheerful helper of her dear mother. She was universally beloved on account of her conscientiousness and sincerity. One of her little brothers named her, though this was some years later, the deputy mother.

"She always looked back with pleasure upon those tranquil days, in which, far from the bustle of the world, she could serve God wdth cheerful zeal, and rejoice in communion with Him. In 1833 a cloud came over her spiritual state, and much of the brightness seemed to have fled; but she learned after a while to understand that our peace does not rest upon our changeful feelings, but upon the redeeming work of Christ. Yet the prayers which have been found among her papers after her decease prove that her soul had not seldom to wrestle with gloomy imaginings.

"Her deeper spiritual experiences seem to have been a providential preparation for the great external change which came into her life in 1833. She was betrothed to Missionary Gobat, who, as he has described the circumstances in his own memoir, received her from the hand of God as his pre-ordained companion for life. Our mother often related to us how surprised she was at the proposal of the missionary, whom she reverenced as a servant of Christ and the friend of her parents. In her betrothal she recognised above all else a call from God, who honoured her by allowing her to labour in His vineyard in Abyssinia; and the keynote of her feeling might be expressed in the words which she repeated in all lowliness of heart: Behold the handmaid of the Lord; be it unto me according to Thy word.

"In the modesty of her retiring disposition our mother had retained a childlike simplicity, which, as we have learned from friends of many years' standing, produced an extraordinarily pleasing impression in the circles to which her new position introduced her.

"We need not recapitulate the story of the marriage and of the years immediately succeeding that event. Suffice it to say, that from May 1834 to December 1836 there was so much privation, difficulty, and suffering crowded into the young life of the missionary's bride, that one cannot think of her without emotion and deep respect. Our father never could speak of the birth of his first child without tears, when he was lying helpless upon his sick-bed, while his young wife, bereft of human aid, must rely solely on the gracious protection of God. And the deep waters surged still higher above their souls when that sweet baby-daughter was recalled after sixteen short months. Our father's illness had violently increased, the hope of recovery became dimmer and more dim, and he decided upon starting for Europe, less with a view to his cure than in the desire to see our dear mother nearer to her kindred. The trials of that journey are indescribable. They nearly exhausted our mother's powers, wdiile they cost the delicate infant its life. Still the mother continued to hope on, and did not let the child out of her arms during the entire voyage down the Nile. In the last night a flicker of hope shot up once more, a certain expression on the face of the dying babe led the mother to believe that the Lord had vouchsafed fresh life. But the father spoke: The grass withereth, the flower fadeth; but the word of our God shall stand for ever. Then the mother knew what he would say, and with hot tears she watched her baby's flight to its Saviour, nor sought to keep it back, well knowing that of such is the kingdom of God

"On the 31st of December 1836, during the great earthquake which ruined Safed, and did much mischief in many towns of Palestine and Egypt, the first little son was born, and received, in memory of numerous bitter trials, the name of Benoni son of my sorrow.

"During the ten years following, our mother accompanied our father with ever-fresh courage to the various scenes of his labours. Five children were born in this interval. On several occasions our mother had serious illnesses, which brought her to death's door. Once she became unconscious, and her last hour was supposed to have arrived. Then she was seen to stretch out her hands, as if to lay hold of something; but she afterwards explained that in that solemn moment she had laid her hands by faith upon the Lamb of God, and committed her sins to Him in peaceful preparation for her call to rest.

"With our father's appointment to the See of Jerusalem in 1846 began an entirely new chapter of our mother's life also. Outward privations decreased in proportion as the comforts of civilised European life found their way to Jerusalem. But other difficulties were plentiful. The various hostilities to which our father was exposed affected her deeply. Her own uncompromising uprightness gave great offence in some quarters. She had not the art of assuming a friendly manner when at heart she was displeased with anybody. She said everything straight out in all its unvarnished reality; and though she possessed the guilelessness of the dove, she had but little of the serpent's wisdom. This repelled some people, and yet, strangely enough, they always came back again. The faithful sincerity of her heart became known, and people would say to themselves, If she does tell us some plain truths now and then, one thing is certain she means them for our good.

"During the three-and-thirty years of her work at Jerusalem, she was a veritable mother to the community, and it was a matter of course that every one in all kinds of difficulties should go to the Lady-Bishop to seek counsel and assistance. The members of the Arab Protestant congregation well knew the way to her audience-chamber. There she has smoothed many a quarrel, and effected many a reconciliation between aggrieved married couples, or between masters and servants. Tor the poor and needy also her heart was ever open, and many who hesitated to go to the Bishop himself found in her a wise and affectionate mediator.

"Two sons and a daughter were born after the removal to Jerusalem. When the youngest child, born at Beuggen, died there in infancy, the mother was dangerously ill. Our father perceived from the doctor's manner that he cherished but little hope. He went down into his study, and poured out everything in prayer. His faith was so strong as to enable him to lay hold firmly upon the promise; and he returned full of trust, and feeling sure that his petitions had been heard. Convalescence began the very next day, and before long our mother was able to superintend her household as usual.

"The seven children whom the Lord had preserved to our parents were not often assembled together under the paternal roof. One or another of the boys was almost always away being educated in Europe. So far as we can remember, it only once happened that we were all at home for several months together. And yet we en- joyed a full and beautiful family life. The absent ones were daily remembered at family prayer, and once in every fortnight, when the European mail came in, our father would hasten upstairs to our mother with the newly arrived letters, in order that she might read them first to him, and then to us children.

"Our mother had quite a remarkable gift for narrating. She could relate sacred and secular stories with such vivacity and copiousness of detail, that children were always enchanted by it. Her vocal powers were also of great service in our education, and the numerous hymns which she taught us are an abiding legacy. She was by no means sentimental, and she never found it easy to give expression to her thoughts in language. When one of her children, tormented by doubts, once came to her in great mental distress, she pressed into his hand, with a look of indescribable affection but with a certain bash fulness, a slip of paper upon which she had written the words: " Tliis is a faithful saying, and worthy of all acceptation, that Christ Jesus came into the world to save sinners, of whom I am chief." We were more especially struck in her later years by the thoughtful, active love with which she treated every one with whom she came in contact.

"If she took a long drive, she was certain to know at the end of it every detail concerning the family affairs of the coachman, and was sure to send an extra coin to his sick child, or something of the kind. If at a watering-place, she sought to become acquainted with everybody, and to rejoice each one's heart, not only by her sympathy for his sufferings, but most likely also by a little gift from Jerusalem.

"In her own house she served her fellow-creatures chiefly by extensive hospitality. Sometimes, if rainy weather set in, and a number of travellers could find no room in a hotel, while they could not well remain in tents, she would invite them, all and sundry, and entertain them for several days. A Bishop who had fallen ill at a hotel, and with whom we were but slightly acquainted, was received into our house, where he lay for three weeks ill of Syrian fever, and remained during three additional weeks of convalescence. One lady writes: How thankful am I to have seen your mother in her later years! I was more delighted than ever with her kindness, and astonished at the humility with which she spoke of my three months' sojourn under her roof, as if it were she who owed thanks to me. All this is not set down for her glorification, for of that she would disapprove, but to the glory of God, and as a pattern to many who selfishly disregard the Apostolic injunction: Be not forgetful to entertain strangers; for thereby some have entertained angels unawares.

"O Lord, so runs one of her MS. prayers, let me be a mother in Israel, a priestess in Thine house and in my own family. Let me be a true Mary, sitting at Thy feet. Let me be a Mary like unto that handmaid of Thine who pondered Thy sayings in her heart.

"The family circle had gradually become narrower in the pleasant house on Zion. The four daughters were married, two in Jerusalem and two in Switzerland. Benoni, the first-born son, had gone before his parents; his widow lived in England with her children and the second son; the youngest was at home.

"In 1878 our beloved parents made ready once more to visit Europe, in order, as our mother repeatedly said with a cheerful smile, to see their children, relations, and friends for the last time, bid them farewell, and then return to Jerusalem to die. Our father, notwithstanding his little less than eighty years, was still fresh and active; our mother was bent and fragile. The summer of that year brought us much happiness. Amongst other things, a wish cherished for years by our mother saw its fulfilment. She beheld the quiet little village of Haslithal, of which her grandfather Siegfried had been pastor, and where her mother, when a little girl, had narrowly escaped being carried off by a vulture. This would have been the fate of the child had not the valiant pastor shot the bird at the very moment when it was about to pounce upon its intended prey.

"Our father and mother were preparing for their return to Palestine when the former was attacked with apoplexy. From that time our mother made every exertion to rally her strength in a last effort, in order to be to our father in his last days such a companion and nurse as he needed He recovered rather quickly, and it was considered safe to comply with his- longing desire to begin the journey to Jerusalem. A few days previously he said to one of his daughters, To-day I have been passing my whole life in review before my mind's eye (I speak of my life since my conversion, for before that event it was a living death), and I find in it nothing but a continuous chain of the Lord's mercies.

"The journey to Jerusalem was accomplished under many difiiculties, though prosperously on the whole; still our father's strength was broken down. At one time he seemed to be regaining some of his former vigour; and on Easter Day he re-entered for the first and last time his beloved Christ Church, in order to celebrate the feast of the Lord's Supper with his flock. That was the final act of his life-work. In the following week he became very ill, and it was evident that his Lord was calling him to a speedy rest from his labours. Early on the morning of the fourth Sunday after Easter, May 11, 1879, he fell gently and peacefully asleep.

"Our mother was now lonely and broken down. She writes: My feelings are of a very mixed character. I am thankful to God for all the great mercy which He has shown to your dear papa during his life long; I also thank Him that I have been permittted to serve Him for five-and-forty years side by side with your father, to enjoy so much tender affection from him and through him, to tend him and watch his peaceful departure, and to feel certain that he is now at home for ever with the Lord. But the feeling of forlornness, of an unspeakable void, is very oppressive. At first I suffered from bodily illness, so that I was sadly homesick for my dear husband, who was always so sympathetic. Your brothers and sisters are very kind, and do all they can to show their love and sympathy for me. Give my love and kisses to the dear children. I ought to love them doubly now; yet, as love never faileth, their grandpapa doubtless loves them still. May the Lord be with us all, and may He fill up the great gap. Continue to love and pray for your deeply afflicted and lonely Mother.

"But her loneliness was not to be of longj duration. That home-sickness for the one who had gone before affected her whole organisation. She could no longer rouse herself to any continuous occupation, and her memory failed in a marked degree. At intervals she could be very cheerful, perhaps when she was talking of our father's going home, and trying to picture to herself how happy he must now be. But bodily weakness increased; feverish attacks and great prostration supervened. She allowed herself to be persuaded to remain in bed and rest, but it was only for a few days. Eternal rest w as at band. Her children Hannah and Samuel were with ber wben the last conflict began. For some time she rolled her head from side to side like a child who has inflammation of the brain. Then she became quite still, and the bystanders did not know the precise moment of her departure. On August i, 1879, at half-past nine in the morning, the Good Shepherd took her home in perfect peace.

"Our dear mother, writes Hannah, has expressed no last wishes. When I once told her I hoped she would get better, she said, I have nothing more to do here, and I am unable to do anything more. On the Wednesday I read some hymns to her, and she asked for one in particular, but could only remember the subject of it. I found it; it was one of thanksgiving. When I came to a passage expressing gratitude even for grief and tribulation, she remarked that it was a beautiful hymn, and that it behoves us to be grateful for everything. The thought of Dr. Barclay, already named as our father's successor, occupied her thoughts much, and she prayed for him fervently, even in her dreams.

"Owing to the state of the weather, the funeral took place on the evening of the day of departure. The beloved remains were borne from the house at six o'clock. The service was conducted by the Eev. Mr. Hall of Jaffa. Her grave had been prepared beside that of our father, beneath an olive-tree. At the conclusion of the service. Pastor Eeinicke said a few words on the text, "Charity (love) never faileth." Michael Kawar also spoke briefly in Arabic, and finally Bishop Megherditsch, in somewhat broken English, but out of the fulness of his heart.

"The full moon shone into the open grave, and the return from the cemetery was extremely solemn. So far Hannah.

"Yes, truly love never faileth. God be thanked for such parents, of whom it may justly be said, Whose faith follow, considering the end of their conversation."

THE END.

PRINTED BY BALLANTYNE, HANSON anD CO. EDINBURGH AND LONDON.

PUBLISHED BY JAMES NISBET CO.

THE EMPIRE OF THE HITTITES. By William Wright, B. A., D. D. With Decipherment of Hittite Inscriptions by Prof. A. H. Sayce, LL. D.; a Hittite Map, by Col. Sir Charles Wilson, F. R. S., c., and Capt. ConDER, R. E.; and a complete set of Hittite Inscriptions, revised by Mr. W. H. Rylands, F. S. A. Eoyal 8vo, cloth, 17s. 6d.

OVER THE HOLY LAND. By the Rev. J. A. Wylie, LL. D., author of "The History of Protestantism." Crown 8vo, cloth, 7s. 6d.

"He gives what will be readily accepted as a tolerably complete picture of the land; he tries to expound the rationale or philosophy of the country in its singular adaptation for its great moral and spiritual ends; and he makes the land a commentary on the Bible and a witness for it." Leeds Mercia-y.

"The volume will be found to contain a very readable account of Palestine as it presents itself to a Biblical traveller." Aberdeen Free Press.

PALESTINE EXPLORED, with a View to its present Natural

Features, and to the prevailing Manners, Customs, Rites, and Colloquial Expressions of its People, whicli throw Light on the Figurative Language of the Bible. By the Rev. James Neil, M. A., formerly Incumbent of Christ Church, Jerusalem. Crown 8vo, 6s. cloth. "The work is very readable." Nonconformist.

"We cordially congratulate Mr. Neil on the results of his combined knowledge of the Land and the Book, and heartily desire for his valuable and interesting volume a wide and prompt circulation." Record.

"The author has accomplished his task very thoroughly and successfully in producing a work full of interest and skilful instruction." Literary World.

"A highly interesting account of divers customs and features of Eastern nations and countries, which serve to throw light on passages of the Bible not clearly understood by Western nations." Graphic.

THROUGH BIBLE LANDS: A Narrative of a Recent Tour in Egypt and the Holy Land. By Philip Schaff, D. D. With Illustrations. Crown 8vo, 6s. cloth.

"The attractions of the book are considerably increased by the numerous excellent illustrations." Belfam News Letter.

WILD FLOWERS OF THE HOLY LAND. Fifty-Four

Plates printed in Colours, drawn and painted after Nature by Hanna Zeller, Nazareth. With a Preface by the Rev. H. B. Tristram, Canon of Durham, and an Introduction by Edward Atkinson, F. L. S., F. Z. S. 4to, 21s. cloth gilt.

"Not the least of the features which will render this volume welcome to-the English reader is the frequent recurrence of some English weed or flower which has long become familiar in our gardens." Daily Nev: s.

"The representations of the native flora of Galilee are exquisite." Morning Post.

"The fifty-four plates contained in this volume ai-e all gems, delicate in outline, brilliant in colouring; the eye rests upon each in turn with admiration and pleasure." Record.

"A volume of very carefully printed drawings in colour of the very flowers on which the eye of our Saviour must so often have rested iu childhood." (? m piic.

LONDON: JAMES NISBET CO., 21 BERNERS STREET, W.

9 781153 146579